Limited Government

This book explores why, despite increased government spending on income-support, health and education, the costs of public goods are rising and their quality is declining. Charting the rise of big government, the author identifies a growing divergence between public-sector ideals and the realities of troubled political economies grappling with debt, deficits, ageing populations, improvident social insurance, declining education test scores and multiplying health costs. *Limited Government* analyzes in detail the social and political factors in major economies that drive up public spending, as well as the relationship between spending and outcomes. By developing an alternate model of public finances, and engaging in a critique of the managerial society, the author emphasizes the positive effects of self-management, social self-organization and technological automation, arguing that high-quality, low-cost goods are the result of nations that save, not states that tax. A sociological account of public finances, *Limited Government* outlines how governments can spend less and yet help ensure good broad equitable standards of health, education and income security.

Peter Murphy is Adjunct Professor in the School of Humanities and Social Sciences at La Trobe University, Australia and Adjunct Professor in The Cairns Institute at James Cook University, Australia. He is the author of *Auto-Industrialism: DIY Capitalism and the Rise of the Auto-Industrial Society* (2017), *Universities and Innovation Economies: The Creative Wasteland of Post-Industrial Societies* (2015) and *The Collective Imagination: The Creative Spirit of Free Societies* (2012).

Limited Government

The Public Sector in the Auto-Industrial Age

Peter Murphy

Routledge
Taylor & Francis Group
LONDON AND NEW YORK

First published 2019
by Routledge
2 Park Square, Milton Park, Abingdon, Oxon OX14 4RN

and by Routledge
52 Vanderbilt Avenue, New York, NY 10017

First issued in paperback 2020

Routledge is an imprint of the Taylor & Francis Group, an informa business

British Library Cataloguing-in-Publication Data
A catalogue record for this book is available from the British Library

Library of Congress Cataloging-in-Publication Data
Names: Murphy, Peter, 1949- author.
Title: Limited government: the public sector in the auto-industrial age / Peter Murphy.
Description: 1 Edition. | New York: Routledge, 2019. | Includes bibliographical references and index.
Identifiers: LCCN 2018024839 | ISBN 9781138894631 (hbk) | ISBN 9781315179896 (ebk)
Subjects: LCSH: Expenditures, Public. | Finance, Public. | Liberalism.
Classification: LCC HJ7461 .M87 2019 | DDC 336.3/9–dc23
LC record available at https://lccn.loc.gov/2018024839

ISBN 13: 978-0-36-758509-9 (pbk)
ISBN 13: 978-1-138-89463-1 (hbk)

Typeset in Times New Roman
by Deanta Global Publishing Services, Chennai, India

Contents

Tables

Acknowledgments

While I was writing this I benefited greatly from conversations with John Carroll, Peter Dansie, Peter Fenwick, Ken Friedman, Trevor Hogan, Vrasidas Karalis, Simon Marginson, Greg Melleuish, Anders Michelsen, Michael Moore, Brian Nelson, John O'Sullivan, Ken Phillips, David Roberts, John Rundell and Keith Windschuttle.

Thanks to the editors of *Quadrant* magazine for their kind permission to draw on material from 'The Legend of the Nurturing State', *Quadrant*, July–August 2016.

1 Introduction

Limited government

A century of spending

The facts speak for themselves. In 1830, the United Kingdom spent 10 percent of its GDP on public outlays.[1] The country had a GDP that was a little over 0.4 billion pounds. Industrial capitalism rapidly expanded the size of the country's wealth. By 1860 Britain's GDP had risen to 0.7 billion pounds. In the meantime, government spending had fallen to 9 percent of GDP. By 1890 GDP was 1.4 billion pounds and spending a still-modest 10 percent. Yet after the 1890s, something changed. In the first 15 years of the twentieth century, public outlays rose to an average of 15 percent of GDP. From that period onwards, public expenditure kept climbing.

The biggest leaps in twentieth-century public spending were connected to the First and Second World Wars (Table 1.1). Public expenditures invariably spike during wars. But in the twentieth century, having risen they did not return to prewar levels once hostilities were over. This broke with previous experience. In the past, mass conflicts like Europe's deadly Thirty Years War (1616–1648) did not lead to a permanent increase in the size of the government. So something else aside from the effects of war was at play as the twentieth century unfolded. The fiscal consequences of the great wars of the century were folded into a larger and historically distinctive structural dynamic. The public sector in the major international economies expanded dramatically and persistently (Table 1.1). Britain spent 27 percent of its GDP on public outlays in the 1920s and 1930s. Then 36 percent in the 1950s, 39 percent in the 1960s, 49 percent in the 1970s and 51 percent in the 1980s. It declined in the late 1980s to 46 percent. This paved the way for the longer-term average of 46 percent through the 1990s and 2000s. From 2010 to 2017 this dipped slightly to an average of 44 percent. The trajectory across the decade was downward. Elsewhere, in other major economies, public spending grew from an average of 22.8 percent of GDP in 1937 to 27.9 percent in 1960 to 43.1 percent in 1980.[2]

The growth of the state was not uniform across the board. Some segments ballooned. Over the long run, other parts hardly grew at all. We see this if we compare the cases of defense, welfare, pensions, health and education spending along with the remainder (general expenditure). In 1900, public spending on these

Table 1.1 Public sector spending

Year	US Public Spending		UK Public Spending		Germany Public Spending		Australian Public Spending		Singapore Public Spending	
	US President	Total spending % of GDP	UK Prime Minister	Total spending % of GDP	German Chancellor	Total spending % of GDP	Australian Prime Minister	Total spending % of GDP	Singapore Prime Minister	Total spending % of GDP
1880		3.0	**Gladstone**	8.5	**Bismarck**	11.3				
1881	**Arthur**	2.9		9.2		12.3				
1882		2.4		9.4		13.6				
1883		2.6		8.7		13.9				
1884		2.4		9.1		14.2				
1885	**Cleveland**	2.6	**Salisbury**	9.4		14.8				
1886		2.2	**Gladstone + Salisbury**	9.6		15.3				
1887		2.3	**Salisbury**	8.9		16.7				
1888		2.3		8.8		16.9				
1889	**Harrison**	2.3		8.7		16.9				
1890		2.4		8.5	**Caprivi**	18.1				
1891		2.6		8.6		18.8				
1892		2.4	**Gladstone**	8.6		18.7				
1893	**Cleveland**	2.7		9.0		18.1				
1894		2.9	**Rosebery**	8.7	**Chlodwig**	19.0				
1895		2.5	**Salisbury**	8.9		18.2				
1896		2.5		8.8		18.6				
1897	**McKinley**	2.5		9.0		18.4				
1898		2.9		8.7		19.5				
1899		3.5		9.5		18.2				
	108%^		***97%^***		***127%^***					

1900		2.9		11.9	**Bülow**	19.4				
1901	**T. Roosevelt**	2.6		11.9		20.4	**Barton**	1.2		
1902		2.3	**Balfour**	11.9		21.0		2.5		
1903		2.2		9.8		20.1	**Deakin**	2.8		
1904		2.6		9.3		18.4	**Watson + Reid**	2.6		
1905		2.3	**Campbell-Bannerman**	8.9		17.9	**Deakin**	2.6		
1906		2.0		8.5		18.7		2.5		
1907		2.0		8.2		19.2		2.4		
1908		2.6	**Asquith**	8.4		20.0	**Fisher**	2.8		
1909	**Taft**	2.3		8.8	**Bethmann-Hollweg**	21.6	**Deakin**	2.4		
	92%^		***111%^***		***105%^***					
1910		2.3		9.2		21.2	**Fisher**	2.7		
1911		2.2		9.0		20.8		2.7		
1912		2.0		9.2		19.2		2.9		
1913	**Wilson**	2.0		9.0		39.2	**Cook**	2.9		
1914		2.2		27.0				3.0		
1915		2.1		44.3			**Hughes**	5.0		
1916		1.6	**Lloyd George**	71.3				7.2		
1917		3.8		70.1				8.9		
1918		19.3		57.0				8.9		
1919		25.0		37.7				9.7		
	258%^		***351%^***				***225%^***			
1920		8.5		27.2				8.0		
1921	**Harding**	8.2		30.4				6.9		
1922		5.9	**Law**	28.0				5.9		
1923	**Coolidge**	4.9	**Baldwin**	28.1			**Bruce**	4.9		
1924		4.4	**MacDonald**	27.3				5.1		
1925		4.2	**Baldwin**	26.5	**Luther**	12.3		5.6		
1926		3.9		28.4	**Marx**	14.4		6.2		
1927		3.8		26.9		12.8		6.0		

1928		3.8		26.7	**Müller**	14.3		6.4		
1929	**Hoover**	3.7	**MacDonald**	26.5		14.6	**Scullin**	6.3		
	82%^		***80%^***				***112%^***			
1930		4.4		27.6	**Brüning**	16.7		6.9		
1931		5.5		30.0		13.1		10.9		
1932		8.9		31.0	**Papen**	13.1	**Lyons**	10.4		
1933	**Roosevelt**	9.4		28.9	**Hitler**	12.0		7.4		
1934		11.2		26.5		13.6		9.0		
1935		10.0	**Baldwin**	25.9				8.6		
1936		11.0		26.1				8.0		
1937		9.4	**Chamberlain**	24.9				7.5		
1938		8.9		25.8				7.3		
1939		10.6		24.3			**Menzies**	7.9		
	174%^		***98%^***				***137%^***			
1940		10.0	**Churchill**	31.9				9.5		
1941		11.3		53.5			**Curtin**	14.3		
1942		21.8		59.9				18.6		
1943		40.9		65.9				26.2		
1944		44.4		67.1				26.1		
1945	**Truman**	45.7	**Attlee**	71.7			**Chifley**	24.2		
1946		29.3		65.9				20.5		
1947		18.0		55.6				17.1		
1948		14.2		41.4				14.3		
1949		16.7		36.9			**Menzies**	14.0		
	283%^		***203%^***				***220%^***			
1950		15.4		37.3	**Adenauer**	27.4		13.3		
1951		14.6	**Churchill**	32.6		30.4		14.0		
1952		19.8		36.8		30.7		15.5		
1953	**Eisenhower**	21.2		36.8		30.7		14.0		
1954		20.3		38.4		31.4		12.6		
1955		18.0	**Eden**	32.5		30.3		12.2		

1956		17.6		34.9		29.9		11.9		
1957		18.2	**Macmillan**	36.2		29.0		12.3		
1958		19.3		37.6		29.4		12.2		
1959		19.6		36.2		29.7		11.4	**Lee, K.Y.**	
	73%^		***65%^***				***69%^***			
1960		29.7		36.8		23.4		24.2		
1961	**Kennedy**	30.9		35.1		29.7		25.8		
1962		31.1		37.2		30.0		25.1		
1963	**Johnson**	30.9	**Douglas-Home**	40.9	**Erhard**	30.1		25.4		
1964		30.3	**Wilson**	35.9		30.0		25.9		
1965		29.8		37.6		29.4		28.3		
1966		30.7		38.8		29.4	**Holt**	28.0		
1967		32.6		43.2	**Kiesinger**	30.2		28.8		
1968		33.0		43.6		30.1	**Gorton**	27.7		
1969	**Nixon**	32.6		42.3		31.2		27.1		
	169%^		***108%^***		***98%^***		***206%^***			
1970		33.7	**Heath**	46.0	**Brandt**	40.4		27.7		
1971		33.8		45.0		41.9	**McMahon**	28.4		
1972		33.6		46.0		42.8	**Whitlam**	29.4		
1973		32.8		47.3		43.5		28.9		
1974	**Ford**	34.1	**Wilson**	52.1	**Schmidt**	47.3		33.5		
1975		36.6		53.1		51.8	**Fraser**	35.5		
1976		35.6	**Callaghan**	53.7		51.1		36.2		
1977	**Carter**	34.7		51.3		50.7		37.0		
1978		33.9		50.6		49.3		36.3		
1979		33.9	**Thatcher**	49.7		49.2		35.8		
	109%^		***126%^***		***159%^***		***123%^***			
1980		36.1		52.5		50.3		36.7	**[Lee, K.Y.]**	15.3

1981	**Reagan**	36.8		56.4		51.5		37.2		17.9
1982		39.5		56.0	**Kohl**	52.0		40.8		16.2
1983		39.7		55.3		50.9	**Hawke**	41.4		16.5
1984		39.0		55.4		50.2		43.2		18.8
1985		39.9		53.8		49.6		43.9		18.0
1986		40.2		49.4		48.5		43.8		22.7
1987		40.2		47.2		48.7		41.0		27.0
1988		39.4		44.4		48.3		39.5		19.0
1989	**Bush 1**	39.5		43.7		47.0		39.1		17.6
	113%^		***103%^***		***106%^***		***123%^***			
1990		40.6	**Major**	44.8		47.4		40.4		17.1
1991		41.6		45.9		48.9	**Keating**	42.2	**Goh**	17.9
1992		42.2		48.0		50.3		41.7		16.5
1993	**Clinton**	41.5		48.1		51.3		41.9		14.6
1994		40.5		47.7		51.0		41.9		10.9
1995		40.6		47.5		58.4		40.9		11.9
1996		39.9		45.8		52.5	**Howard**	39.4		16.1
1997		38.7	**Blair**	44.1		51.6		37.5		13.6
1998		37.7		42.9	**Schröder**	51.4		37.3		15.7
1999		36.9		41.7		51.4		36.7		14.8
	102%^		***88%^***		***103%^***	***51.4***	***98%^***		***78%^***	
2000		36.3		39.5		48.3		37.6		15.8
2001	**Bush 2**	38.2		42.5		50.7		37.0		18.3
2002		38.7		43.1		50.9		36.2		16.3
2003		38.9		44.1		51.5		36.3		16.0
2004		38.6		44.9		49.9		36.2	**Lee, L.H.**	14.5
2005		39.0		46.2	**Merkel**	49.8		35.3		12.6
2006		38.7		46.2		48.2		35.0		13.1

2007		39.7	**Brown**	46.1		46.3	**Rudd**	34.9		12.2
2008	**Obama**	41.8		50.1		46.8		37.4		14.6
2009		45.2		53.3		50.8		38.6		14.4
	108%^		***100%^***		***95%^***		***91%^***		***99%^***	
2010		45.1	**Cameron**	53.4		50.4	**Gillard**	38.4		12.6
2011		43.7		48.2		47.1		36.7		12.9
2012		41.4		44.3		44.3		34.7		12.6
2013		39.8		44.1		44.8	**Rudd**	34.7		12.6
2014		39		42.5		44.5	**Abbott**	35.2		13.5
2015		39.3		41.3		44.1		35.7		16.7
2016		39.7	**May**	40.6		44.2	**Turnbull**	37.5		18.74
2017	**Trump**	35.8		39.4		44.7		36.8		19.14
	102%^		***96%^***		***96%^***		***102%^***		***100%^***	

^percentage increase over the previous decade.

Sources: IMF, Historical Public Finance Dataset 1800–2011, government expenditure as % of GDP plus government interest payments on debt as % of GDP (cf. ourworldindata.org/public-spending for calculation methodology); US and UK 2012–2016, ukpublicspending.co.uk, usgovernmentspending.com; Australia 2012–2015, Singapore 1980–2015, Germany 2012–2015, IMF Government Finance Statistics Yearbook 2016; Singapore 2016–2017, UK 2017, US 2017, Australia 2016–2017, Germany 2016–2017, IMF Fiscal Monitor.

in the UK consumed 3.87, 0.57, 0, 0.3, 1.36 and 8.05 percent of GDP respectively. In 2016, spending on the same devoured 2.39, 6.02, 8.25, 7.40, 4.48 and 12.1 percent of GDP.[3] Across the century, defense spending declined while general expenditure increased quite modestly. In contrast, the share of GDP spent on welfare, pensions, health and education expanded radically: 10-fold, 80-fold, 24-fold and 3-fold respectively. The classic core of the state—as it had been constituted in the nineteenth century—was smaller at the beginning of the twenty-first century than at the start of the twentieth century. Amongst other things mechanization had made armies less expensive. Meanwhile the income-support and healthcare functions that the state acquired early in the twentieth century grew to such an extent that they dwarfed the old classic core.

The growth of state spending and public employment had a dampening effect on economies. Industrialism—in combination with modern capitalism, large-scale urbanism and the public sphere—had a catapulting effect on modern economies after the 1770s. What resulted was a massive and historically unprecedented expansion of wealth driven by increases in productivity. The fruits of this wealth were broadly distributed to populations through rising real levels of household income. A great upward spiral occurred. Increased affluence drove greater wealth that sought higher productivity that produced added real wealth that resulted in more prosperity that was reflected in greater purchasing power. But the pace of this beneficial upward spiral was slowed by one thing. Beyond a certain virtuous level, public spending inhibits economic activity (Table 1.2).

Good public spending is a function of necessity. Most human needs can be satisfied by multiple providers. But a limited number of needs are best suited to one provider. Private armies bring chaos, not order. Likewise private police forces. Neither are very efficient. Similarly, it would cause bedlam if a plaintiff and a defendant in a court of law could rest their cases on different systems of law. Nor does it make sense for me to build my own highway or try to control the spread of infectious diseases. As a matter of practicality, some things in life are best suited to a monopoly provider, namely the state. The state can directly provide these or else can license a private operator to do so. But even if the latter proves more efficient, there is still only one underlying payer. A private-toll, i.e. privately taxed, highway may well avoid cost-inflating construction feather-bedding. Even so, the state remains the ultimate owner of the highway.

But with the benefits of the state also come costs. Beyond a limited range of functions, the costs begin to outweigh the benefits. Why is this so? *First*, every dollar that the state raises has a cost.[4] Taxation has to be complied with, administered and enforced. This is an expensive way of raising revenue. Much more so than savings and investments. *Second*, the primary media of the state—instructions and rules—are time consuming compared with the media of promises and patterns that are widely used in markets and industries. Laws that are based on general principles are efficient. But the micro-rules of government regulation are not. Overall, government spending is significantly more wasteful than private spending. The problem is not so much that public sector employment is 'unproductive' as Adam Smith (1723–1790) put it.[5] Rather its productivity is low

Table 1.2 US state and economy, averaged indicators for specified time periods

Time periods	Public spending as % of GDP	State sector (government) employment as % of total nonfarm employment	Education and health services as % of total nonfarm employment	Number of pages of US *Federal Registry* regulation book	GDP per capita (USD constant 2010 prices)	GDP per capita increase or decrease on previous time period	Annual multifactor productivity percentage growth
1891–1913	2.5				$7,147		1.26
1913–1928	6.6				$9,486	133%	1.51
1928–1950	15.9	12.9		9,074	$12,706	134%	3.36
1950–1964	21.9	15.1		11,598	$18,165	143%	1.75
1964–1972	32.1	17.2		20,059	$23,989	132%	1.53
1972–1979	34.5	18.5	7	53,449	$28,200	118%	0.98
1979–1988	38.4	17.4	8.5	60,646	$32,871	117%	1.01
1988–1996	40.7	16.9	10.6	62,100	$39,049	119%	1.18
1996–2007	39.2	16.1	12.2	75,147	$47,678	122%	1.95
2007–2016	41.0	15.7	15.5	80,743	$50,546	106%	0.50

Sources: IMF, Historical Public Finance Dataset 1800–2011; Rose, Table 7.3; Belman, Gunderson, Hyatt, Table 2; Anderson, Table 2.6; US 2012 Census of Governments: Employment; US Bureau of Labor Statistics, Employment, Hours, and Earnings, 2012; Tucker, Table 1; Gordon, 2010, Table 4; OECD multifactor productivity, annual growth rate (%), 1985–2016; OECD, Public administration, defence, education, health, social work, % of value added, 1970–2016; Economic Report of the President, series 1950–2016.

(Tables 9.1, 9.2, 9.3, 9.4 and 9.5). By applying machinery to production, industrial capitalism unlocked the secret of productivity. But public-sector organizations routinely resist the logic of industrial society. Consequently, the larger public-sector employment is, the greater the drag on a nation's economic productivity. This affects its wealth, prosperity and general well-being.

From natural rights to purposive organizations

Through the nineteenth century an invisible ceiling applied to public expenditure, at around 10 percent or less of GDP. There were exceptions, like Bismarck's Germany (Table 1.1). But the exceptions proved the rule. Ten percent of GDP was the natural limit of limited government. It meant, in effect, a 'night watchman' state devoted to defense, law, order and essential public infrastructure. It had the same means of acting as any state has. It could compel behavior by law or force. What made it different was that it mobilized such means in the service of a clearly defined set of purposes. The function of the minimal state was to protect persons, property and promises and, where necessary, provide public works when private works did not suffice. Whether the state acted by means of law or force, it did so in principle for a limited range of purposes. But where did such purposes come from? Ultimately, they are rooted in the doctrine of modern natural rights formulated by the seventeenth-century English philosopher John Locke (1632–1704).

Locke's key proposition was plain and simple. The state existed to protect an individual's 'life, liberty, and estate'.[6] In a more expansive formulation of this he proposed that state power was properly limited to the preservation of the 'civil interest' of an individual. This was a person's 'life, liberty, health, and indolency of body; and the possession of outward things such as money, lands, houses, furniture, and the like'.[7] Indolency referred to the absence of pain. The American Declaration of Independence (1776) restated Locke's sentiments in hard-boiled prose: 'We hold these truths to be self-evident, that all men are created equal, that they are endowed by their Creator with certain unalienable Rights, that among these are Life, Liberty and the pursuit of Happiness.'

Like all general principles, the idea of the natural rights of the individual was subject to interpretation. In some twentieth-century interpretations the right to life was transformed into a 'right to health care'. In other interpretations 'life' suggested a moral duty of the state to outlaw abortions. In still other interpretations 'life' was translated into a 'right to a minimum living income'. In the nineteenth century, the idea of property was subtly refigured to include skills and talents. What followed from that was the assertion that individuals had a natural 'right to an education'. Education provided by the state was deemed necessary to develop the gifts of every person into express and useful talents. In such ways, the doctrine of natural rights evolved into a doctrine of social entitlements and human rights. Classic liberalism turned into social liberalism. What accompanied this was the evolution of the small state into big government.

Lockean liberalism was built on the idea of natural rights. 'Nature' implies something unchanging. Yet Locke's concept, reinterpreted over time, was dynamic. The modern idea of individual natural rights differed from the classic idea of nature. The former prescribed the legitimate ends of the state. The latter drew attention to the shape and form—the *kosmos* or order—of society.[8] All societies are part-order and part-organization. The distinction between natural rights and natural order reflects two views of society. One says that what matters is organized action. The other says that what's important is society's self-organizing pattern-order.[9]

There is a degree of overlap between these two views. A society invariably contains both order and organization. The key question then is: in what proportion do these factors properly co-exist? What is the right mix of the two? In the twentieth century, organization had the upper hand. In the century before, pattern-order dominated. Neither of these histories tell us what mix will dominate in the future.

In the nineteenth century—and before that in the eighteenth and seventeenth centuries—the liberal party, that is, those who looked to natural rights, paid little attention to the question of the *eidos* (the form, shape and pattern) of society. They preferred instead to direct attention to society's organizations and in particular to the state. In so doing, the advocates of natural rights sought to limit the state—society's largest organization—to the pursuit of specific enumerated ends. Such ends, however, had a tendency to inflate. So over time, the classic liberal party evolved into the party of social liberalism. The small state with circumscribed ends gradually morphed into a big state with expansive ends. The liberal party turned into its illiberal opposite.

In theory, classic Lockean–liberal limited government is an organization that employs legal direction and physical compulsion for defined purposes. It does so against individuals and organizations, including other states, that rely on force or fraud or deceit to attain their ends. The state uses compulsion where necessary to protect individuals in emergencies and against enemies and dishonest or violent persons. Otherwise, it observes the principle of non-interference. Governments with limited purposes are less oppressive and less able and willing to interfere with the liberty of individuals to do as they choose subject to the liberty of other individuals. That is to say, limited government is not paternalistic. It does not tell individuals what to think or say, how they should live their lives or what they should spend their money on as long as those individuals don't interfere with the liberties of others. It respects the independence of persons. The nineteenth-century French liberal Benjamin Constant called this the 'liberty of the moderns'.[10]

The philosophy of modern natural rights provided what seemed initially to be a powerful justification for limited government. The state existed for the specifically defined purposes of protecting each individual's natural right to life, liberty and property subject to the life, liberty and property of others. The state also recognized artificial persons in addition to natural persons. Non-state organizations by analogy possessed life, liberty and property. That was the theory. As to the practice: over time the meaning of 'limited' expanded. It began principally with real persons but grew to include many fictional persons. Universities, schools, hospitals, clubs, associations, firms and corporations expanded in scale and influence. This accelerated in the course of the twentieth century, which became the age of organizations. In step with this, limited government became increasingly unlimited.

Pattern order

Attributing defined purposes to the organization of government is not the only underlying principle of limited government. Adam Smith argued that the state should be limited to four key functions: defense and the administration of justice in the first instance, a contribution to public infrastructure and education offset by user fees in the second instance.[11] Yet Smith's outlook was not simply a re-statement of Locke. Smith's idea of a natural order of things was distinct from Locke's natural-rights-based state. Smith turned attention away from state organization to society's pattern-order.

Imbued with natural rights, Locke's individuals are free to make choices. They can make good choices or bad choices. In principle, the state does not interfere with their choices except when those choices interfere with other individuals' power to choose. Government is not omniscient. The officers of the state do not know better than the citizens, subjects or legal residents of a state. Locke observed that individuals had the 'power to think, or not to think; to move, or not to move, according to the preference or direction' of their own mind. Adam Smith agreed but also observed something else in addition to this.

Locke's limited government is concerned with relations between individuals. The state applies and enforces laws (i.e. general rules of conduct) to stop individuals behaving violently or fraudulently against each other. The state exists in order to uphold peaceful, civil and honest dealings between individuals whether they are acting alone or else part of an organized body. From the single individual, solitary person and sole trader to the family business and partnership to the firm, corporation, charity, hospital, school and university, the principle is the same. It encompasses real persons and legal persons, actual individuals and artificial ones. In a free society, individuals are not subject to the paternalism of the state. They are (mostly) free from the state's direction. They have the liberty to consume, trade, produce, invent, dress, think and speak as they choose. The state exists in order to reconcile the freedom of one person, organized or unorganized, with that of another, by prohibiting force and fraud in their many and varied guises.

Locke's individuals have a two-fold relationship to the world. Either they are unfree or free. When they are unfree they are caught up in some social or political hierarchy. Hierarchies vary. They include clan, tribal, patrimonial, feudal, legal-rational and procedural hierarchies. When persons act freely, they decide on purposes and initiate courses of action for themselves. They cooperate with others by making promises and contracts, and they compete with others by the means of industry and invention. Yet, as Adam Smith recognized, this kind of free action cumulatively amounts to something more than simply relations between individuals. As liberty grows, it also scales. Free action acquires features that are collective as well as individual in nature.

Large-scale free collective action of this kind is different from the 'collectivism' of the twentieth-century command economy or its distant relation the interventionist state. The command economy was an attempt by totalitarian states to subject all social activity to a single all-consuming political hierarchy. As its name suggests, everyone in a totalitarian society is subject to its commands and instructions. It dictates literally what people can produce, who can produce it, what persons can buy, at what price, and what they can view, hear, and say.

The interventionist state is much more piecemeal in its approach. It's a polyarchy. It generates multiple official hierarchies to regulate diverse kinds of activities. These range from local government planning committees to national environmental authorities to international customs unions. Each of these are organized as legal–rational bureaucracies. They are subject to rules and procedures. No one of these distinctly modern procedural hierarchies absorbs the whole of society. Rather, each regulates part of it. In addition, non-government organizations proliferate side-by-side with government organizations both in the public sector and private sector. These appear in the guise of firms, charities, universities, sports clubs, hospitals and schools. They enact procedures and codes. These rules authorize or prohibit an ever-widening range of action. Combined, government and non-government organizational hierarchies in the twentieth century generated a new kind of 'rule by rules'.

Free action on a large scale is different in nature from either totalitarian collectivism or liberal interventionism. Nonetheless, it has a collective character. It is more than individuals acting with initiative, ambition, industry and judgment to achieve purposes and reconcile freely undertaken purposeful actions with the free purposeful actions of others. The liberty of persons to think, move, do and forbear also has a systematic character. This means that the free choices of individuals—the natural liberties they exercise, interacting with others, cooperatively, competitively, in tension and harmony—is meshed into remarkable systems of large-scale social order. The state finds it difficult to create or direct these systems. Rather, they are self-organizing or autopoietic.[12] They self-assemble in ways that their participants are often not even aware of. They shape behavior but mostly in tacit ways.

Human beings are self-conscious. They are aware of the world around themselves and they are aware of this awareness. They set goals, possess intentions, form ambitions and pursue them. To minimize clashes of purpose and ambition, and in order to combine for common goals, they utilize hierarchies and rules. But beyond hierarchies and rules, they also cooperate through patterns and forms.[13] Where hierarchies and rules are explicit, patterns and forms are implicit. Where the former are intentional, visible and overt, the latter are implied, invisible and unspoken. One is direct; the other indirect. Patterns and forms can be made explicit. They can enter into deliberate decision-making. But just as often they work quietly in the background.

Take the case of choosing a restaurant. Imagine a person on Main Street looking for somewhere to eat. There are numerous options. Explicit criteria are weighed up ('I think I'd like a Chinese meal tonight'). But other tacit factors enter into the decision. The person walks down the street looking at the alternatives. Some restaurants are crowded. Others are nearly empty. The Chinese one is 95 percent full. What started out as the likely favorite is dismissed. People like to eat in places that are neither too empty nor too full. Around 60 percent table occupancy is the most desirable. This is a pattern that shapes human behavior.

So then, if patterns shape human behavior, what shapes patterns? How do we explain morphogenesis? Patterns reconcile opposites. They take contraries of all kinds and join them together in pleasing ways. In the case of restaurant patronage, the preferred table-occupancy pattern reconciles emptiness and crowding. A venue that is 10 percent or less occupied can induce in us a mild sense of the *horror vacui*, the fear of empty space. Conversely, over 70 percent occupied, we start to become more uncomfortable at the thought of squeezing in. We tend to feel most comfortable around the 60-percent-full point where fullness and emptiness are in a kind of equilibrium.

Pattern order affects most human behavior. A social media marketing company asks: what is the right mix of promotional content, owned content and curated content?[14] Its answer: 10:30:60. Something similar applies to color schemes for interior decoration. Tripartite schemes are often aesthetically pleasing: 10 percent accent color, 30 percent secondary color, and 60 percent primary color.[15] The tie, shirt, suit jacket combination follows the same proportionality. As does the ratio of fixed items, accessible space and furniture in an attractively laid-out lounge room. 10:30:60 is also a way of proportioning by volume cement, sand and aggregate in a concrete mix for building foundations.

What makes the division of something into (*a*) 10 percent (*b*) 30 percent and (*c*) 60 percent parts so resonant? Unit *a* is one third of unit *b*; unit *b* is one half of unit *c*. In themselves, neither of these fractions, *a*/*b* or *b*/*c*, is of great explanatory interest. The ratio of these fractions, however, is interesting. It is close to 1:1.6. It approximates the golden ratio, φ, *phi*. Whether it is arranging a lounge room or choosing business clothes to wear, the mind mixes three elements in ideal proportions. Such proportions resonate through art, society and nature. The point being that such schemata are not unusual. In fact, they are pervasive if often tacit in human experience. Human beings deploy them usually without explicitly knowing what they are doing. We often feel uneasy when we depart from these inexplicit patterns that are built into the fabric of nature, even if we can't necessarily say why.

Income-support, health and education

The large growth of the state in the twentieth century was premised on the assumption that state-organization was better than self-organized order. Organization was key to income-support, healthcare and education. So the state entered these fields in a large way. It began to provide retirement pensions, welfare income, hospitals, doctors, schools and universities. It did this directly itself or else indirectly by subsidizing public and private organizations, or by regulating these. It funded the expansion of non-government public and private sector organizations along with the expansion of government. This was paid for by increasing levels of taxation. The taxation state increasingly supplanted and crowded out the savings-based provision of health, education and retirement income.

The public provision of income-support, healthcare and education was popular with voters. Yet the consequences of the state funding of these goods often proved less popular. Take the case of income-provision (see chapter twelve). On the surface it sounds good. Yet state pensions can never rise beyond a fairly austere minimum because state money is inert. It is not investable. As in the examples above, nature's 10:30:60 is also a method of calculating private retirement income. Ten percent of such income is typically sourced from money that is saved during a person's working life; 30 percent from the investment returns before retirement; and 60 percent from investment returns during retirement. So while the state might be benevolent in its intention, the consequence of state pensions is to immiserate retirement income. State-provided income is a function of zero-sum taxation rather than growth-orientated saving and investment. Purposive organization rarely matches the performance of pattern order.

Cities are one of the great examples of pattern order. Their flexible patterns house millions of people. Historically, in the major economies, the 'multiple' of 'median house price to median income' was in the 2s and 3s.[16] It took the equivalent of somewhere between 2 years and 4 years of household income to pay off a house. Today, in many major economies, the multiple has risen to 8 or more.[17] There are two reasons for this.[18] One is the relatively poor productivity of the domestic housing industry. The second is that national, state and local government spending expanded four-fold in a century. This expansion required money, specifically tax money. Some taxes are explicit; others are hidden. Governments like to hide taxes if they can. Voters like the idea of state-provided goods. They are less happy to be taxed to pay for them. So governments institute stealth taxes. This explains the increased cost of housing. Governments impose on housing heavy property taxes or lengthy regulatory processes with fees attached to them. The natural proportion of three years of household income to pay off a house is distorted and undermined by governments hungry for revenue.

Publics are another prime example of self-organizing order. Modern life is built on the printed word. Books, newspapers and magazines, and the high literacy that underpinned them, grew up spontaneously over the centuries after the invention of Gutenberg press. A society that is well read benefits from increased levels of creativity and invention, pattern thinking and disciplined reasoning, and from the cognitive character traits of persistence, focus and concentration. Government funding of classrooms expanded three-fold in the twentieth century (chapter eleven). Did society's capacity to read expand accordingly? Not at all. Today, children read less. Adults read less. Word proficiency has sunk in the course of the century. In many advanced societies, student reading, writing, science and mathematics test scores have been static or have declined in recent decades while government spending on schools has risen dramatically. This suggests a major misallocation of resources to an institution (the classroom) that does not improve learning.

What about the other major area of government spending, health? Healthcare was revolutionized in the twentieth century due to the development of effective pharmaceuticals, notably in the decades between 1920 and 1970. The associated rise in life expectancy is a clear indictor that clinical medicine was a major twentieth-century success story. Organizationally, though, it was the reverse story. As clinical performance increased, so did real costs. These escalating costs were not the result of better clinical practice but rather the burgeoning of purposive organization in the medical and health field (see chapters nine and ten). Cumbersome organizations waste time and resources. Dysfunctional organizations disrupt and debilitate work. In step with this, large organizational third-party payers (insurers, government departments, hospitals) captured the health dollar. Their corresponding record of controlling costs and encouraging efficient lean high-quality health delivery was poor.

Large-scale markets, including health-consumer markets, are a prime example of modern self-organizing order. Markets are probably the most commonly cited example of autopoietic order. But the argument of *Limited Government* does not assume that markets alone can fix the problems of supersized government expenditure. Industries, cities and publics play key roles in self-organizing order along with markets. If we look at education, for example, there is the case of school vouchers: government tax coupons that parents can use to send their child to private or religious schools of their choice. Vouchers employ tax money that otherwise would be used to teach the child in the public-school system.[19] Yet education vouchers have not made a big difference in education performance.[20] Nor have charter schools: publicly funded independent schools exempted from government department rules. The reason is that these all offer a single undifferentiated 'good', namely classrooms, which in fact may be as much 'a bad' as 'a good'.

Industries, cities and publics normally interact with markets to create markedly different offerings. Some succeed, some fail. Vouchers, however, are an organizational pseudo-market. Like charter schools, vouchers for private schools offer 'school choice'. What they don't offer is 'learning choice', including alternatives to classroom instruction. For more than a century in education (chapter eleven) there has been a fixation on classrooms. Longitudinal evidence suggests that the classroom model has not been very successful. Yet government-sponsored pseudo-markets have done little to support or enable alternatives to schooling or hybrids of school and non-school learning. Perhaps this might change with the development of educational savings accounts.[21] These are not coupons for a predetermined good but rather tax funds repatriated by governments to mandated parental savings accounts. What makes a crucial difference is that such savings accounts can be used not only for classroom tuition but for a broad range of educational services including textbooks, tutors, library-based or studio-based learning, home study, online courses, and so on.

Public happiness

Pseudo-markets are dominated by third-party payers. Those who use or consume a good don't pay for it directly. This creates economic and social distortions because first-party payers are always more interested in costs and outcomes than are third-party payers. Government is the dominant third-party. It collects tax revenue and spends it. For this reason there is a strong case to transition the contemporary state from a tax state to a savings state. In a savings state, what is nominally tax money is ring-fenced in individual savings accounts dedicated to spending on education, health and retirement. These are all inescapable expenditures. The state mandates these so that feckless citizens do not become an unnecessary burden on others. But beyond that minimal requirement, individuals can transfer money from education to health to retirement accounts as their needs change. They can invest their ring-fenced money for retirement and spend it on the type of education and healthcare they want for themselves and their family.

But that then raises the question: what is the *type* of education and healthcare on offer to consumers? What constitutes education or healthcare is as much a function of the autopoietic drive of publics and industries as it is of markets. What this means, in effect, is that if the good on sale in the education marketplace is classrooms then markets are not going to improve student performance significantly because the classroom is not a very effective way of inducing learning. Classrooms substitute institutional doings for intellectual activity. Likewise in health: it is better if consumers directly purchase healthcare. But if the choice in the health market is one clumsy organization versus another clumsy organization then market efficacy is diluted. Markets work best when they are matched with industries that are lean. Slim, wiry, sinewy, spare, trim organizations reduce the kinds of spiraling costs that have afflicted healthcare since 1970. The slender organization appears when ratios replace rules and patterns replace procedures. That is, when autopoietic forms are substituted for directives, policies and planning.

In the last century, advanced societies moved from the mass-industrial to the post-industrial age. Employment shifted from manufacturing to service jobs. The health and education sectors grew enormously. Now the auto-industrial age beckons.[22] It is characterized by increased technological automation not just in agriculture and manufacturing but increasingly in service industries, affecting not just entry-level work but also white-collar, professional and managerial work. However, the 'auto' in auto-industrialism is not just about machines, though these are significant. 'Auto' is also a mode of working. Societies offer three basic styles of working: patrimonial, procedural and pattern types. The first entails personalized familial–kin, master–servant and patron–client hierarchies. The second is the twentieth-century-style bureaucratic hierarchy based on rules, policies and procedures. The third is work that is structured around aesthetic-like patterns. The latter insert the 'auto' into auto-industrialism as much as do machines that automate repetitive human actions.

The 'auto' in auto-industrial is a mirror of nature. Nature can be thought of as a set of mathematically beautiful structures. *Phi* is one example. *Phi* plays a role in the way flower petals are packed; shell, galaxy and hurricane spirals form, trees branch, and DNA molecules and human bodies are proportioned. *Phi* is one of the many pattern types that recur in nature, society and art. Bands, branches, cracking, fractals, flows, oscillations, spirals, symmetries, slaloming, tiling and waves have physical, biological, social, economic, political, design and art counterparts. Society organizes itself autopoietically using pattern-creating contrasts, cycles, fractals, power laws and ratios that structure unions of opposites often by means of pleasing proportions.[23] All of these are ways of creating relations between contrary quantities and forces. They bind the antitheses of large and small, length and width, trunk and branch, hub and spoke, sedentary and mobile, inner and outer, centripetal and centrifugal, anterior and posterior, stability and change, and so on, into a recognizable, meaningful, lucid order.

Each of the great modern self-organizing social systems—markets, industries, cities and publics—tap into these ways of creating order. These are large-scale systems. They involve millions of participants. Their effectiveness relies on generating order that is beautiful.[24] Patrimonial and procedural bureaucracies can't do this. Rule-governed, policy-defined institutions can't do it either. What beauty signifies are the ratios, proportions and symmetries that persons find satisfying. This is irrespective of whether they happen to be in a high- or low-status group or a large or small group. What *Limited Government* argues in essence is that public happiness is a function of the extent and efficacy of social self-organization. It is only when organizations and institutions defer to the autopoietics of markets, industries, cities and publics that we can expect the problems of the contemporary public sector to diminish.

Notes

1 http://www.ukpublicspending.co.uk/
2 Petrisor and Lupu, 101–102.
3 http://www.ukpublicspending.co.uk/. See 'Major Spending Programs in 20th Century'.
4 Robson, 2005.
5 Smith, 1776, book 2, chapter 3.
6 *Two Treatises on Government*, 1689.
7 *A Letter Concerning Toleration*, 1689.
8 Strauss, 1953, 122–213.
9 Hayek, 1973.
10 Constant, 110.
11 Smith, 1776, book 5, chapter 1.
12 A search on Google's N-gram Viewer indicates that the term auto-poietic comes into regular use after 1970. Common use of the term self-organizing begins in 1955.
13 Murphy, 2007, 2005.
14 www.rallyverse.com
15 Just as colors that are separated by the golden ratio of 1:1.61 on the light spectrum often are aesthetically pleasing when put together.
16 Cox and Pavletich, 2017, 1.3; 2012, 6; Richards, 2008, graph 7.
17 Fox and Finlay, 2012, graph 4.
18 Murphy, forthcoming.
19 Charter schools are state-funded but independently run.
20 'Extensive research on educational vouchers in the United States over the past 25 years shows that gains in student achievement are at best small.' Carnoy, 2017. 'We find no overall impacts on college enrollments' except for African-Americans. Vouchers were not associated with an improvement in reading or math performance. Chingos and Peterson, 2012. 'My overall takeaway from the literature is that voucher programs

probably do a little bit of good. But the emphasis is on the word "little"... ' McCardle, 2017. Likewise US charter schools mostly do 'not generally deliver greater learning gains than similar students' in traditional public schools, with the exception of minority students in poverty (CREDO, 88).

21 Cunningham, 2016; Malkus, Peshek, Robinson, 2017.

22 Murphy, 2017.

23 On cycles, see Schumpeter, 1939; Scheslinger, Sr., 1949 [chapter 4, 'The Tides of National Politics']; Kondratieff, 1979 [1926], Freeman, Clark and Soete, 1982; Van Duijn, 1983; Scheslinger, Jr., 1986; Tylecote, 1992; Freeman and Louçã, 2001; Atkinson, 2004; Piereson, 2015; Polybius, 2010 [circa 118 BC]; on power laws, see Gabaix, 2016; Jones, 2015; Rozenfeld, Rybski, Gabaix, Makse, 2011; Giesen, Zimmermann, Suedekum, 2010; Luttmer, 2007; Ding and Wang, 2007; Newman, 2005; Adamic and Huberman, 2002; Bouchaud, 2001; Levy and Solomon, 1997.

24 On beauty as a social self-organizing principle, see Murphy, 2001, 2014.

Bibliography

Adamic, L.A. and B.A. Huberman. 2002. "Zipf's Law and the Internet." *Glottometrics* 3: 143–150.

Anderson, J.E. 2012. *Public Finance: Principles and Policies*. Mason, OH: South-Western.

Atkinson, R.D. 2004. *The Past and Future of America's Economy: Long Waves of Innovation that Power Cycles of Growth*. Cheltenham: Edward Elgar.

Belman, D., Gunderson, M. and D. Hyatt, eds. 1996. *Public Sector Employment in a Time of Transition*. Madison, WI: Industrial Relations Research Association.

Bouchaud, J-P. 2001. "Power Laws in Economics and Finance: Some Ideas from Physics." *Quantitative Finance* 1, no. 1: 105–112.

Carnoy, M. 2017. *School Vouchers Are Not a Proven Strategy for Improving Student Achievement*. Economic Policy Institute, Stanford University, February 28.

Chingos, M. and P. Peterson. 2012. *The Effects of School Vouchers on College Enrollment: Experimental Evidence from New York City*. The Brown Center on Education Policy at Brookings Harvard's Program on Education Policy and Governance.

Constant, B. 1998. *Political Writings*. Cambridge: Cambridge University Press.

Cox, W. and H. Pavletich. 2017, 2012. *Demographia International Housing Affordability Survey*. Christchurch: Performance Urban Planning.

CREDO. 2013. *National Charter School Study*. Palo Alto: Centre for Research on Educational Outcomes, Stanford University.

Cunningham, J. 2016. "The Next Generation of School Vouchers: Education Savings Accounts." *National Conference of State Legislatures*, August 18.

Ding, N. and Y.G. Wang. 2007. "Power-Law Tail in the Chinese Wealth Distribution." *Chinese Physics Letters* 24 no. 8: 2434–2436.

Fox, R. and R. Finlay. 2012. "Dwelling Prices and Household Income." *Reserve Bank of Australia Bulletin*, December Quarter.

Freeman, C. and F. Louçã. 2001. *As Time Goes By: From the Industrial Revolutions to the Information Revolution*. Oxford: Oxford University Press.

Freeman, C., J. Clark, J. and L. Soete. 1982. *Unemployment and Technical Innovation: A Study of Long Waves and Economic Development*. London: Frances Pinter.

Gabaix, X. 2016. "Power Laws in Economics: An Introduction." *Journal of Economic Perspectives* 30, no. 1: 185–206.

Giesen, K., A. Zimmermann and J. Suedekum. 2010. "The Size Distribution across all Cities—Double Pareto Lognormal Strikes." *Journal of Urban Economics* 68: 129–137.

Gordon, R. 2010. *Revisiting U. S. Productivity Growth over the Past Century with a View of the Future*. Working Paper 15834. Cambridge, MA: National Bureau of Economic Research.

Hayek, F. 1973. *Law, Legislation and Liberty, Volume 1: Rules and Order*. Chicago, IL: University of Chicago Press.

Jones, C.I. 2015. "Pareto and Piketty: The Macroeconomics of Top Income and Wealth Inequality." *The Journal of Economic Perspectives* 9, no. 1: 29–46.

Kondratieff, N. 1979 [1926]. "The Long Waves in Economic Life." *Review (Fernand Braudel Center)* 2, no. 4: 519–562.

Levy, M. and S. Solomon. 1997. "New Evidence for the Power-Law Distribution of Wealth." *Physica A* 242: 90–94.

Locke, J. 2016 [1689]. *Two Treatises on Government* and *A Letter Concerning Toleration*. Oxford: Oxford University Press.

Luttmer, E. 2007. "Selection, Growth, and the Size Distribution of Firms." *Quarterly Journal of Economics* 122, no. 3: 1103–1144.

Malkus, N., A. Peshek and G. Robinson. 2017. *Education Savings Accounts*. Lanham, MD: Rowan and Littlefield.

McCardle, M. 2017. "We Libertarians Were Really Wrong about School Vouchers." *Bloomberg*, October 24.

Murphy, P. Forthcoming. "Housing Affordability and Tax Gluttony." *Connor Court Quarterly*.

Murphy, P. 2017. *Auto-Industrialism: DIY Capitalism and the Rise of the Auto-Industrial Society*. London: Sage.

Murphy, P. 2014. "The Aesthetic Spirit of Modern Capitalism." In *Aesthetic Capitalism*, edited by P. Murphy and E. de la Fuente, 47–62. Leiden: Brill.

Murphy, P. 2007. "The Art of Systems: The Cognitive-Aesthetic Culture of Portal Cities and the Development of Meta-Cultural Advanced Knowledge Economies." In *Cross-Cultural Perspectives on Knowledge Management*, edited by D. J. Pauleen, 35–63. Westport, CT: Greenwood.

Murphy, P. 2005. "Social Phusis and the Pattern of Creation." *Budhi: A Journal of Culture and Ideas* IX, no. 1: 39–74.

Murphy, P. 2001. *Civic Justice: From Ancient Greece to the Modern World*. Amherst, NY: Humanity Books .

Newman, M.E.J. 2005. "Power Laws, Pareto Distributions and Zipf's Law." *Contemporary Physics* 46, no. 5: 323–351.

Petrisor, M.B. and D. Lupu. 2012. "International Analysis of the Dynamics of Public Expenditure in Modern Society." *Journal of Accounting and Management* 2, no. 3: 97–105.

Piereson, J. 2015. *Shattered Consensus: The Rise and Decline of America's Postwar Political Order*. New York: Encounter Books.

Polybius. 2010 [c.118 BC]. *The Histories*. Oxford: Oxford University Press.

Robson, A. 2005. *The Costs of Taxation*. Sydney: Centre for Independent Studies.

Rose, R. 1985. *Public Employment in Western Nations*. New York: Cambridge University Press.

Rozenfeld, H.D., D. Rybski, X. Gabaix and H.A. Makse. 2011. "The Area and Population of Cities: New Insights from a Different Perspective on Cities." *American Economic Review* 101: 2205–2225.

Schlesinger, A.M., Jr. 1986. *The Cycles in American History*. Boston, MA: Houghton Mifflin.

Schlesinger, A.M., Sr. 1949. *Paths to the Present.* New York: Macmillan.
Schumpeter, J. 1939. *Business Cycles: A Theoretical, Historical and Statistical Analysis of the Capitalist Process*. New York: McGraw-Hill.
Smith, A. 1776. *An Inquiry into the Nature and Causes of the Wealth of Nations*. London: Strahan and Cadell.
Strauss, L. 1953. *Natural Right and History*. Chicago, IL: University of Chicago Press.
Tucker, J. 1981. "Government employment: an era of slow growth." *Monthly Labor Review*, October.
Tylecote, A. 1992. *The Long Wave in the World Economy*. New York: Routledge.
UK Public Spending http://www.ukpublicspending.co.uk/
Van Duijn, J.J. 1983. *The Long Wave in Economic Life*. London: Allen and Unwin.

2 A self-organizing society

Smith and Bastiat

Adam Smith's immortal insight was that the success of dynamic societies rests on self-organizing social systems. Smith talked not just about individual liberties but also about large-scale autopoietic systems. These encompassed expansive markets, free cities, the liberty of industries, the liberty of export, international free trade, and the freedom of navigation and discovery. Each of these macroscopic social systems complemented the microscopic workings of individuals, their liberties and purposeful activities. They involved the fruitful interaction of large numbers of persons most of whom were strangers.

How do such systems work? The short answer is that their efficacy and power lie in their paradoxical nature. Smith illustrated this with his famous comment about the investors of capital.[1] In pursuing their own interests, he observed, the owners of capital promote the interests of society. Each one of them might be self-regarding yet markets and industries operate in such a way as to turn self-interest into mutual interest. This happens because self-organizing systems work by transforming antitheses into unities. They do this via the medium of paradox. In a paradox, A is not-A. Smith noted that self-interested actions create common goods. In markets, price signals enable self-regarding motives to be converted into mutually beneficial outcomes. An owner of capital wants to get the largest return on money invested in a venture. It turns out paradoxically that the best way of achieving this is not to raise prices and thereby sell fewer goods but rather to reduce prices and sell more goods. In order to achieve the paradox of a greater return on the basis of lower prices, the investor is obliged to find cheaper ways of manufacturing, transporting or retailing the goods on offer. This is what makes modern societies 'dynamic'. The search for a larger profit yields a smaller cost, thanks to innovations in technology and organization.

Transforming A into not-A is not an explicit action. Rather, it occurs in systems guided by what Smith called the 'invisible hand'.[2] Smith did not invent the concept of the hidden hand. Rather, it was a secularized interpretation of Calvinist theology. Calvinism was a minority Protestant religion. Its intellectual sway, though, extended well beyond its adherents and entered into the broader intellectual culture of modernity.[3] Smith grew up in a household with moderate Calvinist

Church of Scotland views.[4] His comparison of markets with the hidden-hand of God is a secular translation of Calvinist providence.[5] He was not by any means the first to draw the analogy between the operation of markets and the workings of providential nature. Smith's immediate inspiration for this was the Dutch-English doctor and writer Bernard Mandeville (1670–1733).

Mandeville grew up in a professional family in Rotterdam that produced multiple generations of lawyers, doctors and Reformed Church ministers. Dutch Calvinist society had a tradition of lampooning its own religion. Both the impulse to satire and Calvin's providence end up in Mandeville's work.[6] Secularized providence is not an effect of God per se but rather the paradoxical working-out of human passions over long periods of time.[7] The principal aim of Mandeville's philosophy was to 'rebuke man's pride in his rational self-control'.[8] This is the basis of all subsequent autopoietic views of the world. Smith had reservations about Mandeville's world-view. Nonetheless, he concluded that Mandeville's contrary outlook 'bordered upon the truth'.[9]

This is the truth that existence—or at least the most energetic and spirited part of existence—is paradoxical. This paradoxy is beautifully captured in Mandeville's 1714 work *The Fable of the Bees* when he says that 'The worst of all the multitude/Did something for the common good ... This, as in musick harmony,/ Made jarrings in the main agree;/Parties directly opposite,/Assist each oth'r, as 'twere for spight... ' Mandeville's observations about the power of paradox—its capacity to transform one opposite into another—belongs in turn to a broader stream of thought that includes among its number not only Smith but also Plato, Kierkegaard, G.K. Chesterton and the American Founders who placed their faith in the balance of competing powers.[10] In Smith's case the paradox of private benefit and public good allied itself with the paradox of providence, namely that modern liberty rests on providential necessity. Modern societies owe much to free will (free choice, liberty) yet more still to grace.

The notion of economic grace interlaced with its opposite economic freedom echoes the influence of Calvinism on Scottish, Dutch and English thought but also on French thought via the French Protestant Huguenots and, subsequently, the French Catholic but Calvinist-toned Jansenists among whose number included Blaise Pascal, Jean Racine and Alexis De Tocqueville.[11] Eight decades before *The Wealth of Nations*, the French thinker and Jansenist Pierre de Boisguilbert (1646–1714) produced a beautiful description of the operation of autopoietic markets in society.[12] 'Nature, or Providence if you prefer... establishes first of all an equal necessity to sell and buy in all sorts of exchanges in such a way that the pure desire for profit will be the soul of every market for buyer and seller alike; and it is with the aid of that equilibrium or balance that each partner to the transaction is equally required to listen to reason, and submit to it.'[13] The equilibrium of nature—its pattern-order—works as long as 'nature is left alone'. The action of leaving markets alone—*on laisse faire la nature*—means leaving them free of state intervention. This is necessity given its liberty.[14]

In a free market 'proportion prices' prevail.[15] That they prevail is a function of the fallen state of human nature. This Jansenist economic assumption was rooted in the same Augustinian view of the world as Calvinism. Fallen beings are selfish. Yet the exchanges between them have to be just or else they will ebb away. Selfishness and justice are opposites. How are they reconciled? By a providence-like 'superior power' that 'governs invisibly'.[16] What is that power? Paradox.[17] It has different names: God, Providence Nature, order, the market. Common to all these is the power of paradox. Paradox takes a force, quality, or drive (freedom, selfishness) and transforms it into its opposite (grace, justice). That which 'governs invisibly' has the capacity to transform one quality into its antithesis. It does so in surprising and invisible ways. The power of paradox acts in a manner that is unlike the visible, conscious, deliberate and interventionist actions of a Mercantilist, Cameralist or Keynesian state.

Modern self-organizing social systems are set in motion by paradox. These systems generate ingenious conversions of one thing into its opposite. So it is that individual self-regard 'miraculously' generates collective other-regard. The ingenuity of these systems is a source of human happiness. But that happiness in turn is a product of the system's own paradox. For modern societies are permeated by dissatisfaction. Grumbling, complaint, discontent, disappointment, frustration, disgruntlement and unhappiness are common in even the most prosperous of these societies. The more that people have the worse-off often they feel. Adam Smith, in *The Theory of Moral Sentiments*, pointed out that human beings had two ways of looking at the world.[18] They observe things either with dissatisfaction or delight. Dissatisfied souls think of the world as laborious. They regard their fellow human beings as unjust, perfidious and ungrateful. Even those who achieve the objects of their desire still regard each economic season as inclement. They never experience summer showers but always winter storms. They are chronically unhappy. No matter what they accumulate in life they perpetually feel 'more exposed than before, to anxiety, to fear, and to sorrow; to diseases, to danger, and to death.' This view of the world is dyspeptic.

Smith observed what has become a systemic irony in modern life. Modern societies generate enormous prosperity. At the same time they produce a vast array of peevish, cantankerous, testy, peppery, fractious and irritable personalities. The person who is both successful and unhappy is commonplace. Such persons ought to be content and yet are painfully dissatisfied. They have accumulated every convenience. But they find that mental repose and tranquility are elusive. For them, even the greatest power and most fabulous riches in the end appear to produce little more than a few trifling conveniences. Even those need to be 'kept in order with the most anxious attention'. For in spite of every care, these amenities 'are ready every moment to burst into pieces, and to crush in their ruins their unfortunate possessor'.

What does the life of petulant and bad-tempered persons amount to? They study and work hard to excel. But they gain employment in laborious occupations. They serve those whom they hate. They are obsequious to those they despise. Their mistake, Smith concluded, is that they misunderstand the nature of happiness. The objects by which we promote ease, prevent wants and gratify wishes do make us happy. But not in the way that the dissatisfied person thinks. If we just look to conveniences in themselves we will be cruelly disappointed. In the end they will seem to us contemptible and trifling. We will loath everything we once passionately sought. Smith argued that this is because real satisfaction lies in looking at objects of desire in light of 'the beauty of [the] arrangement' that delivers them to us. Satisfaction becomes satisfying rather than tormenting when we 'confound it in our imagination with the order, the regular and harmonious movement of the system, the machine or oeconomy by means of which it is produced'.[19] As long as we can locate our pleasures in this 'complex view', which is attentive to the beauty of the whole, what is trivial is made grand and what is contemptible is made noble.

Smith's great innovation was to observe in society something like a clockwork universe. It produced a deeply satisfying order. This satisfaction is derived not just from the placating of particular ends or desires, though we aim for that. Rather, this is a deeper more hidden satisfaction. It stems from the observation of society's automaticity. Society, or at least some societies, interpolate systems whose complex motion is regular, harmonious, machine-like and beautiful to behold. These systems tick over largely on their own. Self-regulating systems need relatively little adjustment to produce a remarkably lucid macroscopic order out of an infinite number of microscopically small actions all of which are purposeful and none which are geared to produce such an order.

Purposeful action involves arranging means to achieve ends. There are two ways in which human beings achieve their purposes. One is by intentional action and deliberate organization. The second is by participating in pattern-based systems. Intentional action can be either individual or collective in nature. Every individual selects means to achieve ends. Persons calculate, plan, devise, schedule and arrange the resources at their disposal to realize the ends that they have in view. Sometimes, individuals are good at purposeful action; at other times, not so good. Some are canny, others less so. Whatever the case, individual action also has its limits. Beyond a certain point it is no longer efficacious. There are many things that individuals cannot effectively do by themselves. They need the cooperation of others.

There are two ways of achieving such cooperation. One is to join together to create organizations. These are what Thomas Hobbes (1588–1679) called artificial persons.[20] These artificial persons combine multiple individuals to achieve specific ends. A significant number of persons can be compressed together into a single organization. The largest of such organizations are states. Firms, companies, schools, universities, hospitals and charities are other common types of organizations. Every organization, even the most durable ones like states, have goals- or ends-in-view. These mostly are short-lived. Their satisfactions are brief. In contrast, pattern action or pattern order is long-lasting. Its satisfactions are deeper. Its beauties quench desire. The systems that generate pattern order are larger than the largest organizations. Deliberate or purposeful action can never achieve the scale of society's self-organizing systems. The latter coordinate the interactions of an almost infinitely greater number of people.

In 1848, the French classical-liberal economist Frédéric Bastiat (1801–1850), an admirer of Adam Smith, explained the extraordinary reach of these systems.[21] He used the simple example of a man getting up in the morning and putting on his clothes. This fellow has made none of the numerous articles of which his clothes consist. What makes the simple act of getting dressed possible is an infinite chain of labor, industry, locomotion and invention. As Bastiat described, the Americans produce the cotton, the Indians the indigo, the French the wool and flax, the Brazilians the hides. These materials then have to be transported to various towns where they are spun, woven, dyed, and so on. No person can do this alone. In fact, Bastiat suggested, a single person in a single day consumes more than that person could produce by themselves in ten centuries.

Bastiat observed that the things we enjoy are produced by persons whom we will never meet and never know. Self-organizing systems coordinate strangers. This is true not only of markets and industries. Take the case of modern publics. The Internet, as an example, mediates the public opinion of millions of people. Compare that with the organization of a newspaper or a book publisher. Bastiat described the difference between a self-organizing system and a Hobbesian-style artificial person as the difference between a 'natural organization' and an 'artificial organization'. Artificial organizations are composed of natural persons arranged together via hierarchies. Irrespective of the kind of hierarchy it is—whether it is patrimonial or procedural, steep or flat—hierarchies are built on face-to-face relationships. Staff and members to varying degrees know each other. Organizations coordinate staff and members by commands and rules. Compared with the self-organizing systems of strangers, even the largest organizations are small. The largest among them are states. States themselves are composed of multiple organizations—departments, armies, universities, schools, hospitals. As well as states, organizations include everything from companies and firms to councils, boards, charities, endowments, associations and philanthropies. Each of these has an end or multiple ends. They exist in order to achieve a purpose.

Autopoietic systems

Purposefulness is a wonderful thing. Yet, often it misfires. This applies to individuals hoping to achieve goals by themselves. It applies equally to artificial persons. Failure is as commonplace as success. Every year in any major economy, a large percentage of businesses collapse and are wound up. Many of these were once great organizations, even household names.[22] Yet while businesses fail, markets and industries persist. Paradox helps explain this. What artificial persons intend often differs dramatically from what they achieve. Goals-in-view are frequently the obverse of outcomes-actually-attained. Self-organizing systems reverse this paradox. They turn it from a negative into a positive paradox. The annual failure of a portion of businesses is not a bad thing but rather a good thing for markets and industries. It exits businesses that are tired, entropic, badly managed or that act irrationality. Overall, this improves the functioning of markets and industries. The latter are not animated by managerial targets or organizational procedures but rather by the creation of lucid order out of the unpredictable interaction of untold trillions of purposeful actions pursued by millions of natural and artificial persons. Markets and industries, like cities and publics, are geared to patterns, not purposes, and to order, not ends-in-view. They coordinate strangers, not colleagues. They operate at a distance, not near-to-hand.

Autopoietic systems harmonize millions of individual choices and preferences. They interlace these selections in ways that generate elegant order. Self-organizing social systems coordinate and integrate the behavior of untold millions of individuals without the need for organizational hierarchies or defined purposes or elaborate rationalizations of these. This is because they are driven by patterns, not purposes. In a hierarchy, a few decision-makers make top-down strategic decisions. They allocate means and resources, and issue instructions and plans, to achieve a given end. Self-organizing systems are not decision systems. No one 'tells' markets or cities what to do, or if they try this, they fail. Municipal councils periodically legislate limits to the expansion of cities only to reverse their by-laws in due course. Government budgets plan infrastructure spending to expand the rate of economic growth only to find this has little effect. In each case, the pattern behavior of markets and cities overrides the determinations of purposive-rational actors. Goal-attainment is conditioned by pattern-maintenance. The best way of reducing fallible purposive-rational judgment is to distribute decision-making across millions of people. That is what markets, industries, cities and publics do.

Successful purposeful-rational actors adapt to patterns. They adjust, modify, revise, bend and amend their actions to better fit dynamic patterns. They might hope that a stock market will continually rise yet they realize that the persistent cyclical nature of stock markets over-determines that. Millions of buyers want lower prices. Millions of sellers want higher prices. All of their actions, and their hopes, expectations and judgments, are conditioned by the wave-like pattern of markets and their endless oscillations between price resistance and price support. No person or group 'decides' when resistance or support occurs. It just emerges, often seemingly out of nothing.

Self-organizing systems combine contraries paradoxically. Ups generate downs, and downs create ups. The up-party is inseparable from the down-party. In that sense these systems are impersonal. It gives them a distinct edge.[23] They do better in decision-making than do purposeful-rational actors, organized or unorganized, simply because they don't make decisions. Rather, they condition decisions. They validate or falsify them according to whether they are in step with self-organizing pattern-forms.

In this way, society structures itself in an autocatalytic manner. It gives rise to itself. We find golden ratio patterns in stock market support-and-resistance levels and the timing of major stock-price movements. Markets of all kinds are structured in non-linear short, medium and long-term waves.[24] In contrast, individual opinions and judgments such as market predictions tend to be linear rather than oscillating. If things are getting worse, it is assumed they will continue along that trend line and get worse still. But the structure of reality is not linear. Rather, it is super-positional. When things are going down there are less visible forces

Table 2.1 Long waves, US

Cycles & Phases	Mood	Periods	Economic Pivot Points	Era-defining Technology	Percentage of total workforce by industry	Dominant Economic Outlook	Dominant Political Party (Presidency)
Cycle		**1789–1844**		**Iron, water power, mechanization, textiles**			
Up (Spring)	Fragile	1789–1803				Hamiltonian	Federalist
High (Summer)	Confident, ends in recession	1803–1816	**Depression 1815–1821**			Jeffersonian	Democratic-Republican
Plateau (Autumn)	Happy, ends in euphoria	1816–1835			*Agriculture 78%*	Jeffersonian	Democratic-Republican/ Democrat
Low (Winter)	Fearful	1835–1844	**Panic of 1837; Recession 1836–1838, 1839–1843**			Jeffersonian, Hamiltonian	Declining Democrats, rising Whigs
Cycle		**1844–1896**		**Steam power, railways, steel**			
Up (Spring)	Fragile	1844–1859				Hamiltonian	Whig
High (Summer)	Confident, ends in recession	1859–1865	**Recession 1865–1867**			Hamiltonian	Republican
Plateau (Autumn)	Happy, ends in euphoria	1865–1873				Hamiltonian	Republican
Low (Winter)	Fearful	1873–1896	**Long Depression 1873–1879; Panics of 1893 and 1896**			Hamiltonian, Jeffersonian*	Republican
Cycle		**1896–1940**		**Electricity, chemicals, automobiles**			

Up (Spring)	Fragile	1896–1908			*Agriculture 40%*	Progressive	Republican, divided
High (Summer)	Confident, ends in recession	1908–1920	**Depression of 1920–1921**		*Manufacturing 22%*	Progressive	Democrat
Plateau (Autumn)	Happy, ends in euphoria	1920–1929			*Manufacturing 26%*	Jeffersonian	Republican
Low (Winter)	Fearful	1929–1940	**Great Depression 1929–1939**			Hamiltonian, Progressive, Liberal	Democrat
Cycle		**1940–2016**		**Petrochemicals, aviation, electronics, information technology**			
Up (Spring)	Fragile	1940–1964		*Military-industrialization; interstate highway system#*	*Manufacturing 23%; agriculture 7%*	Hamiltonian	Democrat, Republican consenus era
High (Summer)	Confident, ends in recession	1964–1982	**Recession 1973–1975, 1981–1982**	*Post-industrialization begins*		Liberal	Democrat
Plateau (Autumn)	Happy, ends in euphoria	1982–2005		*Information technology era*		Jeffersonian, Hamiltonian	Republican
Low (Winter)	Fearful	2005–2017	**Long Stagnation 2008–2017**			Liberal	Democrat
Cycle		**2017–?**		**Artificial intelligence, ?, ?**			
Up (Spring)	Fragile	2017–?		*Auto-industrialization accelerates*	*Education and health 15%; manufacturing 8%; agriculture 1.5%*	Hamiltonian	Republican

* The two administrations of Grover Cleveland were a Jeffersonian exception to the Hamiltonian norm.

Military-industrialization included the early models for the Internet; the interstate highway system was begun in 1956.

Note on terminology: '***Hamiltonian***' [aka the 'American System' or the 'American School'] = public works spending, tariffs, central bank regulation of credit; 'Jeffersonian' = low taxes, low public debt, low government spending, budget surpluses, free markets; 'Progressive' = public works, economic regulation; 'Liberal' = high public spending, taxes and regulation.

Sources: On cyclical behavior see, Introduction, note 23; Bureau of Labor Statistics, Employment by major industry sector, 2006, 2016, and projected 2026; S. Lebergott, Labor Force and Employment 1800-1960, table 1, National Bureau of Economic Research.

pushing in the opposite direction. The same applies to upward motion. In a stock market, the drive upwards will meet a point of resistance; the drive downward will meet a point of support. Longer-term upward phases incorporate periods of downward movement just as downward phases interpolate upward movements. The overall picture has a fractal-like shape.[25] Micro-periods have the same jagged 'up-down-up-down' pattern as macro-periods. The same pattern repeats at all scales.

Modern technology (industry innovation) has a wave-like character similar to large-scale markets.[26] So do cities and publics.[27] Cyclical motion is one example of the way that patterns meld contrasts (in this case, up-down, growing-shrinking). Wide-reaching pattern behavior is an outcome of the interaction of large-scale countervailing forces including 'bear and bull' stock markets, 'conservative and liberal' public opinion, 'expanding and declining' cities, 'productivity-driven and protectionist' industries, and so on. The nature of modern societies is such that each tendency is met by a counter-tendency. No matter how powerful an 'up' trend is, it will encounter a degree of 'downward' motion. In the longer term, there will be a tipping point and the 'down' movement will become the dominant trend for a period. Eventually, this will reverse.

Antithetical social motion creates waves and cycles of collective behavior (Table 2.1). This is not crowd or herd behavior.[28] Crowds and herds tend to unanimity. Self-organizing systems instead have a *phi*-like structure. A dominant polarity will rarely rise above a 62 percent support ceiling. A subordinate polarity will rarely fall beneath a 38 percent floor. Self-organizing behavior is fractal or super-positional in nature. It does not rely on the conscious judgement of a single individual or a handful of individuals. Nor on uniform crowd psychology. Rather, it is shaped by the actions of millions of individuals behaving (to a large extent) anonymously. Anonymous contrariety builds-in corrections to herd-like behavior whether of peers or packs.

Notes

1 Smith, 1776, chapter IV.2.9.
2 '[The investor of capital] intends only his own gain, and he is in this, as in many other cases, led by an invisible hand to promote an end which was no part of his intention. Nor is it always the worse for society that it was no part of it. By pursuing his own interest he frequently promotes that of the society more effectually than when he really intends to promote it. I have never known much good by those who affected to trade for the public good.' Smith, 1776, chapter IV.2.9.
3 The most influential study of this was Max Weber, 2001 [1905].
4 For the intellectual context of Scottish Calvinism during the Enlightenment era, see Oslington, 2018, 30–36.
5 For a contemporary, mostly secular Neo-Calvinism, see the sociology of John Carroll, 2008, 2001, 1985; see also Murphy, 2018.
6 Dekker, 1992.
7 Hundert, 51.
8 Hundert, 51.
9 Smith, 1759, chapter 4.
10 Murphy, 2001, 2016.
11 Adamson, 1995; Goldmann, 1964; Selby, 2015.
12 Faccarello, 1999.

13 Keohane, 354.
14 Faccarello, 2014, 79.
15 Faccarello, 2014, 78.
16 Faccarello, 2014, 79.
17 An example, glossed by Pabst 113, is the Jansenist paradox of Pierre Nicole and Jean Domat that God admits evil into the world because God uses evil as a remedy, so good things come from wickedness. Or as Adam Smith put it: 'we may admire the wisdom and goodness of God even in the weakness and folly of Man' (*Theory of Moral Sentiments* II). In the same spirit, God 'this benevolent and all-wise Being can admit into the system of his government, no partial evil which is not necessary for the universal good' (*Theory of Moral Sentiments* III).
18 Smith, 1790 [1759], part 4, chapter 1.
19 Smith, 1790 [1759], part 4, chapter 1.
20 Hobbes, Introduction, chapter XVI, XVII, XIX, XXI, XXII, XXIV.
21 Bastiat, 'Natural and Artificial Organizations', 2011 [1848].
22 Foster and Kaplan, 7-8, note that of the 100 largest American companies on the original Forbes list in 1917, by 1987 61 had ceased to exist and a further 21 had fallen out of the top 100. Only 18 remained. Likewise, of the original 500 companies that made up the S&P 500 in 1957, only 74 were still on the list in 1997.
23 Surowiecki, 2005.
24 Elliott, 1938; Schumpeter, 1939.
25 The stock analyst Prechter (1999) developed an industry-analytic social-psychological theory of this stock-price fractal pattern and its parallels with other forms of pattern-based collective social behavior including elections and warfare.
26 Freeman and Louca, 2001.
27 Montgomery, 2007; Stimson, 1999, 2004; Bruscox and Roy, 2015; Schlesinger Sr., 1949; Schlesinger Jr., 1968; Adams, 1986 [1889–1891].
28 In contradistinction to Prechter, 1999.

Bibliography

Adams, H. 1986 [1889–1891]. *History of the United States during the Administrations of James Madison*. New York: Library of America.

Adamson, D. 1995. *Blaise Pascal: Mathematician, Physicist and Thinker about God*. New York: St Martin's Press.

Bastiat, F. 2011 [1848]. "Harmonies of Political Economy, Book 1, Natural and Artificial Organization." In *The Bastiat Collection*. Auburn, AL: Ludwig von Mises Institute.

Bruscox, S. and J. Roy. 2015. "Cycles in Public Opinion and the Dynamics of Stable Party Systems." *Department of Economics Working Papers*. New York: Stony Brook University, October 1.

Carroll J. 2008. *Ego and Soul: The Modern West in Search of Meaning*. Melbourne: Scribe.

Carroll J. 2001. *The Western Dreaming*. Sydney: HarperCollins.

Carroll J. 1985. *Guilt*. London: Routledge and Kegan Paul.

Dekker, R. 1992. "Private Vices, Public Virtues revisited: the Dutch Background of Bernard Mandeville." *History of European Ideas* 14, no. 4: 481–498.

Elliott, R.N. 1938. *The Wave Principle*. n.p.: Monetary Research Limited.

Faccarello, G. 2014. "From the Foundation of Liberal Political Economy to its Critique: Theology and Economics in France in the Eighteenth and Nineteenth Centuries." In *The Oxford Handbook of Christianity and Economics*, edited by P. Oslington, 73–93. Oxford: Oxford University Press.

Faccarello, G. 1999. *The Foundations of Laissez-Faire: The Economics of Pierre de Boisguilbert*. London: Routledge.

Foster, R.N. and S. Kaplan. 2001. *Creative Destruction*. New York: Double Day.
Freeman, C. and F. Louca. 2001. *As Time Goes By: From Industrial Revolutions to the Information Revolution*. Oxford: Oxford University Press.
Goldmann, L. 1964. *The Hidden God: A Study of Tragic Vision in the Pensées of Pascal and the Tragedies of Racine*. London: Routledge.
Hobbes, T. 1991 [1651]. *Leviathan*. Cambridge: Cambridge University Press.
Hundert, E.J. 1994. *The Enlightenment's Fable: Bernard Mandeville and the Discovery of Society*. Cambridge: Cambridge University Press.
Keohane, N.O. 1980. *Philosophy and the State in France: The Renaissance to the Enlightenment*. Princeton, NJ: Princeton University Press.
Montgomery, J. 2007. *The New Wealth of Cities: City Dynamics and the Fifth Wave*. Farnham, UK: Ashgate.
Murphy, P. 2018. "A Neo-Calvinist Sociology: John Carroll's Metaphysical Modernity." In *John Carroll Metaphysical Sociology*, edited by S. James. London: Routledge, 2018.
Murphy, P. 2016. "Christianity's Paradox: Chesterton after Kierkegaard." *Budhi: A Journal of Culture and Ideas* 20, no. 3: 1–21.
Murphy, P. 2001. *Civic Justice: From Ancient Greece to the Modern World*. Amherst, NY: Humanity Books.
Oslington, P. 2018. *Political Economy as Natural Theology: Smith, Malthus and their Followers*. London: Routledge.
Pabst, A. 2011. "From Civil to Political Economy: Adam Smith Theological Debt." in *Adam Smith as Theologian*, edited by P. Oslington, 106–124. New York: Routledge.
Pareto, V. 1965 [1917–1919, 1935]. *Mind and Society: A Treatise on General Sociology*. New York: Dover.
Pareto, V. 1896–1897. *Cours d'Économie Politique* [*Course in Political Economy*]. Lausanne, Switzerland: Rouge.
Parsons, T. 1949 [1937]. *The Structure of Social Action*. New York: Free Press.
Prechter, R.R. 1999. *The Wave Principle of Human Social Behavior and the New Science of Socionomics*. Gainesville, GA: New Classics Library.
Schlesinger, A.M. Jr. 1986. *The Cycles of American History*, Boston, MA: Houghton, Mifflin.
Schlesinger, A.M. Sr. 1949. *Paths to the Present*, New York: Macmillan.
Schumpeter, J. 1939. *Business Cycles: A Theoretical, Historical and Statistical Analysis of the Capitalist Process*. New York: McGraw-Hill.
Selby, D.A. 2015. *Tocqueville, Jansenism, and the Necessity of the Political in a Democratic Age: Building a Republic for the Moderns*. Amsterdam: Amsterdam University Press.
Smith, A. 1776. *An Inquiry into the Nature and Causes of the Wealth of Nations*. London: Strahan and Cadell.
Smith, A. 1790 [1759]. *The Theory of Moral Sentiments*. London: A. Millar.
Stimson, J. 1999. *Public Opinion in America: Moods, Cycles, and Swings*. Boulder, CO: Westview.
Stimson, J. 1964. *Tides of Consent: How Public Opinion Shapes American Politics*. New York: Cambridge University Press.
Surowiecki, J. 2005. *The Wisdom of Crowds*. New York: Knopf Doubleday.
Tullock, G., A. Seldon, A. and G.L. Brady. 2002. *Government Failure: A Primer in Public Choice*. Washington, DC: Cato Institute.
Weber, M. 2001 [1905]. *The Protestant Ethic and the Spirit of Capitalism*. London: Routledge.

3 Ordered liberty

Order and organization

In his 1883 work *Investigations into the Methods of the Social Sciences*, the Austrian economist Carl Menger (1840–1921) distinguished between society's 'natural organisms' and those organizations that result from the 'agreement of the members of society'.[1] He noted that the analogy with organisms was limited and somewhat strained yet it served to make the point that some social bodies are purposefully created and purposefully directed whilst 'organic' systems are the unintended result of historical developments that generate large-scale patterns of behavior. Pattern orders are not the result of deliberate human calculation or positive legislation or even explicit social agreements. Pattern-drivers explain the emergence of law, language, money, markets, competition, communities and states. No matter how much positive institutions are mapped over these phenomenon, in origin they are self-organizing. In a more general sense, some social phenomena are the results of a common will; others are the unintended outcome of human efforts that are aimed at individual goals but that spontaneously generate larger beneficial social structures.

Menger posed the question: how can institutions that contribute to the common welfare come into being without a common will that is directed towards establishing them? While persons may enter deliberately into contracts with builders, no act of deliberation creates either the housing market or markets in general. Menger's best example (in fact his only well-developed example) of how systems emerge spontaneously instead of being explicitly made concerned the case of money. Money, he argued, was not originally legislated or explicitly designed by conscious concerted group action. Rather, it developed unprompted. Persons met to barter goods. Difficulties in exchanging one good for another occurred when a person trading a cow wanted an axe in exchange yet either no one had an axe to barter or else no one wanted a cow in trade. What the frustrated but clever trader did was to look for third-party barterers who were trading goods that pretty much everyone wanted, like precious metals. These goods tended to be portable, divisible, durable and all-round marketable. Gradually, such items become 'money' without the need for any explicit legislation or agreement. Rather, a pattern developed. Some traders found it practical to do trades with third parties whose barter items were easy to store and carry until a future trade could be made. Eventually, these items spontaneously turned into money that everyone used.

Menger's insight was developed almost a century later, with great beauty, by Friedrich Hayek (1899–1992). Hayek was one of the three most important economists of the twentieth century, the other two being Joseph Schumpeter (1883–1950) and John Maynard Keynes (1883–1946). The key for Hayek was the distinction between spontaneous orders and organizations. The latter—the organization—was characterized by intention and deliberate design. Organizations bring persons together for concerted action. Like self-organizing systems, they exist in order to achieve what one person alone cannot achieve. Autopoietic systems do this by anonymously coordinating human activities. In systems that generate spontaneous order, strangers (what Hayek called 'unknown persons') interact using impersonal signaling mechanisms of great flexibility such as prices. Organizations, on the other hand, arrange persons into hierarchies and coordinate those individuals using rules and commands. Organizations have will and purpose. They allocate and distribute resources. Autopoietic systems are self-maintaining. They adapt to changed circumstances. Organizations need constant intervention and restructuring to operate. The kind of 'order' they generate is directed rather than spontaneous. It is the product of will, intention, purposeful design, deliberation or planning.

An organization is a managed body of people that is directed to specific goals. It is purposive. It operates via conscious reasoning. It projects goals and devises plans for achieving those goals. It instructs its staff to follow a plan. It has rules and procedures that establish how the organization's staff or its members shall act in foreseeable circumstances. Organizations stress means and ends that are conscious, visible, deliberate, premediated, considered, plotted, prearranged, projected and scheduled. At least some part of the staff of an organization claim to be experts. They are knowledgeable in the conscious, methodical, orderly achievement of goals utilizing organizational means (rules, procedures and codes). Unfortunately, as is well known to anyone who has belonged to an organization, much if not most of this conscious knowledge, expertise, reason and organization is a waste of time. Very few plans of organizations actually come to pass. Organizations have considerable capacity to mobilize the concerted action of large numbers of people. Instructions, orders, directives, mandates, edicts, demands and commands all work in generating activity. Yet equally, much of that activity to varying degrees is futile, pointless, misdirected, fruitless and ineffective.

Rather than relying on conscious expert knowledge, the operations of autopoietic systems, as Hayek emphasized, to a large extent are instinctive, intuitive and unconscious. He argued that members of self-organizing systems are guided by rules—yet not rules that they are aware of. Autopoietic system rules have a non-conscious character. Accordingly, they generate spontaneous orders that are not predictable. Social actors cannot foresee how an autopoietic system will evolve. Take the case of industry technology. The information technology industry developed in the 1980s and 1990s. Yet no one in the 1960s foresaw its future scale even though the science of computing was already well established. The reason for the unpredictability of such systems, Hayek suggested, is that autopoietic actors rely principles, assumptions and rules that are 'abstract'. They are abstract in the sense that they are not discursive. They are not reducible to words and cannot be made explicit in statements. They do not readily lend themselves to reasoning. Rather they are tacit and intuitive.

Hayek argued not against reason per se but rather against the hubris of reason. This is the assumption that we can dispense with intuitive abstraction and thereby consciously master social processes. When persons think abstractly, they rely on principles that for the most part are implicit. This is quite different from a handbook of rules, a set of instructions, a stock of newspaper information or textbook formulae. Like logic, these lay everything out explicitly. But reason, Hayek suggested, loses its power when it turns its back on its tacit almost inarticulable presuppositions. So what then are these presuppositions? It is easy to understand what drives organizations (hierarchies, procedures, protocols, rules and commands). But what orchestrates and animates autopoietic systems? Hayek noted that many people previously thought these worked like biological organisms. He was skeptical of this even though he did draw the distinction between a self-generating order that 'grows' and an organization that is 'made'. Self-generation or 'growth' supposes that outcomes are unforeseeable. In contrast, the ends of organizations are designated or consciously 'designed'. In autopoietic social systems, persons realize ends that were never part of their intentional plan. Whereas in organizations, persons design ends that they often never realize.

So what then constitutes an order that is not deliberately made? In nature, a crystal takes shape. It emerges following the pattern of a lattice. Each crystal is a unique instance of a general pattern. Likewise the effect of the magnet on iron filings. The appearance of the filings depends on circumstances which we can never fully know, but its general character is determined by 'known laws'. Note the shift in Hayek's analogy with nature. He begins by talking about patterns like lattices or rings. He ends by talking about general physical 'laws'.[2] This terminological slide is revealing. For in his view, order arises spontaneously when persons irrespective of their particular purposes follow the same tacit 'general rules' or 'regularities' of conduct. For Hayek, then, order is based on tacit rules whereas organization is based on explicit rules.

In an organization, rules are specific because they are geared to particular purposes. For example, members of an organization of professionals might be banned from purchasing chemicals. The organization applies this rule to reduce the number of accidents caused by chemical spills (this is the projected goal). The concrete organizational rule (the ban) is the product of reasoning that supposes that industrial accidents are caused by in-house professionals being careless and that the rate of accidents will reduce once the ban is enacted. Rule-based purposive action (regulation) sometimes works but often it doesn't. In the particular case of the chemical-purchase ban, it might be based on a faulty perception of causation. Spills, in fact, may be unrelated to who-purchases-what. Alternatively, the ban may generate unintended consequences. Centralized purchasing may reduce problems with ad hoc unsafe storage and handling, but the increased procedural steps may also reduce the legitimate handling of chemicals because no one wants to fill-out the laborious paperwork. Spills may reduce but primarily because the valid use of chemicals in the workplace has declined, not because the net level of prudent handling of the chemicals has increased.

The centralization of anything—i.e. hierarchy—is mediated through language. At a minimum it requires instructions and orders. Twentieth-century organizations were obsessed with procedural rules. That is to say, organizations are discursive entities. They try and articulate what they do. They message incessantly. They are suspicious of regularities that are tacit. An unarticulated rule is a regularity of conduct that has 'grown' over time rather than being explicitly 'made'. For Hayek, tacit or 'grown' regularities of conduct are the basis of spontaneous orders. He observed that language is a blunt tool. It is often insufficient to express what the mind is capable of taking account of in determining action. Conversely, we are often unable to state in words the subtleties of what we do in practice.[3] In short, explicit rules often fall short of mute regularities. Hayek argued that Anglo–American common law developed as a way of putting silent regularities into words. This system of law did not 'make' law like a parliamentary legislature did. Rather, common law courts 'found' or 'discovered' laws. When kings and, later, parliaments began to 'make' the law (to create something new rather than discover something existing) this deliberate making came up against the limits of discursiveness.

Hayek acknowledged that 'making' law sometimes was necessary to supplement the law that had 'grown'. But extensive law-making invariably takes on the characteristics of organizational rule-making. The latter is no longer simply the attempt to put into words established pre-existing inarticulate practices but rather the attempt to remake those practices through language. That is, treat society as an organization rather than an organism. Instead of being an articulation of inarticulate practice, law becomes increasingly the articulate means of managing and directing society by instructing and commanding it. Hayek's analysis of tacit, unarticulated regularities of conduct is sketchy. These regularities are *not* linguistic. That much is clear. But how do we describe them in positive rather than negative terms? Hayek talks about practices. But if not language, then what gives such practices their all-important 'regularity'?

Pattern order not rules

What puts the order into tacit order? Hayek's conception of regularity or order is law-like. Even though it may be 'found' law, it is still law. Such law-likeness, however we might conceive it, aspires to language. Law finds it's apotheosis in statement. What kind of regularity does not do this? The answer is pattern. Pattern is much closer to the muteness of aesthetics than to the language of the law. Pattern is pre-linguistic. Pattern, shape and form are perceptible without being voluble. They impress without having to say anything in a linguistic sense.

What underlies pattern formation in social systems? The answer, arguably, is the human imagination, specifically the analogical character of the human imagination. Consider again Menger's example of money. Unlike barter, money is not a medium of a simple exchange—say, the cow for the axe. Rather, it is the medium of analogical or proportionate exchange. Analogical exchanges are involved in the deepest forms of society-making, i.e. socio-poietic processes. In an analogical exchange, the cow stands to money as money stands to the axe. If the cow is A, money is B and the axe is C, then it is not so much the case that A=C but rather that A:B::B:C, as Aristotle observed in the *Nicomachean Ethics* where he analyzed how builder A stands to the shoemaker B as a house C stands to a shoe D.[4] Justice in exchange, Aristotle observed, is reciprocity in accordance with proportion.[5] Proportionality, in turn, is a kind of analogy.

The human mind is such that it perceives things analogically.[6] The faculty of the imagination allows it to convert unlike things into like things. The cow, the scarce metal and the axe are distinct tradable goods. Yet they are also stores of value. Each can be converted into the other because they all share a common characteristic even though they have different functions. The divisibility, durability and portability of precious metals means that these metals are especially good for storing value. So much so that this characteristic eventually emerges as the principal use of these metals. At the same time, the metallic coin serves as a metaphor: A stands in relation to B as B stands in relation to C. It also, even more powerfully, serves as a proportionate metaphor: one unit of A (a cow) stands in relation to ten units of B (coins) as ten units of B (coins) stands in relation to three units of C (axes). The work of producing one cow is equated to the work of producing three axes.

The analogical conversions do not stop there. For a paper note may become an analog of the metal coin. As paper is even more portable than metal, it is also more convenient. Around such metaphorical conversions [metal:store of value:paper; cow:coin::coin:axe] are built positive institutions. A society might agree as a matter of positive legislation that paper money has to be redeemable by precious metals. A society might also agree to sever the legislated link between paper money and precious metals such that the analog between them is no longer considered a likeness but rather a practical equivalence such one (fiat paper) eventually replaces what it resembles (precious metal).

Patterns, like analogies, convert unlike things into likenesses. This applies not just to money. Modern societies have four prime self-organizing systems: markets, industries, cities and publics. In each of these, patterns equate what otherwise cannot be equated. These kinds of 'equations' tacitly determine choices in large-scale self-organizing systems. Take the example of where people choose to live. Location is key to cities in the way that innovation is key to industries. Aristotelian ratios are a kind of pattern thinking. They apply not only to commercial exchanges in the ancient polis but to contemporary persons in modern mega-cities trying to work out where to live. A modern application of A:B::B:C is Work-to-Home:Home-to-Shopping::City-to-Next-Comparable-City:City-to-Weekend Retreat, as in 60 minutes travel:10 minutes travel::240 minutes:40 minutes = 6:1::6:1. This is a tacit comparability. No one calculates this explicitly. But like so many self-organizing calculations, it is done intuitively, in the faculty of the imagination. Patterns equate what otherwise cannot be equated. This is what the human imagination does. It makes lightning-fast tacit conversions.

Markets, industries, cities and publics

Modern capitalism involves not one but several systems of capital. The most commonly cited is market capitalism. This system is steered by profit-and-loss. If actors in the marketplace, principally businesses, do not make a profit, they eventually perish. The interaction of profit-and-loss, like the closely related antipodal mechanism of supply-and-demand, has a remarkable clarity about it. That said, market capital is not the only prime kind of capital. There is also ingenuity, or innovation, capital. Its axiological pivot is efficiency-and-waste. Technological advances improve efficiency and reduce costs.[7] Technologists are often indifferent to the profit motive but highly attuned to reducing inputs while increasing outputs. The latter indirectly generates profits or avoids losses, sometimes far in advance of ordinary everyday market capitalism.

A third kind of capital is location capital. Cities represent the most intense form of location capital. Their axiological pivot is improvement-and-decay. Improvement is not the same as profit, even though it can yield substantial capital gains. A lot of the capital in a city is tied up in owner-occupied domestic housing. For the most part these units are not businesses. The value they represent to their owners is their improved value, namely their aesthetic qualities, ranging from comfort, ease and pleasantness to picturesqueness and beauty. The capital value of non-commercial dwellings and buildings can increase or decrease. Often, this happens cyclically as neighborhoods rise and fall and rise and fall in value. Against this larger rhythm of place, the improved value of an individual dwelling can be diminished or retained over time or added to or depreciated according to the efforts of owners. In addition to market, industry and location capital, there is a fourth kind of capital, semantic capital. Its axiomatic pivot is not profit-and-loss, efficiency-and-waste, improvement-and-decay but rather meaning-and-noise.[8] Societies accumulate meaning; they also fritter it away with antipodal noise. Publics fluctuate between significance and insignificancy.

As well as price systems and technology systems, modern societies generate spontaneous order through location systems and semantic systems. Each of these permit swift action at a distance. In contrast, whether they are neo-patrimonial or procedural in character, states operate through hierarchies. These encourage action that is 'close to hand'. Authorities allocate resources and give permissions. Accordingly, approval to access a service is frequently defined in terms of spatial nearness. A child can be enrolled in a public school in the 'close-to-home' zone A but not in the 'further-from-home' zone B even though the quality of schools in zone A are poor compared to those in zone B. A tariff—which is a tax on goods—is applied to goods that come from overseas but not to those produced locally. Public patients are approved to use a provincial or national healthcare service, but they will not be rebated for their expenses if they go to an international provider to avoid waiting times or service queues or to benefit from an equivalent or better standard of care at a cheaper price.

In modern societies, millions of people combine in anonymous systems using patterns, forms and shapes rather than organizational directives, rules and procedures. For classrooms, there are reading publics. For firms, there are markets. For urban planning, there are self-organizing cities. For hospital organizations, there are lean waste-reducing patterns of interaction. When we think of a social organization, we typically mean a body that issues instructions or commands, procedures or plans, with the view of achieving some goal. Companies and firms, armies and states, universities and hospitals, political parties and pressure groups are commonplace examples of purposive organizations.[9] They direct behavior with the hope of achieving stated ends. Self-organizing systems, in contrast, do not direct behavior. Nor do such systems have defined ends. They are not purposive. Rather, they generate order. They create and observe aesthetic-like patterns.

A state, any state, all states—including modern democratic governments—are organizations. As such, they are purposeful. They set goals. All state action supposes that the goals of the state, what it plans, will be achieved. Intention and consequence, aim and outcome, are perfectly aligned. This fallacious assumption is the basis of Shakespearean comedy and tragedy. No matter how often the fallacy is pointed out, it seduces human belief. Voters and pressure groups in modern mass liberal democracies routinely confuse intention and outcome. The will to believe that some dime-a-dozen plan represents a definitive result is intense. Voters readily believe governments or parties when they promise that they can 'create jobs' or 'increase growth'. Pressure groups lap up the same magical thinking. They want to hear from the government that the state can 'step in' and 'save' firms or industries when an economy is performing poorly. This is a psychological mirage. No amount of government intervention, spending or subsidy can overcome the implacable cycles, ratios and power laws of a modern economy that work 'behind the backs' of all purposive actors in society.

Modern societies mix self-organization and other-direction. Sometimes, other-direction helps self-organization. Classic examples are when states enforce free contracts or the freedom of the seas. But, being purposeful organizations, states also overreach. As do firms and universities, councils and hospitals. Purposive organizations like to manage things. They operate via instructions, commands, rules and codes. They try and substitute these for the pattern-driven self-organization. But they cannot replace autopoietic systems. The idea of limited government is a way of conceptualizing this. It supposes not simply that governments have defined purposes but that even these defined purposes are limited by the ordered liberty of self-organizing social systems.

Notes

1 Menger, 1985 [1963/1883], books 3 and 4.
2 Hayek, 1973, 39–40.
3 Hayek, 1973, 76–77.
4 Aristotle, chapter 5.
5 The long-term evolution of the model of justice-as-proportionality is described in Murphy, 2001.
6 Murphy, 2012, 80–82.

7 Here, I part company with the Austrian School of Economics. It stresses that prices are established through subjective value. It is true that markets allow subjective value-judgements ('do I think this product is good value?') to establish prices. Yet in addition to markets, there are also industries, as Joseph Schumpeter stressed. This means that there is the potential of industry innovations (technological and organizational innovations) to simultaneously reduce costs and improve the quality of production, leading to a reduction in prices. Market competition applies pressure on producers to innovate. Yet there are also internal entrepreneurial drives within industries to find ingenious ways of increasing efficiency. When these are successful the effect is paradoxical. There is a reduction in cost and an increase quality at the same time. The Austrian School of Economics (Carl Menger, Eugen von Böhm-Bawerk, Ludwig von Mises and Friedrich von Hayek) built on the subjective theory of value that was originally introduced by William Stanley Jevons, Léon Walras and Menger. The concept of an entrepreneurial industry began with Schumpeter's *The Theory of Economic Development* (1911) and culminated in his *Business Cycles* (1939) and *Capitalism, Socialism and Democracy* (1942). Schumpeter's legacy was carried on principally by business theorists, prominent among them Peter Drucker (the nephew of the Austrian legal theorist Hans Kelsen). Drucker's work is well represented in the collection *Innovation and Entrepreneurship*, 2015 [1985].

8 The philosopher G.W.F. Hegel accurately described public opinion as a mix of truth and endless error.

9 As a result, political parties lean towards economic mercantilism even if rhetorically they support free markets and industry innovation. This is because, as organizations, they are naturally sympathetic to organizations and are predisposed to view the world as a matrix of offices, positions, careers, allocations, benefits and hierarchies.

Bibliography

Aristotle. 2000 [c.340–350 BC]. *Nicomachean Ethics*. Cambridge: Cambridge University Press.

Drucker, P. 2015 [1985]. *Innovation and Entrepreneurship*. London: Routledge.

Hayek, F. 1973. *Law, Legislation and Liberty, Volume 1: Rules and Order*. Chicago, IL: University of Chicago Press.

Menger, C. 1985 [1963/1883]. *Investigations into the Method of Social Science with Special Reference to Economics*. New York: New York University Press.

Murphy, P. 2012. *The Collective Imagination: The Creative Spirit of Free Societies*. Farnham: Ashgate.

Murphy, P. 2001. *Civic Justice: From Ancient Greece to the Modern World*. Amherst, NY: Humanity Books.

Schumpeter, J. 2010 [1942]. *Capitalism, Socialism and Democracy*. London: Routledge.

Schumpeter, J. 1939. *Business Cycles*. New York: McGraw-Hill.

Schumpeter, J. 1983 [1911]. *The Theory of Economic Development*. New Brunswick, NJ: Transaction.

4 Social liberalism

Free-to-choose versus let-it-be liberalism

In the nineteenth century classical liberals supported low taxation, modest public spending and free trade. After 1850, though, the philosophical winds began to blow in the opposite direction. It would be another half century before states began what became in the course of the twentieth century a prolonged, deep and pervasive shift from small government to big government. Various philosophical currents contributed to this shift, including socialism and communism. In the long run, though, it was liberalism itself that most shaped state practice. It did so by turning its classic tenets into progressive ones.

In his *Principles of Political Economy* (1848), the liberal philosopher John Stuart Mill (1806–1873) observed that there are limits to government. The point to be determined, though, is where are the limits to be placed? Mill's answer to his own question would prove influential. When a government 'provides means of fulfilling a certain end', such as teachers for the purpose of general education, then so long as government leaves 'individuals free to avail themselves of different means', government intervention is defensible.[1] Mill did not address questions of the scale, efficacy, productivity or efficiency of such taxpayer-funded 'means'. What mattered was that individuals were free to choose non-government means if they so desired.

Classical liberals today assume much the same when they argue that if tax revenue is used to fund state schools then it also ought to be used to fund non-state (charter, religious or independent) schools or else provide vouchers to help parents purchase places for their children at non-government schools. Effectively, the limit of government is that government funds non-government alternatives to government services. This, though, implies no ceiling on government spending. It assumes no criteria for the efficiency or effectiveness of government spending. It ignores the question of the level of productivity of government-funded activity, be it private or public. It does not ask what happens to an economy when taxpayer funds are invested in low-productivity occupations rather than high-productivity ones. It poses no questions about whether the raising of tax revenue becomes so large a percentage of a country's gross domestic product that it causes the country's tax base to shrink. It does not ask itself whether government spending on the non-government sector in fact ensures only the most nominal limit on government.

In the 1840s, government intervention, Mill noted, was rare.[2] In no sense could he have imagined that 150 years later government spending on health, education and income-support would constitute the bulk of public spending. Nonetheless, Mill's *Political Economy* signaled a shift in classic liberal thinking. This change would be built on. Later nineteenth-century 'new liberals' of various kinds laid the philosophical groundwork for the left-liberal, social-liberal, progressive-liberal and radical-liberal currents that proliferated in the twentieth century. From T.H. Green in the 1870s to Lester Frank Ward in the 1880s and 1890s and John Hobson in the 1890s, social liberalism challenged classic liberalism. Social liberals backed the expansion of state compulsion (taxation) as long as Mill's criterion was satisfied and there were alternatives to state services. Those alternatives could be funded or subsidized by the state. As long as private schools, private hospitals and private retirement funds existed, irrespective of their size, scope or efficacy, social liberalism saw no problem in the relentless expansion of the public sector.

In contrast to the liberal democracies, Communist China and Soviet Russia opted for socialism, with debilitating consequences. Western economies adopted a mix of efficient markets and inefficient state services and grants. They substituted government regulation and subsidization for central planning. State socialism and bureaucratic capitalism competed with each other globally from the 1920s to 1980s. Due to the marked superiority of industrial capitalism, the state-socialist model eventually collapsed. China replaced its command economy with a system of authoritarian state capitalism. Russia adopted a mix of illiberal Caesarist democracy and oligarchic kleptocracy based on resource extraction.

Classic liberal ideas spread in the first half of the nineteenth-century. Liberal-progressive philosophies spread in the second half of the nineteenth century. Neither of these competing philosophical currents had much discernable impact on the fiscal make-up of major states in the nineteenth century. The size and scope of government remained tenaciously small through the ups-and-downs of philosophical taste and party choice (Table 1.1). So how much effect did any of these ideas really have?

The post hoc justification for social-liberal state expansion grew out of Mill's definition of liberalism. He argued that governments should not interfere with an individual's freedom to choose. The same principle of liberty was evident in the work of Adam Smith. Yet if we compare Smith and Mill, what we see is that Mill does not assume the ingenious principle of automaticity that Smith assumes. Smith presumed the principle that governments ought to leave the automaticity of society to work freely. Mill did not. 'Free-to-choose' was not the same as 'let-it-be' (*laissez faire*).

Mill's philosophy did not signal the end of models of the automatic society, by any means. Herbert Spencer in the 1850s through the 1880s and William Graham Sumner in the 1870s through the 1890s offered influential defenses of the modern type of self-organizing society. Nevertheless, by the end of the 1890s the popularity of such defenses was in decline. From the 1890s through the 1970s there was also a lot of talk about socialism. Most intellectuals during this period favored some vague kind of socialism. Few, though, went beyond nebulous nostrums. They talked hazily about 'nationalizing' businesses or government 'planning'. The idea that government 'organization' should swallow self-organizing society spread widely. But it was the milder social-liberal version of this that had the greatest practical impact on Western political economies.

Long-dead economists

Social liberals—from Leonard Hobhouse in the 1910s to John Maynard Keynes in 1920s, 30s and 40s and William Beveridge and T.H. Marshall in the 1940s to John Kenneth Galbraith in the 1950s, 60s and 70s—shaped the dominant social philosophy of mid-twentieth-century Western states. Variants of classical liberalism (latterly called neoliberalism) competed with socialism, social liberalism and radical liberalism through the 240 years between 1770 and 2010. Yet how much did any of these philosophies drive events? To what extent did they generate significance rather than just noise? The nineteenth century is one giant experiment that helps answer this question. Most of the arguments for or against big-government fiscal largesse were already circulating in the 1800s. And yet public spending remained tenaciously modest and broadly constant across the nineteenth century (Table 1.1).

War and peace were the principal variables, with wars increasing state spending temporarily. Political party outlooks changed over time, but spending levels as a percent of GDP remained broadly static. In the Britain of the nineteenth-century, we had conservative governments that identified variously with free trade (Robert Peel), one-nation democracy (Disraeli), and laconic abstention (Lord Salisbury). Yet none of these twists and turns had much discernable impact on the fiscal sociology of the state. Neither, for that matter, did Gladstone's Liberal Party. The mirror-reverse of this took place in the twentieth century. In the first two decades of the twentieth century, a quiet tectonic shift occurred. State spending suddenly 'took off'. From that point onwards it expanded repeatedly. Social liberalism provided handy post facto justifications for the growth of the state. But it is unlikely that such ideas in themselves caused the propulsive expansion of the scale and scope of government in the twentieth century. Deeper social and social-psychological forces were at work.

The era of big government begins during the two decades from 1900 to 1920. Why? One explanation is that various socialist, progressive and radical-liberal theories of society take hold at this historical juncture. As an explanation of events, this is a variation on Maynard Keynes' quip that 'practical men who believe themselves to be quite exempt from any intellectual influence, are usually the slaves of some defunct economist'. But while these theories provided after-the-fact rationalizations of new fiscal habits, the popularity of these theories is not necessarily an explanation of why small or big governments came to exist in the first place.[3]

Conversely, in the middle of the twentieth century there was a global revival of classic-liberal political economy. Many distinguished theorists were associated with this resurgence, notably Friedrich Hayek and Milton Friedman. Friedman proposed a 'neo-liberal' state. This was Locke's liberal night-watchman state with several functions added. The state, Friedman argued, had responsibilities to ensure free competition (by outlawing monopolies), the relief of acute misery and distress, and the elimination of the private creation of money (by monopolizing the provision of money in the interest of a stable monetary system).[4] The state accordingly should not seek to replace self-regulating markets. The price system efficiently coordinates the activities of millions of people. It cannot replace this elegant tacit autopoietics with planning, direction and regulations without causing substantial harm.

Liberalism in the twentieth century, Friedman rightly observed, had come to mean the opposite of what it had meant in the nineteenth century.[5] Social liberals, he acknowledged, wanted to do good. But their intentions repeatedly led to bad consequences. Liberal-progressive big government had become subject to the rule of negative paradox. By seeking to alleviate visible short-term harms it routinely caused serious but less visible long-term social injury. That said, the neoliberal revival had only a relatively modest impact on the long-term size of government spending. It mildly decreased the scale of government spending, decade on decade: in the US in the 1990s and 2000s; the UK in the 1980s and 1990s; Germany in the 2010s; Australia in the 1990s and 2000s (Table 1.1).

Liberty and providence

So what happened in the first two decades of the twentieth century to create a major shift in society's tacit fiscal ethos? Why did we go from a century of fiscal restraint to one of fiscal largesse? Why did philosophical arguments that didn't work in the 1870s and 1880s suddenly start to work in the 1900s and 1910s? Possibly, progressive liberals and social liberals got better at making their case. But this implies a voluntarist view of society that supposes that government behavior is set in motion by powerful ideas. If that was the case then we would have seen a much greater rolling-back of the size of the state in the neoliberal decades of the 1980s and 1990s. But in truth, the direction a modern society takes is less deliberate and more anonymous than the Keynesian 'long-dead economist' theory suggests.

Lord Salisbury, the great nineteenth-century British Prime Minister, expressed the matter in his typically pithy manner: 'You can no more act against the operation of great economic laws than you can act against the laws of the weather'.[6] By the beginning of the twenty-first century, social-liberals had decided that human beings, by using coal power, in fact could change the climate. They also thought that by spending billions in public subsidies on wind and sun power these climate changes could be averted. In the middle of the twentieth century, liberal-progressives typically objected to the idea that human beings dominated nature. A half century on, they thought that human beings did control nature. By this point, the progressive-liberal belief in voluntarism had reached boiling point. So much so that it became a common belief that governments could intervene to change global temperatures even though the most potent determinant of the earth's climate is the sun, over which human beings have no control.

The human desire to act against the laws of nature in the name of various kinds of anthropomorphism is strong. This is particularly true in the case of large-scale socio-historical laws. Modern societies and economies are organized around rhythmic cycles and periodical phases. These expand and contract. Societies move from agriculture to manufacturing to services and beyond. Populations shift from country to city to megacities. Periodicities of this type cause tensions that are palpable. Social patterns are recurrent. But such recurrence involves a paradoxical combination of continuity and change. Social patterns persist and repeat. But this persistence and repetition is accompanied by punctuations and periodic big shifts. Psychologically, these shifts generate dissatisfaction and grievance. This is because a portion of any population will see the visible negatives of a shift but not the longer-run less visible positives.

Those who recognize positives even amidst the pain of change have an intuitive grasp of natural law. These individuals have some sense of stoical cycles, predestination, fate, destiny, fortune and necessity. These various world views sum-up how individuals adapt well to the larger shifts that occur in societies. Stoicism, for example, says: act on what you can control; accept and adapt to what you cannot control. The mix of doing and adjusting helps people keep calm in the midst of chaos. It soothes and settles anxieties.

In the eighteenth and nineteenth centuries, limited-government advocates recommended a subtle mix of nature and freedom. Adam Smith imagined modern capitalism as a coalescence of freedom and the providential hidden-hand of the market. Frederic Bastiat similarly envisaged a mix of providence and liberty. Classicism and Christianity provided images of stoical, patient, resilient human beings. Both secular and religious thinking owed something to these images. Stoics are not passive individuals but, rather, prudential ones. They act on what they control and adapt to what they cannot control. Modern liberal-democratic societies are a mix of what is controllable and what is automatic. A person in an economic downturn cannot change the economic cycle. But they can move location from a region without jobs to one with jobs.

By the end of the nineteenth century, though, the nature–providence part of this equation was beginning to disappear.[7] In the middle of the nineteenth century, Karl Marx argued that capitalism was bad because it operated behind the backs of individuals, outside their control.[8] In Marx's own day this kind of argument largely fell on deaf ears. The notion that social actors could intervene to alter big-picture cycles and phases, however, started to take hold in the first decades of the twentieth century. It was not that the philosophical arguments for this were new (they weren't). Rather, the nature–providence component of the broader culture was in decline.

Consider, for example, the heated debates among American Calvinist Presbyterians around 1900 about how Calvinist they actually were.[9] Sharp division emerged over whether Calvinism was too fatalistic, whether the Augustinian doctrine that everyone was born in original sin was right and just how far the freedom of the will went. Parties devoted to the idea that salvation was determined in advance parted company with Presbyterians, who thought that salvation was more contingent on human action. On the surface this was an intellectual, in this case theological, battle. But it was also part of a larger attitudinal shift away from the notion that there were things in society that none of us controlled. The shift was echoed in intellectual debates but those debates themselves were expressions of the wider society drifting away from a providential toward a voluntaristic view of the world.[10]

The consequence of this shift was ironic. Rather than social actors feeling more in control, they began to feel less in control of the world. One of the advantages of the providential world-view is that if persons recognize that there are things they do not control, they are less apt to panic and run-amok. Their acceptance of their 'lack of control' leads paradoxically to a sense of 'greater control' over their own lives. A person cannot control whether an event like a recession occurs. But that person can calmly and realistically adapt to the event. Anxiety is a nebulous fear that we cannot control future events. By accepting the proposition that there are many events that we cannot control but we can abide, we reduce anxiety. Assuming we control events yet then finding that we don't control them only increases anxiety. A lack of control over what we wrongly think we control induces forms of psychological depression.

Naturally, some untoward events beyond human control cause suffering. But human beings can also prepare themselves for such suffering. They can imagine the uncontrolled events and rehearse the things that are in their control that allow them to adapt to, cope with or alleviate events they don't choose. Human beings don't will the climate or the weather. Rather, through storm and sunshine they adjust, bend, accommodate, fit, modify and acclimatize. All of this assumes a stoical demarcation between things we control and things we don't control. In the twentieth century, the urge to control grew. The stoical let-it-be decreased. As it did, the state grew. The enlarged state falsely promised control. It would intervene and fix things.

Notes

1 Mill, book V, chapter XI, 1848.
2 Mill, 1848, chapter 11, remarked that 'when a government, instead of issuing a command and enforcing it by penalties, adopts the course so seldom resorted to by governments … leaving individuals free to use their own means of pursuing any object of general interest, the government, not meddling with them, but not trusting the object solely to their care, establishes, side by side with their arrangements, an agency of its own for a like purpose.'
3 Friedman, 1993, asked whether ideas were perhaps not important, answered in this way: 'So ideas are important, but they take a long time and are not important in and of themselves. Something else has to come along that provides a fertile ground for those ideas.'
4 Friedman, 1951.

5 Friedman, 1955.
6 Roberts, chapter 17.
7 The use of the term 'providence' reaches a high point between 1640 and 1800, and 'fate' in the late eighteenth and early nineteenth century. Secular substitutes like 'social law' and 'destiny' escalate in use during the nineteenth century as does the religious term 'predestination'. The entire cluster of terms declines in use from the early twentieth century onwards. There are some exceptions like the term 'hidden hand' whose use increases through the twentieth century, but the relative incidence of the term or the like is miniscule. Google N-gram analysis.
8 'Just as in religion the spontaneous activity of the human imagination, of the human brain and the human heart, operates independently of the individual—that is, operates on him as an alien, divine or diabolical activity—so is the worker's activity not his spontaneous activity. It belongs to another; it is the loss of his self.' Marx, *Economic and Philosophical Manuscripts of 1844*.
9 Thuesen, 172–192.
10 This shift was strongly echoed in Talcott Parsons' 1937 study of social theory, *The Structure of Social Action*, which charted a transition from nineteenth-century 'positivistic' social theory to twentieth-century 'voluntaristic' models of society. In the former, individuals orientate themselves empirically; in the latter, self-expressively. Positivistic actions occur independently of individual sentiments while voluntarist actions pivot on them. The positivist outlook is receptive of and adaptive to empirical reality rather than seeking to control and will that reality. Positivism focuses on understanding, forecasting and adapting to society's nonsubjective conditions rather than transforming those conditions in line with subjective ends and values.

Bibliography

Friedman, M. 1993. "Why Government is the Problem." *Essays in Public Policy* 39.

Friedman, M. 2012 [1955]. "Liberalism, Old Style." in *The Indispensable Milton Friedman: Essays on Politics and Economics*, edited by L. Ebenstein, 11–24. Washington, DC: Regnery .

Friedman, M. 2012 [1951]. "Neo-liberalism and its prospects." In *The Indispensable Milton Friedman: Essays on Politics and Economics*, edited by L. Ebenstein, 3–10. Washington, DC: Regnery.

Mill, J.S. 1848. *Principles of Political Economy, with some of their Applications to Social Philosophy*. London: Longmans, Green.

Parsons, T. 1949 [1937]. *The Structure of Social Action*. Glencoe, IL: Free Press.

Roberts, A. 2012 [1999]. *Salisbury: Victorian Titan*. London: Faber and Faber.

Thuesen, P.J. 2009. *Predestination: The American Career of a Contentious Doctrine*. New York: Oxford University Press.

5 The anxious society

Providence and control

In the late eighteenth century, a historically distinct type of society emerged. It was built around a number of self-organizing pattern-based social systems, principally markets, industries, cities and publics. These extended human freedom markedly. They expanded the human capacity to exchange, invent, live and speak without direction. The power of hierarchies accordingly declined. The converse of this was that the scope of providential-like cycles and phases expanded. Markets, technologies, cities and opinions rise and fall and rise and fall. They are not linear or progressive but rather cyclical, looping and recursive. They rotate up and down and up and down (Table 2.1).[1] In the down phases come waves of social anxiety and pessimism.[2] With pessimism comes the assertion of the desire to control. Out the door goes stoicism; in the door rushes the will to regulate, direct, command and dictate.

The most visible 'down' eras are the recurring Kondratieff-wave-style economic winters.[3] Concern, fear, panic and depressed feelings accompany these decades. Deflation, high unemployment, bank failures and currency crises are typical of cyclical winter phases. Decade-plus periods of social instability, voluble discontent, political fracturing, populism, revolution, terrorism and the like follow pivotal low-points. 1785, 1836, 1893, 1929 and 2008 were classic lowlight years signaling sharp historical turning-points. Intersecting with this, at a still-deeper social level, is the unfolding of the stages of industrial society. The 1890s is illustrative. It was the interregnum between the railway age and the mass production era. The shift from agriculture to manufacturing and from country to city accelerated as the turn of the twentieth century approached. Structural shifts of this type—e.g. from primary to secondary industry and from rural to urban life—are part of the natural law of industrial societies. The stages of industry development, like the cycles of capitalist economies and the step-like rural–urban–conurban growth dynamics, work away in a largely automatic fashion. They create long-run prosperity out of short-term disruption. The periods of greatest stress coincide with the economic winter lows. These are politically charged points. They concentrate human pessimism.

Societies in the nineteenth century were not quiescent about the low points of economic cycles and developmental stages. There were revolutions, agitations, complaints and dissatisfactions. Yet for all that, the nineteenth-century state fiscally played a limited role in seeking to control society's cycles and phases. It made laws, provided courts and funded essential public infrastructure. But otherwise it did not generate a leviathan of departments and agencies in order to "make work" to try and reverse employment downturns. It did not pretend to be able to obviate large-scale cycles and structural transitions. Even socialists, including Karl Marx, expected the state to wither away. Instead, the reverse happened.

By the beginning of the twentieth century, in Western societies, the providential world-view had begun to slip away. What had once been common sense became uncommon sense. Providence, be it benevolent or injurious, stopped being assumed. The change was tacit and cultural. The effect of this on individuals was to encourage in them the belief that society was something external, alien and hostile. Against this hostile power, voters and citizens turned to the state. The state, it was thought, could intervene to ameliorate the workings of the natural laws of society. The new common attitude was that if prosperity dipped it was the business of government to 'fix things'. What this denied was that there were large-scale pattern-driven social systems that were self-fixing. This did not mean they were not disruptive or that at points in time they did not cause social stress. What it did mean was that pattern-based systems created long-term self-correcting pluses for each short-term minus they generated. In pattern systems, invisible cooperation ensues from visible competition as do public benefits from private interests. As the term suggests, patterns fuse contrasts and oppositions. Downturn is translated into upturn.

Persons have two basic ways of interacting. First, they can interact by following directions or rules that anticipate explicitly what they should do. These include orders, commands, instructions, regulations, statutes, decrees, imperatives and rulings that are generated in order to control and manage human action. In the twentieth century, as the state grew, the per capita volume of imperatives and rules increased vastly. This was a sign of the rise of what eventually became known as the managerial society.[4] Pre-industrial societies were dominated by personal hierarchies. These included tribal and patrimonial hierarchies of various kinds. Twentieth-century managerial society substituted impersonal bureaucratic hierarchies for the personal hierarchies of pre-industrial society. Personal authority was replaced by procedural authority. Councils were supplanted by committees. In another influential variant, the managerial society was fused with patrimonialism to create neo-patrimonial societies, outwardly industrial but inwardly dominated by patron–client relationships.

In between the decline of pre-industrial society and the rise of the bureaucratic society, pattern-based social systems (markets, industries, cities, publics) proliferated. These had historical precedents. As noted, mostly pre-industrial societies were built around personal hierarchies. But there were exceptions to the rule. The most important of these were cities. Exception cities substituted, to varying extents, pattern-based systems for personalized social hierarchies.[5] This did not mean that traditional order-giving or patron–client-style hierarchies disappeared from the exception cities. But the influence of personal hierarchies did diminish in places ranging from Athens and Rome to Venice and London. These encouraged or permitted strangers to interact using tacit patterns rather than explicit instructions. Classic examples of this were economies in which impersonal markets set prices rather than government legislating them. The ancient Athenian state controlled the trade in grains but otherwise the city's trade was relatively free. It is estimated that the volume of international trade in the Mediterranean grew 30-fold from the eighth to the fourth century BC. Long-distance trade is inter-state trade. Given that means multiple rule-jurisdictions, such trade can only grow significantly where tacit pattern interaction between buyers and sellers to a significant degree replaces rules or orders.

Pattern-based interaction generates unions of opposites. It melds contrasting behaviors such as short-term transactions and long-term relationships or personal trust and contractual business commitments. The strength of pattern-based interactions is their paradoxical or uncanny nature. Things that normally are set apart in ordinary social situations are unified in pattern-driven social systems. Impersonal trade is a mix of competition and cooperation. Sellers compete amongst themselves for buyers on the grounds of low price and high quality. Sellers in turn cooperate with buyers on the same grounds, thereby creating mutual benefit. Patterns are impersonal in the sense that they don't address anyone in particular. That is why they are effective in stimulating relations between people who don't know each other, namely strangers.

How do patterns coalesce competition and cooperation, low price and high quality? That is, how do they unify antitheses? They sympathetically meld contraries into unities through media such as symmetry, ratios and proportions. These are the natural laws of society. They are 'natural' in the sense that they are present in nature as well as society. They are 'laws' in the sense that they are chiefly responsible for automaticity in both nature and society. Principally, they organize relations between contrary qualities: they interlace big and small, abundance and lack, addition and subtraction, alike and forbidden, argument and agreement, background and foreground, beginning and ending, building and destroying, buying and selling, certainty and probability, cooperation and competition, change and constancy, compulsion and volition, danger and security, distance and nearness, enemies and friends, exports and imports, speed and slowness, future and past, planting and harvesting, lending and borrowing, lightness and heaviness, breaking and mending, artifice and nature, occasionally and frequently, outside and inside, poverty and wealth, quiet and noisy, rest and work, rural and urban, sending and receiving, sick and healthy, success and failure, unity and division, violence and gentleness, whole and part.

There are two basic prevailing attitudes in modern societies. One says that we must 'intervene' in order to 'fix' problems. The second says, 'no, leave it alone, it will fix itself.' The argument here is not that only one of these matters. There is a time and place for intervening. There is also a time and place for leaving things be. As Aristotle observed, society is animated by two complementary principles: action and contemplation. Sometimes, we do have to fix things. Sometimes, things are self-fixing. Melding the two requires an understanding of their symmetry and their right proportion. Action and contemplation are a subset of a much larger set of ambidextrous qualities that, when well integrated, constitute the background ticking clock-work mechanism of a modern society. The ability to artfully combine work and rest, cooperation and competition, distance and nearness, and so on, is crucial to high-functioning societies. The more that this occurs quasi-automatically, the more fluidly these societies work.

Automaticity is key to the emergence of the modern autonomous society. Most societies in human history have been, and continue to be, heteronomous. They are organized around various kinds of personalized social hierarchies. These include tribal, patrimonial, charismatic and neo-patrimonial kinds. This way of thinking about society is deeply entrenched in the human psyche. It has remained so in the modern age. But the modern era also saw the rise of a series of exceptional societies. These gravitated toward autonomy at both the individual and collective level. At the individual level, they encouraged human independence and self-reliance. At the collective level, they looked to large-scale social automaticity. The latter was a lithe way of organizing vast numbers of individual micro-choices and decisions into large-scale social systems. Cities, markets, industries and publics aggregate and coordinate innumerable free decisions by patterning them. These systems orchestrate, via the 'natural laws' of ratio and proportion and the like, the contrary demands and pressures of insiders and outsiders, importers and exporters, producers and consumers, inventors and copiers, and so on.

Natural laws are complemented by positive laws. Positive laws are those 'discovered' by courts or laid down by parliaments and other law-making institutions. Markets and industries, cities and publics operate within such legal frameworks. These specify certain conditions of operation. Notably, laws forbid social actors to use force or fraud in their interactions. They require persons to keep their lawful promises, and so on. The principal function of positive law is to reduce the impediments to the natural systems of ordered liberty. As Lord Salisbury observed, 'all Parliament can really do is to free the energies and support the efforts of an intelligent and industrious people'.[6]

But even such legal principles are broad and abstract in nature. They don't try and anticipate any particular concrete course of action. This is quite different from administrative regulation. As the state grew in the twentieth century, so grew the desire for regulatory control. This control principally took the form of rules made by bureaucracies and advocated by lobbies (Table 1.2). Bureaucratic regulatory rules try to be omniscient in detail. They try and anticipate everything that might possibly go wrong in human action at the micro level. Such forward-looking omniscience is doomed to failure. It ends by smothering human energy and wasting social time. Heteronomous societies gravitated towards instructions and orders. Twentieth-century managerial societies, in contrast, leaned heavily towards rules and procedures. Rules are created with the intention of correcting perceived problems. But rules lack the fluidity and litheness of the 'natural laws' of ratio, proportion, symmetry and the like. The latter are continuously adaptive. Rules, in contrast, are inert. As time passes, they increasingly become obstructive. They frustrate and hinder productive human activity. The bureaucracies that create rules often claim an all-seeing knowledge. But in practice such knowledge is far from omniscient. No rule can possibly anticipate all future circumstances and eventualities. Rules are concrete and thus inflexible. 'Natural law' is abstract and thus lissome. It adapts to unforeseen circumstances, allowing action to remain svelte, limber, lively and nimble. It readily accommodates unknown persons acting in unforeseen ways in unanticipated circumstances.

But the obvious retort to this is: no one is in charge. No one is controlling outcomes. No one is codifying what will happen. No one is planning the future. No one is directing events. No one is intervening in the course of human affairs to make things better. All this automaticity happens 'behind the backs' of individuals. It operates independently of each specific individual as it aggregates and coordinates the preferences of all individuals by sorting them into patterns. The competitive person is obliged to cooperate and the cooperative person is prompted to compete. To the degree that this patterning of action occurs independently of each individual, it is alienating (according to its critics). Today, the value of a currency moves downwards favoring exporters and disfavoring importers. A year later, the pattern reverses. Importers are favored. This swinging up and down is not a function of any specific individual but rather of the micro-decisions of millions of unknown persons. Their free will produces patterned necessities: waves, cycles, rotations, phases, and so on. The purchasing power of a currency represents the proportionate strength of the economies of different countries at any given time. As central banks often have to admit, it is very difficult to artificially change the underlying real ratio of economic power that exists between countries. Intervening, to turn weakness into strength or else to water down a too-strong currency, is difficult to do successfully.

The alternative to intervention is observation followed by adaptation. 'Natural law' supposes that social actors in the first instance are observers. They look at social systems in the same way that an observer contemplates a work of art. They look at it in order to intuitively discern the implicit pattern of the work or system. The pattern may be coherent and legible. It may be incoherent and illegible. There are poor artworks just as there are poor social systems. Observers watch how various pertinent factors align, and the degree to which factors such as danger and security, speed and slowness, buying and selling, breaking and mending can be patterned in a way that satisfies and is intuitively plausible. Observers are not passive. They adapt to the patterns they see. They may be happy with the trade-offs between contrary factors. When they are less happy, they adapt. Adaptation is not intervention. As the value of a currency increases, the importer does not ask for exchange controls (rules) but rather understands that the higher the value of the currency, the higher the price of the goods imported, the fewer the goods sold, and so the need to temporarily reduce or diversify the importer's business until the currency pendulum swings in the other, more favorable, direction. Like a diaphragm, the importer's business shrinks and expands.

The observation–adaptation model of social action began to fall into disfavor in the late nineteenth century. This was bound up with a growing discomfort with the pattern-order of modern autonomous societies. New heteronomous social models emerged in competition with the autonomous society model. There was the totalitarian cluster (Communism, Fascism and National Socialism), a neo-patrimonial cluster, as well as neo-antediluvian theocracies, oligarchies and tyrannies. Alongside all of these were the variants of the managerial society. The latter was organized hierarchically. But unlike other kinds of heteronomous societies that pivoted on personalized hierarchies, the managerial model emphasized impersonal rules and procedures. Policies replaced instructions; committees supplanted patron–client relations; qualifications emerged in place of loyalty; expert knowledge of rules superseded personal connections.

Most twentieth-century societies were either totalitarian, neo-patrimonial or neo-antediluvian in character. Some influential exceptions were in varying degrees autonomous societies. From the late nineteenth century onwards, though, autonomous societies faced the question: to what degree might they transform into managerial societies? Autonomy was attractive in principle. In practice, though, ambivalence grew. This ambivalence was not just intellectual. It was cultural. It percolated through society as a whole. It was expressed in the accelerating late nineteenth-century divestiture of previously influential religious concepts of providence and destiny and their semantic overlap with concepts of foresight and prudence, economy and frugality. The mix of foresightedness, discernment, thrift, moderation, saving, fortune, necessity and predestination began to crumble. In its place arose an increasing emphasis on ideas of voluntarism and planning. Rather than pattern-driven social action, forethought turned to goal-driven actions and setting out rules that organized behavior into sequenced planned steps.

Neurasthenic society

The remarkable Bourbon Democrat, Grover Cleveland, was twice elected US President during the long downturn that stretched from the mid-1870s to mid-1890s. Cleveland battled tariffs and pork-barreling. He vetoed an astonishing number of rent-seeking Congressional laws. He was not alone in this either. The periods in office of the great conservative British Prime Minister Lord Salisbury (three times between 1885 and 1902) were distinguished by a deep skepticism about government utopias and an equally deep stoical confidence in the providential workings of markets and industries.

Modern economies are cyclical. They oscillate through long waves of economic upswing and downswing. When markets and industries contract, which they do periodically, there are two possible responses. One is for societies to hold their nerve while the economic cycle moves from winter to summer. The second is for the government to try and reverse the effects of downturns by expanding the state. The nineteenth century relied largely on strategy one, the twentieth century on strategy two. The definitive turning point occurred in the United States in 1932 when Grover Cleveland's spiritual successor, Al Smith, ran against Franklin Roosevelt in the Democratic Party primary. Smith lost overwhelmingly. He went on to be a rallying point for conservative Democrats opposed to Roosevelt's massive expansion of government spending, the New Deal.

In the twentieth century, fiscal conservatives were those who said: do not expand the state. It is already large enough. There are sufficient staff to carry out its key functions without adding more in real terms. The classic liberals of the nineteenth century argued for small government in an age when small government was taken for granted. In the twentieth century, liberals on the whole converted to social liberalism and identified with big government. A small number of principally conservative governments resisted this. Governments that arrested or reduced total government spending as a percent of GDP occurred only a handful of times in a century: during Calvin Coolidge's presidency in the 1920s; the Bill Clinton and George W. Bush years in the 1990s and 2000s; Winston Churchill's years as Chancellor of Exchequer in the 1920s Baldwin government; the Churchill–Eden era in the 1950s; Margaret Thatcher's premiership in the 1980s; Australia's Menzies government in the 1950s and John Howard's prime ministership in the late 1990s and early 2000s; and Germany's Merkel government in the 2010s (Table 1.1).

The conservative argument for limited government has two parts. First, reduced government spending increases economic growth. This requires also a conservative culture. Think of it this way: modern industrial economies are not progressive but rather cyclical. They oscillate up and down. Industries grow and decline, appear and disappear. Character allows individuals to adapt well to the cyclical ups and downs. Perseverance is necessary for the downcycles and initiative for the upcycles. Independence and self-reliance are the concomitant of limited government. The character traits of patience, forbearance, nerve, prudence and endurance are necessary for dealing with the inherent waxing and waning of modern economies.

The American Founders included 'the pursuit of happiness' as one of the three ends of government. They did so because the phrase signified all that was unbroken, sturdy, firm, stable, fixed, reliable, dependable and durable in human desire. It was John Locke who originally coined the phrase. In *An Essay Concerning Human Understanding*, he observed that the pursuit of happiness was the foundation of liberty. By happiness he meant the careful and constant pursuit of true and solid happiness. If we engage in that, he argued, we liberate ourselves from the tyranny of inconstant desires and random cravings. True and solid happiness makes us free. Conservative constancy, persistence, endurance and continuity is the key to liberty. Winston Churchill agreed. His motto was never give in.

What then changed in the forty years between Grover Cleveland's election in 1893 and Franklin Roosevelt's in 1932? Simply put, there was a general societal loss of nerve. In his 1911 book *Political Parties*, the German sociologist Robert Michels noted how in the era just before World War One the eudemonic spirit of the nineteenth century had started to recede in favor of those who made 'a profession of discontent'.[7] Some of these personality types are familiar from history: the demagogues, humbugs and charlatans. More interestingly though Michels also observed the growth in the number of 'neurasthenics' and *mauvais coucheurs*.[8] The former lacked the ability to cope with anything but trivial tasks. The latter were inclined to protest at the slightest hitch.

Neurasthenia was a catch-all nineteenth-century psychological term for anxiety, irritability and depression. It had clinical and social meanings. In Western societies, in the twentieth century, it fell out of favor as a clinical classification. But in countries like China it was retained. In any event, whether clinical terms were broad like 'neurasthenia' or more specific like 'mood disorders', 'anxiety', and 'depression'—and whether (like 'anxiety') these had an express social aspect or (like 'depression') they were biologically anchored terms,[9] the underlying condition of nervous *angst* became increasingly common in countries in the twentieth century as their GDP per capita grew.[10] Anxiety and/or depression became the era-defining diseases of the twentieth century. But just as crucial, accompanying medically defined anxiety and depression was a much broader, more diffuse spectrum of social anxiety. The great mid-twentieth-century poet W.H. Auden called his own era the Age of Anxiety.[11] There was a shift in the tenor of many of the most successful modern societies from happy to unhappy. Their dynamism generated stress, tension and nervousness. Over time, the need to placate social anxieties led to widespread compulsive eating, non-medical drug consumption and an addiction to public spending.

The most anxious society was also the most successful one: America. Unsurprisingly then, the term neurasthenia originated in the United States.[12] It was popularized by the American neurologist George Beard, who first used the term in 1869. It was the condition of persons who lacked sufficient 'nervous energy' to deal with the pace, growth, teeming and expectations of modern societies. Modernity made some people sick. It induced in them irritability, anxiety, depression, vertigo, indigestion, insomnia, lethargy and impotence.[13] It left them in a state of nervous exhaustion. Principally, Beard argued, this occurred amongst 'brain-workers'. It was a phenomenon of the desk, the pulpit and the counting-room. If tuberculous was the condition of the day-laborer, then nervy anxiety, Beard suggested, was the condition of the in-door knowledge worker.

Beard proposed multiple causes of this.[14] Among them were eating too fast, stimulants and narcotics, and stress. Opiates, the drug of choice a century before, induced sleep. These had been replaced by tea and coffee, which kept users awake. Then there was the use of watches. These compelled users to be 'on time' and excited the nervous habit of constantly 'checking the time'. Next, there was steam power, the telegraph and vastly increased long-distance travelling. These amplified the expanded pace and scale of life. Telegraphy transmitted information about big life-changing events around the world instantly. Through newspapers, the horrors and sorrows of one place suddenly became familiar everywhere. Big cities concentrated harsh, jarring sounds. Knowledge-work expanded as women entered the workforce as telegraphists and typists, the consequence of new technology. The stock-market innovation of buying on a margin intensified economic insecurity just as it multiplied the possibilities of enrichment. Then there were the cultural stresses. In modern life, accepted ideas turn-over with increasing rapidity. Promised discoveries, Beard quipped, keep millions of capital and thousands of capitalists in constant suspense and distress.

As modern life expands possibilities and horizons, so it does risks and disappointments. Persons can rise in position. Yet they can also fall or (often worse) imagine themselves falling. Modern ambition promises great advancement, yet with it painful striving, uncertain outcomes, agony and stress. Some embrace this with alacrity; others view it with alarm. The latter look for salvation from angst. This is not salvation of a religious after-life kind but rather redemption of a secular this-life kind. Worldly salvation comes in the form of all kinds of social security (safety, protection, care) provisioned by the state. This is often the result of a misunderstanding of the nature of modern freedom. At its core, modern freedom is paradoxical. Free persons make commitments that bind them. Their liberty ties them, obliges them and often necessitates them. They freely enter into contracts that they must honor. They choose vocations that last decades. They make statements that they are obliged to justify and argue for. They move far and wide in order to settle long and lastingly. This is what animates modern self-organizing markets, industries, publics and cities. This is quite unlike fretful liberation from anxious cares and concerns. Yet for many, the fundamental liberty that they seek is release from the inherent psychological stresses, burdens and worries of modern life.

If forethought is key to a modern civilization, then, in a world riddled with anxiety, thinking turns apprehensive. It dwells on terrible contingencies and ugly possibilities. The thought of 'what about tomorrow?' conjures images of starvation, impoverishment, devastation, apocalypse, destruction and catastrophe. As these become ever-less practical possibilities, they become ever-stronger mental images. Forecasting descends from statistical objectivity and becomes instead the anticipation of sorrow and distress. The future is lurid and miserable.

While some individuals are exhausted by modern life, Beard noted, others are exhilarated by it. The latter have surplus nervous energy. They seemed to go on endlessly, never fatigued. Others, in contrast, fret over trifles. As John Locke remarked, happiness requires delayed satisfaction and a tight rein on explosive emotions. As John Calvin postulated, it demands hard work and a sense of seeing things through in spite of difficulties. Those who are exhausted by modern life are susceptible to emotional outbursts. Similarly, the expectation of hard work is experienced by them as nerve-racking overwork. Life is experienced as vertiginous.

The social-psychological condition that Beard described 150 years ago sounds familiar. In the late nineteenth century, neurasthenia was also called 'Americanitis'. It was, in effect, an inflammation of the mind and body that America, the prototypical modern society, caused. By the time Michels wrote *Political Parties*, the coping mechanisms typical of eudemonic (happy) personalities were in decline, and not just in the United States. This trend accelerated over the next century. The personality traits of perseverance, persistence, tenacity, determination, tirelessness, the courage to continue and suchlike atrophied. Insecurity, anxiety and nervousness grew. With these came political movements trading in grandiosity and megalomania, the flip-side of insecurity. Even severe economic downturns began to be labelled after psychological depressions.[15]

As a critical mass of neurasthenic social psychology formed, states were asked to 'do more'. Already in 1911, Michels noticed a sharp increase in the demand for official positions. He attributed this to the 'ever-increasing precariousness in the position of the middle classes'.[16] The long downturn from the mid-1870s to mid-1890s was over. It was replaced instead by a lengthy period of economic and emotional fragility. The economics of the period, Michels noted, put a lot of pressure on 'smaller manufacturers and traders, independent artisans, farmers, etc.' The precariousness of their situation, though, was as much social-psychological as it was material. Growing social anxiety generated demands. 'All those whose material existence is threatened ... by modern economic developments', Michels noted, 'endeavor to find safe situations for their sons, to secure for these a social position which shall shelter them from the play of economic forces'. In response to such demands made by increasingly nervy populations, states began to offer an expanding pool of secure positions. Governments started to proffer salves and balms for ever-more edgy, jumpy and panicky national sensibilities. The underlying irony was that these same societies were enjoying a historically unprecedented level of per capita wealth. Paradoxically, greater prosperity induced wider-spread panicking. The demands of successful modernity induced in some, even many, a shift from calm to alarm. In others, the old eudemonic traits continued unchanged. Societies split between the happy and unhappy, the satisfied and dissatisfied, the composed and the agitated.

Neurasthenic behaviors are common in the culture today. On American college campuses we encounter a small army of phobic students agitating for 'safe places' and 'trigger warnings' to protect them from the slightest upset. Older self-help moral cultures have declined in influence. The threads of Augustinian, Thomist, Stoical, Epicurean or Aristotelian character are frayed. Thomas Jefferson's 'pursuit of happiness' has been replaced by an expectation that individuals will be 'insulated from anxiety'. Instead of patiently adapting to the inherent ups and downs of modern life, many people now instead get angry. Anger turned inwards (depression) leads to drug addiction. Anger turned outwards is an expression of powerlessness. As anxiety spirals, the elites, the political class, globalization, bankers, Jews, Mexicans, Chinese, past presidents, current senators (fill in the blanks) are wheeled out for ritual blame. Exclamation replaces argumentation. Fretful fulmination substitutes for calm justification.

George Beard observed of American-style democratic political campaigning that it appealed most to those of a nervous rather than eudemonic temperament. He underlined the point with an anecdote. Someone Beard had successfully treated for anxiety approached him. His ex-patient said that he was getting interested in politics. There 'are great issues before us,' the fellow exclaimed, 'and the neglect of politics on the part of intelligent men was the ruin of their nation.' To which Beard replied rather astutely, 'My friend, presidents and politicians are chips and foam on the surface of the sea; they are not the sea ... fold your arms and go to bed, and most of the evils of the world will correct themselves.'[17] Beard was spot on.

Notes

1 The dating of long waves, such as in Table 2.1, can only be approximate. By their nature, waves are super-positional. Each up or down wave-motion interpolates its opposite. Waves subsume multiple technology, investment, infrastructure and inventory cycles, each with their own up-down periodicity.
2 '...in downward phases of long waves, large groups of people display behaviour that can be interpreted as anxious and, conversely... this behaviour decreases when the wave rises.' Gaus, 42.
3 First conceptualized by the Russian economist Nikolai Kondratiev (1892–1938) who was executed in one of Stalin's purges.
4 Burnham, 1941.
5 Murphy, 2001.
6 Roberts, chapter 17.
7 Michels, 1968 [1911], 251.
8 Michels, 1968 [1911], 251.
9 Horwitz (2010: 121) describes how the diagnostic condition of 'anxiety', with social connotations related social stress and tension, was marginalized in the 1970s through the 1990s in favor of the biologically based condition of 'depression', due to the pressure of family lobby groups in the United States. 'Family advocacy groups became a major lobbying force in the [National Institute of Mental Health] ... These groups, like the National Alliance for the Mentally Ill, were primarily composed of family members with children suffering from severe mental illnesses. They lobbied the NIMH to shift its focus from broad social research to the study of the biological underpinnings of and treatments for specific mental disorders. These efforts culminated in a 1982 directive from Congress ordering the NIMH to stop its support of social research...'
10 Hidaka, 2012; Klerman and Weissman, 1989.
11 Auden, 1947. The poem was book-length. It was the inspiration for Leonard Bernstein's 1948/1965 work *The Age of Anxiety (Symphony No. 2 for Piano and Orchestra).*
12 Beck, 2016.
13 Schuster, 2011.
14 Beard, 1881.
15 The earliest use of the term 'economic depression' in the Google database of books occurs in Callender, 1909, an academic history of the American economy.
16 Michels, 1968 [1911], 188.
17 Beard, 1881, 124.

Bibliography

Auden, W.H. 1947. *The Age of Anxiety: A Baroque Eclogue*. New York: Random House.

Beard, G.M. 1881. *American Nervousness*. New York: Putnams.

Beck, J. 2016. 'Americanitis: The Disease of Living Too Fast', *The Atlantic*, March 11.

Burnham, J. 1941. *The Managerial Revolution*. New York: John Day.

Callender, G.S. 1909. *Selections from the Economic History of the United States, 1765-1860: With Introductory Essays*. Boston, MA: Ginn.

Gaus, H. 2001. *Why Yesterday Tells of Tomorrow: How the Long Waves of the Economy Help Us Determine Tomorrow's Trends*. Antwerp: Garant.

Hidaka, B.H. 2012. "Depression as a Disease of Modernity: Explanations for Increasing Prevalence." *Journal of Affective Disorders* 140, no. 3: 205–214.

Horwitz, A.V. 2010. "How an Age of Anxiety Became an Age of Depression." *The Milbank Quarterly: A Multidisciplinary Journal of Population Health and Health Policy* 88, no. 1: 112–138.

Klerman, G.L. and M.M. Weissman. 1989. "Increasing Rates of Depression." *JAMA: The Journal of the American Medical Association* 261, no. 15: 2229–2235.

Michels, R. 1968 [1911]. *Political Parties: A Sociological Study of the Oligarchical Tendencies of Modern Democracies*. New York: Free Press.

Murphy, P. 2001. *Civic Justice: From Ancient Greece to the Modern World*. Amherst, NY: Humanity Books.

Petrisor, M.B. and D. Lupu. 2012. "International Analysis of the Dynamics of Public Expenditure in Modern Society." *Journal of Accounting and Management* 2, no. 3: 97–105.

Roberts, A. 2012 [1999]. *Salisbury: Victorian Titan*. London: Faber and Faber.

Schuster, D.G. 2011. *Neurasthenic Nation: America's Search for Health, Happiness, and Comfort, 1869-1920*. New Brunswick, NJ: Rutgers University Press.

6 The managerial society

Intellectuals

Patronage appointments were a staple of pre-modern states. The nineteenth-century liberal state gradually replaced patrimonial with procedural bureaucracies. Robert Michels was a keen observer of this change.[1] Michels was a socialist but also a critic of bureaucracy. As such, he observed things about the new meritocratic bureaucratic state that others overlooked. Notably, that early in twentieth century it began to create a new class of 'intellectuals'. It started to hire staff to help in its own 'self-defense', recruiting employees to work on what Michels in 1911 tellingly called 'the legend of the state'.

The word 'intellectual' only comes into wide usage in English after 1900. What turn-of-the-century governments did, in effect, was to create a new apparatus to publicize, market, defend, promote, analyze, report on, certify and document the state. Eventually, these legend-makers migrated to the state-funded post-industrial health and education sector. By the middle of the twentieth century, this broader public sector had begun to proliferate alongside government. By the end of the century, the legend-makers made-up a sprawling class devoted to policy, management, consulting, advocacy, strategy and analysis in a range of government, quasi-non-government, public sector, corporate, industry, association, arts and think-tank bodies. They worked for pollsters, electoral offices, political campaigns and lobbyists—touting ideas, peddling influence and seeking to leverage the state and shape public opinion. The members of this class were not classic *philosophes*. Yet neither were they just white-collar workers. Rather they were something in between.

The legend of the state has many authors. Even so, demand for these jobs always exceeds the supply. As a consequence, Michels observed, society ends up with two classes of intellectuals. There are those who succeed in securing public employment and undertake to defend the state. Then there are those on the outside who became by default the 'sworn enemies' of the state. Today, you find many of these outsiders with web blogs and Twitter accounts, on opinion sites or doing PhDs. This class is restless. Its members habitually criticize and carp. They are exponents of outrage, anger, affront, incense, annoyance and indignation. At least they are until they get lucky and finally receive a good public post or a comfortable slot in the pressure-and-influence industry. Michels pointed out the paradox that this implies. The managerial state continually increases. Yet it can never expand as rapidly as the discontented elements of the middle class want it to.

The larger the public sector gets, the less compatible it is with the general welfare. Yet it alone can promise secure positions for educated members of the anxious middle classes. This implies a vicious circle. More so for the fact that the state in the main now also educates the children of the middle class. In doing so, it tacitly pledges that this education will end in a good job. Yet, periodically, this promise is doomed to fail. In essence, what it entails is a state-run Ponzi scheme. Whenever this scheme falters, the intellectual proletariat gets in a rage. This happened in 1968 with the international student revolt. It repeated itself in 2011 with the Occupy movement. The latter was populated by individuals with large student debts and poor middle-class career prospects. In 2016 in the United States the same social group flocked to Senator Bernie Sanders' Democratic presidential campaign rallies. Their anger was soothed by Sanders' promises of nationalized health care and gratis college tuition.[2] These further entailed an implicit promise of endless jobs in an ever-larger, never-costed, infinitely benign public health-and-education industry.

The roots of this are long and deep. State expansion after 1900, or in Germany's case after 1890, (Table 1.1) was part of a larger social development. This might be best described as the spread of the ideology of managerialism. One of the earliest and best observers of this phenomenon was the American philosopher James Burnham. In *The Managerial Revolution* (1941) through to *Suicide of the West* (1964) Burnham charted the emergence of a new status-power class. This class flourished by messaging rather than markets and by politicking rather industry. From 1910 to 2010, the state in key societies expanded massively. As it did, the mechanisms for lobbying, grants and allocations also expanded dramatically. The economic weight of occupational and business licensing, government contracting, and subsidization of uncompetitive businesses expanded. The terms and conditions for the private use of public resources multiplied. Private goods were increasingly treated as public goods. Income from government tax, pooling and allocation began to compete as a percentage of GDP with income from work, savings and investment. As this occurred, the number and size of politically connected rent-seeking businesses and organizations grew, both as a cause and an effect of the expanding state.

Top-decile inequality followed in train. As the French social-democratic economist Thomas Piketty has noted, those who have contributed most over time to the volume of top-decile asset accumulation have been organizational supermanagers.[3] This class is found not only in companies but in all social sectors, including big universities, big charities, big government, etc., not to forget the revolving door between these. The status-power class has evolved not only on the basis of supersized income and assets but also even more crucially on the basis of shared values, attitudes, tastes, mating, marriage and the ideology of managerialism. These latter factors were as important for the creation of this politically connected, group-bonded, rank-obsessed, status-power class as was money.

At first glance, it might appear that modernity favours ties of money and finance rather than status and rank. But, in fact, status hierarchies have remained remarkably persistent in the face of the cash nexus. That is not to say that money is not important to the managerial power class. Yet so is status. The status of this class is not defined by inheritance or bloodline nor by virtue or deeds. Nobility, honesty, integrity, courage or prudence play little role in the way it validates itself. Rather, its status is defined by education. It claims to 'know more' than others do. It asserts that it is smarter, shrewder and cleverer than other social classes. Which might also be a way of saying that it is slicker, glibber and more superficial than other classes. This is because status-defined intelligence is a kind of brightness that is directed to securing a cognitively defined social ranking rather than the genuine fruits of discovery and inquiry.

Education, especially higher education, is the status marker of the managerial power class. Rank is defined by the status of the university that a person has attended and the level of university degree that person has attained. Postgraduate degrees of all kinds are favoured by the managerial power class. Its members marry individuals of a similar educational background. At university, the status-power class adopts shared tastes, attitudes and values. The dominant value-set is a mix of procedural rationalism and rhetorical progressivism. The first represents organizational power; the second, social power. Its technique is to find progressive arguments for regulations and allocations that enhance its power. Regulation and allocation are utilitarian in nature. But because it is status-driven, the power class has a strong need to wrap its claims and demands in sweeping progressive verbalisms.

The status-power class espouses predominately left-liberal ideas. This is hardly surprising, as its well-being depends on politicking rather than on markets or other self-organizing social systems. What is crucial to it is its capacity to extract, from the state, restrictive licenses to operate, tariffs and other barriers to competition, friendly regulations, tax exemptions, monopolies, subsidies, grants and budgetary allocations. In simple terms, it pursues various kinds of crony capitalism. The principal political technique of the managerial class is to lobby and pressure the state. The desired effect is to channel tax revenue into subsidies, grants and allocations for businesses and organizations—both public and private—and to create, via regulation, procedural barriers to new, less-well-funded, competitors succeeding. Over time as big government has expanded the scale and scope of regulation, the beneficiaries have been big business, big universities, big hospitals and the like.

The proliferation of elaborate procedures and rules lies at the core of the ideology of managerialism. In turn, a paradox lies at the heart of the status-power class. It applauds the idea of impersonal power. It claims forthrightly that it acts in the name of rules, policies, regulations, guidelines, standards, directions and the like. Yet its power is built on expansive hierarchies. These, it claims, are models of impersonal power. These are, rightly enough, legal-rational in design. Yet what is evident on closer inspection is the highly personal nature of these impersonal procedural pyramids. For unlike self-organizing systems, which rely to a very significant degree on the interaction of strangers, hierarchies, including procedural hierarchies, unavoidably involve personal ties between superiors and subordinates. Commands or instructions may be disguised as policies and rules. They may be wrapped up in awkward pseudo-impersonal language. Loyalty to superiors may be old hat. But the personal connection remains ineluctable. Thanatocratic bureaucracies in genocidal states illustrate the extreme of this. Instructions are carried out bureaucratically ('I was just following orders') but the malicious hierarchs give permission to underlings to do horrible things, unleashing the inner demons of subordinates.

Observation versus intervention

Economic and moral independence, personal industry, self-formation and self-mastery are keys to successfully enduring the wave-like character of modern economies. That, at least, was the commonplace view in dynamic societies in the nineteenth century. A new, contrary, attitude began to form in the early twentieth century. It held that the key to social well-being was not independence but rather procedural intelligence or planning. This vision propelled the growth of government. In the hope of organizing society, the state hired, or else subsidized, knowledge, expertise, qualified staff, university graduates and brain trusts. It employed increasing numbers of symbol-wielding functionaries. Their job was to produce justifications, defenses, evaluations, strategies and rationalizations of state action and public-sector organization. They crafted programs that then employed burgeoning numbers of white-collar and pink-collar workers.

Along with this grew conceit. The swelling knowledge class convinced itself that it knew things that could save the world. Promising redemption and deliverance does not make for modesty. Over time, the knowledge class became increasingly self-important, smug, vain and superior. Society paid a price for its conceit. For the knowledge class, in fact, knew considerably less than it claimed. The depression years of the 1930s illustrate this. Between Calvin Coolidge's last full year in office (1928) and Franklin Roosevelt's second year in office (1933), government in America grew 250 percent. The more conservative British grew government by less than 10 percent in the same period (Table 1.1). The relative merits of this are clear. Double-digit unemployment lasted in America till 1940; in the UK, till 1936. Peak-to-trough output declined in the US by a precipitous 46 percent; in the UK by 16 percent. In the 1930s, US public spending as a share of GDP was massively less than the UK. It would not 'match' the UK until the years of the Obama presidency. Yet no big leap in peace-time government spending—whether it was Hoover and Roosevelt in the late 1920s to early 1930s, the Eisenhower–Kennedy–Johnson surge in the 1960s or the Obama-era spurt—averted the economic winters of the 1930s, 1970s/early 1980s and 2010s. Still, the lack of efficacy of greater spending did not diminish voter belief in its power. If anything, the poorer it performed the more individuals trusted in its talismanic power.

The underlying reason for this was cultural. The *laissez-faire* notion that modern societies function best when they function autonomously declined visibly after 1900. An aversion to in-built social automaticity grew. John Dewey summed up this atmosphere in his 1922 lectures on *Experience and Nature*.[4] America's foremost progressive philosopher, Dewey was a subtle, probing thinker. Like a litmus-test paper, he registered the metaphysical shift of outlook that took place in liberal democracies after 1900. He dubbed the attitude of the autonomous society 'aesthetic'. He attributed the origin of the 'aesthetic' world-view to the ancient Greeks.[5] This was the point-of-view of the observer rather than the interventionist. The old liberalism of the nineteenth century had been contemplative, he argued. The new liberalism of the twentieth century thought it obligatory to intervene in the world rather than simply observe it and adapt to it. Dewey defined the difference between the old and new liberalism in terms of their attitudes to design. In the new liberalism, design was thought of as the conscious aim of society rather than the expression of society's objective order and architectonic form.[6]

The old liberalism of the nineteenth century was self-consciously modern. Yet its respect for society's autonomous self-organization meant that its defense of individual liberty, choice and decision was tacitly built on the 'aesthetic' outlook of the patient observer who chronicled society's natural oscillating ups and downs. Nineteenth-century liberalism retained a tacit sense of society as an objective order independent of any specific individual or organized group of individuals, not least the state.[7] The aesthetic order of economy and society arose from pattern-forms that echoed deep-set nature-like self-organizing capacities.[8] Economic and social patterns grew out of the 'aesthetic-like', forming, shape-giving wellsprings of symmetry, proportion, ratio, rhythm, cyclicality, capillarity, clustering, meshing, oscillating, waving, counterbalancing, equilibrating, scaling, fractal repetition, similitude, homology, homomorphism, affinity, aggregation, banding, layering, modularity, branching, switching, curving, quantum superpositioning, knots, nodes, flows, grids, nets and the like. Art, society and nature alike embody these fundamental structuring principles. Such pattern-principles are invisible simplicities that set in motion visible complexities. They are 'beyond change' in the sense that they are the kind of durable structural principles that generate dynamic motion when applied to modern industries and cities, markets and publics. These ordering principles are also 'beyond change' in the sense that they are fundamental mechanisms of nature as well as society or art.

In contrast to the objective order of the adaptive observer, the new progressive liberalism of the twentieth century emphasized 'conscious aims constructed and entertained in individual minds independent of nature'.[9] The attention paid to 'conscious aims' was crucial. This was not only the dividing line but also the semantic bridge between the old liberalism and the new liberalism. Nineteenth-century liberalism expressed a powerful sense of the individual unencumbered by old pre-modern hierarchies. Accordingly, the liberal individual had subjective tastes, values and preferences and freely made decisions based on these. Massed together though, these subjective preferences slotted into objective systems. The systems were objective in the sense that they sorted and arranged millions of preferences in a coherent way. They did this via an intuitive aesthetic economy that on the whole artfully reconciled the competing demands of individuals for large and small, fast and slow, cheap price and high quality, near and far, quiet and noisy. At the core of this lay mechanisms that were more tacit than conscious. Individuals are drawn to things that implicitly are 'beautifully' arranged. Obliquely and subliminally they turn away from what looks or feels 'ugly' or 'disproportionate' or fit no 'ideal ratio'.

Liberal progressives emphasized conscious planning. They believed in the deliberate organization of means to achieve explicit ends. These ends are what John Dewey called 'ends-in-view'. Once an 'end-in-view' is secured, intellectuals define new ones. This structure of behavior is progressive and linear. It moves in a straight line endlessly upwards and onwards toward the future, securing evermore ends-in-view. But this assumes that societies in fact move in a straight line. Yet what if they don't? What if they move in a cyclical or rotating fashion? This does not necessarily mean that they don't advance. Rather it means that advancement involves backwards as well as forwards movement. Expansion entails contraction, and contraction unleashes expansion. In short, society and history are double coded. They are ambidextrous.

Jean Charles de Sismondi in his *Nouveaux principes d'économie politique* (1819) observed the periodic ups and downs of market economies. The classic-liberal economist Charles Dunoyer turned this observation into a theory of economic cycles. Dunoyer concluded that economies are subject in a nature-like way to alternating phases of 'activity' and 'relapse'. The alternation of activity–relapse–activity–relapse is a good way of understanding the dynamism of modern societies. It is premised on the pendulum-like motion of forwards–backwards–forwards–backwards. This is not one 'end-in-view' (achieved) followed by another 'end-in-view' (to be achieved). Rather, cyclical motion assume limits. The up-phase of a cycle reaches a limit or terminus point. It then cycles down. And so on.

John Dewey thought that a person who accepted cyclical limits looked upon things much like an 'aesthetic' or contemplative observer does. The observer is someone who watches the rhythm of cycles, including economic and social cycles, yet makes no concerted or determined effort to change the cycle. Adapt to it, yes, but not change it. Adapt to winter or summer but not expect to change the seasons. Dewey argued that this attitude was typical of classical Greek social thinking. 'Modern' thought and behavior, he contended, was different. In the modern case, ends are not the termini of nature-like social processes. Rather they are the 'creation of private mental operations guided by personal desire'.[10] Such ends are not conclusions. They are not the 'telos' of human action. Rather they are goals that are projected so as to organize the means to attain those goals. The old-fashioned end (that is, the conclusion or limit) can only be possessed contemplatively, that is, by someone accepting that a boundary or limit or termination of human action has been reached. Who says, in effect, 'we can go this far but no further.'

One of the weaknesses of modern organizations is that they have difficulty recognizing limits. So in the case of a company, its market share or its profitability is projected always to increase; for a university, its enrolment will always grow; for a financial journalist, the share market will always do better. When these projections prove not to be true, then the reverse applies: everything is forecast to get worse in a linear manner, down, down, down interminably. The cyclical model of the economy supposes instead that as things rise up there are also counter-vailing forces pushing them down, and as things sink they are accompanied also by rising trends. The point being that both downturns and upturns are limited. At a certain point up and down reverse themselves. The end (=limit) of a social process is different from the end (=goal) of an individual or organization. The old-fashioned end (=stopping point) is objective rather than subjective. Such ends are outside the power of individuals or institutions to determine through conscious, deliberate, organized action. Goals and strategies are the product of calculated intentional reflective choices. In the past two centuries, both liberals and anti-liberals have placed a lot of faith in organized action. Plans, stratagems, schemes, blueprints, proposals and schedules have all been in fashion. Such methodically structured action is valuable in many circumstances. But can it substitute for cyclical action? No. Can it substitute for pattern action? No.

The view of Dewey, who spoke for all progressive-liberals, was that objective termini were so out of date that they belonged to the age of Plato and Aristotle. Already in the era of Francis Bacon, in the late sixteenth and early seventeenth century, the aesthetic and contemplative view of economy and society had started to be replaced by a scientific and instrumental view of things. How quaintly old-fashioned that anyone might suppose in the twentieth century that there were finales or windups cyclically built into large-scale social operations or that actions organized by knowledgeable persons with specific 'goals-in-view' could not control the larger society's periodic, cyclical and pattern-based systems. Voluntarism—the sense of intended, intentional, controlled, deliberate and chosen action—trumped the view of the world that society has its own natural laws and that economies have in-built automatic and periodic mechanisms that are readily observable and not reversible but that can be adapted to. For the latter, adjustment, variation and acclimatization overshadows change, reform and reorganization.

Self-employment versus organized enterprise

Self-organizing systems need only the limited assistance of the state to enforce free contracts, the freedom of the seas and the like. The power of autopoietic systems lies in their paradoxical nature. Adam Smith illustrated this with his famous comment about merchants. In pursuing their own interests, merchants promote the broader interest of society. The invisible hand that orchestrates commerce causes them to promote an end that forms no part of their intention. Progressive-liberals, in contrast, emphasize conscious aims and designs. They envisage a world in which events and outcomes can be explicitly planned. The state is important in their view because it is a conscious collective actor. It sets goals and creates methods to achieve its ends. It organizes staff and resources along with rules and procedures to implement its plans and strategies.

In a managerial society, the state may be the largest but it is not the only significant organization. Social-liberal societies are polyarchies.[11] They have multiple centers of organizational power. This contrasts with authoritarian or totalitarian regimes. The latter try to absorb all of society into one organization. Instead, the progressive-liberal society of the twentieth century developed plural centers of organizational power. Liberal polyarchies are societies in which big government, big corporations, big business, big charities and big science coexist. These organizations possess a strong family resemblance. Each acts and interacts through elaborate legal-rational structures.[12] There is a sharp distinction between these organizations and self-organizing social systems. The latter coordinate the actions of strangers at a distance through abstract patterns and principles. The former orientate to explicit detailed projected purposes. These are pursued by means of bureaus, rules, procedures and budgets.[13] If we compare the individual firm and the market order, firms are 'islands of conscious power' located in an 'ocean of unconscious cooperation'.[14]

At the core of an organization is its offices. These are structured hierarchically and subject to rules and procedures. Modern organizations are procedural hierarchies. By their nature, hierarchies organize persons into relationships of superiority and subordination. Each immediate level works in relatively close proximity. By default everyone knows the other. In modern organizational hierarchies this personal aspect is offset by an impersonal dimension. In procedural hierarchies superiors direct subordinates via policy more so than by command. Instructions are issued, but they are couched in impersonal-sounding language. Despite that, all organizations, whether modern-procedural or traditional-patrimonial ones, are pecking orders. That is, they are status institutions. They place persons in ladder-like positions that have a higher or lower status. At the same time, organizations are peer bodies. Their members are sensitive to the approval of their peers, however these are defined.[15] Organizations encourage group-think. Sycophancy, anxious pleasing, peer pressure, placatory behavior, servility, subservience and self-serving conformism commonly occur in organizations.

In 1975 Michael Oakeshott observed that there are two powerful and contrary dispositions in human character.[16] One is the disposition to be self-employed; the other to join a common enterprise. In the first case, persons see themselves and others as self-determining beings. In the second case, the emphasis is on sharing a common stock of resources and talents. This distinction drove politics in the twentieth century. It underpinned two ways of being. One saw society as a set of organizations, or in the totalitarian case, as a single organization. The other saw society as a composite of millions of self-employed persons creating macroscopic pattern order via microscopic interactions.

As Oakeshott's colleague Kenneth Minogue further observed, common enterprises, that is, organizations, expect servility of mind in return for security of being.[17] They offer protection and safety in exchange for spiritual dependence—that is, subordination to a common enterprise. Organizations are managed entities. They command and control staff and resources. That control symbolizes risk-reduction. It promises security, surety and indemnity in the form of employment tenure, rule-driven work, guaranteed benefits, predictable career paths and qualification-based status. The condition of this institutional predictability is intellectual dependency. The consequence of this dependence is self-conscious, self-pitying, self-righteous, sentimental sufferance. In an autonomous world, the emphasis is on independence. Self-employment is distinguished by spontaneous cooperation and unself-conscious absorption in activities.[18] Spontaneous cooperation denotes the autopoietic behavior of markets, industries, cities and publics. Absorption is another word for vocation. It is what the psychologist Mihaly Csikszentmihalyi calls 'flow'. It is the autotelic ability to concentrate deeply on a demanding activity for long sustained uninterrupted periods of time.[19]

Autopoietic action is distinct from the organized action of firms and corporations, cartels and lobbies, institutions and unions, schools and universities. In organizations, unself-conscious vocational activity is over-determined by self-conscious strategic calculation and all-too-self-aware behavior. A commonplace example of the latter is virtue-signaling, which reached plague proportions in both private and public organizations as the post-industrial era matured. In parallel with this, organizations routinely cripple autotelic behavior. They disrupt 'flow', disturb concentration, interrupt attention, create distractions and destroy focus. They are anti-absorption machines. This has especially negative effects on creation and innovation, which more than anything are the result of human persistence and doggedness.

As Minogue observed, in cooperative moments, absorbed by an activity, persons merge into something greater than themselves.[20] When they are absorbed in activities, individuals don't think of these as a means to an ulterior end. Rather, they act for no other reason than to be absorbed in the activity.[21] This is freedom. It is freely entered into. It is free from external considerations. But, as Minogue also noted, like all great instances of freedom, this freedom is only freedom when, paradoxically, it is given up.[22] It is not given up, as in the case of an organization, for direction. It is not given up for custom or duty or rule-following. Rather it is given up for commitment. Persons enter freely into the spontaneous cooperative pattern orders of markets, industries, cities and publics. In doing so, they commit themselves. They bind themselves to fulfill contractual promises, concentrate and persist in difficult and demanding work, turn free mobility into durable settlement and match opinions and judgements with arguments and explanations.

Along with the large corporation, big government was key to the organizational age. This era started to take definitive shape by the 1920s.[23] By the 1990s it had reached its apogee. In the 2010s it was showing signs of decline. Auto-industrialism was beginning to replace organizational staff on a significant scale.[24] Small businesses, micro-manufacturers, sole traders and partnerships were increasing in number relative to firms and corporations (Table 12.2 and 12.3). This did not mean that organizations were disappearing or becoming inconsequential. However, they were subtly reducing in relative volume and social weight. Self-employment was increasing its share of household income and percentage of the total workforce.[25] In step with this was the declining level of active participation in formal and increasingly management-dominated social organizations like churches, sporting clubs, charities, service groups, parent bodies, ethnic associations, hobby bodies, fraternal associations, professional bodies and the like.[26] As interest in these shrank, persons opted instead to participate in markets, industries, cities and publics.[27]

Organization is a matter of intentional design. An organization consciously sets goals and in a deliberate planned manner seeks to achieve those goals. Whether an organization and its staff actually achieves the goals it sets is a separate matter. In organized action, consequence routinely is disconnected from intention. Once intentions and goals are set down, rarely does anybody ever check to see if they are realized. Nothing is emptier than an organization's 'strategic goals' or 'strategic plan'. The primary concern of the managerial society is not achievement, even if goal-setting is central. Setting goals is important in an organization because this sets in motion conscious sequences of action. An organization acts deliberately. Its ambition is that nothing occurs automatically or inexplicitly 'behind the back' of individuals. This is a matter of self-conscious behavior not objective outcomes.

In short, what organizations like to do is to message they have established a goal. Organizations are subjectively goal-orientated. Such goals once set, though, rarely come to pass. Rather than actual achievement, what organized action imparts to social actors is a sense, more often than not a false sense, of being 'in control'. Committees meet, managers decide, boards resolve, policies are made, instructions and directives are issued. All of these imply that the organization is 'doing things' that will realize its objectives. But actions that derive from policy frequently have little or no effect. This is because too often they fail to comprehend the pendulum motion of the large, barely visible, tacitly operating, self-organizing markets, industries, cities and publics that they have to interact with. Organizations live in perpetual hope that explicit policy goals will override the implicit automaticity of self-organizing systems. Organizations put their faith in a kind of control that they don't actually possess.

Such control purportedly is a function of knowledge. The more presumed knowledge, the greater the expertise, the more imposing is the capacity for controlling outcomes. This theory of society leads to conceit. The knowledge class—made-up of state officials in the first instance; later on public sector, corporate and not-for-profit intellectuals—thinks of itself as omniscient. It is knowledgeable, therefore it is right, and so it should decide matters. Lord Salisbury observed this attitude. He noted how the Whitehall civil servant typically thought that 'he himself is the best person to decide'.[28] Yet such self-anointed expertise often torpedoes common sense. As Salisbury later observed of the British legislature: 'Parliament is a potent engine, and its enactments must always do something, but they very seldom do what the originators of these enactments meant'.[29] Deliberate intentional documented self-aware plan-making—so valued in the twentieth century—promised a kind of all-seeing social control. But this never came to pass. Rather, all too often good intentions lead to bad consequences. All-seeing ends in blindness.

Notes

1 Michels, 2017 [1911].
2 The hard-left leader of the British Labour Party, Jeremy Corbyn, campaigned in a similar vein in the UK general election of 2017. Both were unsuccessful.
3 Piketty, 2014, 265, 304, 315–316, 334, 378.

4 The definitive form of these lectures was published in 1929.
5 He was not wrong in that. See Murphy, 2001. Leo Strauss (1950: 123) pointed to the role that *eidos*—the shape, form and character of a thing—played in classical (Platonic–Aristotelian) natural right as opposed to modern (Lockean) natural right.
6 Dewey, 1958 [1929], 95.
7 This liberalism was rooted in conservative realism. As Richard Weaver (2001 [1960], 477) put it, 'a conservative is a realist, who believes that there is a structure of reality independent of his own will and desire. He believes that there is a creation which was here before him, which exists now not by just his sufferance, and which will be here after he's gone .... Though this reality is independent of the individual, it is not hostile to him. It is in fact amenable by him in many ways, but it cannot be changed radically and arbitrarily. This is the cardinal point. The conservative holds that man in this world cannot make his will his law without any regard to limits and to the fixed nature of things'.
8 Classic accounts of the self-organizing forms of nature include Goethe, 2009 [1790], Thompson, 1961 [1917], Mandelbrot, 1985, Kauffman, 1993, Holland, 1995, Carroll, 2007.
9 Dewey, 1958 [1929], 95.
10 Dewey, 1958 [1929], 101.
11 Galbraith, 1952; Dahl, 1958.
12 Galbraith, 1967, ix, 115, 162, 176, 186, 204, 207, 209, 2015, 280, 337, 347, 380, 381 dubbed these 'techno-structures'.
13 On the difference between organizational hierarchies and self-organizing markets see Williamson, 1985. Thompson, 2003, examines the idea of networks as a 'third way' between hierarchies and markets.
14 Robertson, 1923, 85.
15 Minogue, 2001 [1963], 155.
16 Oakeshott, 1975, 324.
17 Minogue, 2010.
18 Minogue, 2001 [1963], 51–52.
19 Csikszentmihalyi, 1990.
20 Minogue, 2001 [1963], 52.
21 Minogue, 2001 [1963], 159.
22 Minogue, 2017 [1984].
23 Berle and Means' theory of the replacement of ownership control of corporations with management control dates from 1933; Ronald Coase's theory of the firm dates from 1937.
24 Murphy, 2017.
25 In the United Kingdom, the Office for National Statistics in 2012 reported that since 2008 the cohort of self-employed workers had grown by 367,000 while the group of wage-and-salary employees had declined by 434,000. London, the UK's richest sub-national economy, had the largest percentage of self-employed workers (18 percent). The North-East of England, one of the poorest regions in the UK, had the lowest percentage (11 percent). In Australia Monash University's Department of Management *Ipro Index 2015* 7th annual survey concluded that self-employed professionals choose to work that way because of the variety of work (70 percent), the sense of freedom (71 percent) and flexible hours (70 percent), not for reasons of job loss (0 percent). Eighty-five percent said they were happy when working intensely; 81 percent indicated that they were immersed in their work.
26 Putnam, 2000.
27 Carroll, 2017, examines the Australian case and the key role that cities and city life play in substituting for organizational participation.
28 Roberts, chapter 17. Salisbury's comment dates from 1882.
29 Roberts, chapter 17. Salisbury's comment dates from 1891.

Bibliography

Berle, A.A. and G.C. Means. 1933. *The Modern Corporation and Private Property*. New York: Macmillan.

Burnham, J. 1941. *The Managerial Revolution*. New York: John Day.

Carroll, J. 2017. *Land of the Golden Cities: Australia's Exceptional Prosperity and the Culture that Made It*. Redland Bay: Connor Court.

Carroll, S. 2007. *Endless Forms Most Beautiful*. London: Phoenix.

Coase, R.H. 1937. "The Nature of the Firm." *Economica* 4, no. 16: 386–405.

Csikszentmihalyi, M. 1990. *Flow*. New York: Harper.

Dewey, J. 1958 [1929]. *Experience and Nature*. New York: Dover.

Galbraith, J.K. 1967. *The New Industrial State*. Boston, MA: Houghton Mifflin.

Galbraith, J.K. 1952. *American Capitalism: The Concept of Countervailing Power*. Boston, MA: Houghton Mifflin.

Goethe, J.W. 2009 [1790]. *The Metamorphosis of Plants*. Cambridge, MA: MIT Press.

Holland, J.H. 1995. *Hidden Order*. New York: Basic Books.

Kaufmann, S.A. 1993. *The Origins of Order: Self-organization and Selection in Evolution*. New York: Oxford University Press.

Mandelbrot, B. 1982. *The Fractal Geometry of Nature*. San Francisco, CA: W.H. Freeman.

Michels, R. 1968 [1911]. *Political Parties: A Sociological Study of the Oligarchical Tendencies of Modern Democracies*. New York: Free Press.

Minogue, K. 2010. *The Servile Mind: How Democracy Erodes the Moral Life*. New York: Encounter Books.

Minogue, K. 2017 [1984]. "The Conditions of Freedom and the Condition of Freedom." In *On Liberty and its Enemies: Essays of Kenneth Minogue*, edited by T. Fuller. New York: Encounter Books.

Minogue, K. 2001 [1963]. *The Liberal Mind*. Indianapolis: Liberty Fund.

Murphy, P. 2017. *Auto-Industrialism: DIY Capitalism and the Rise of the Auto-Industrial Society*. London: Sage.

Murphy, P. 2001. *Civic Justice: From Ancient Greece to the Modern World*. Amherst, NY: Humanity Books.

Oakeshott, M. 1975. *On Human Conduct*. Oxford: Clarendon Press.

Piketty, T. 2014. *Capital in the Twenty-First Century*. Harvard: Harvard University Press.

Putnam, R. 2000. *Bowling Alone: The Collapse and Revival of American Community*. New York: Simon and Schuster.

Roberts, A. 2012 [1999]. *Salisbury: Victorian Titan*. London: Faber and Faber.

Robertson, D. H. 1923. *The Control of Industry*. London: Nisbet.

Thompson, G.F. 2003. *Between Hierarchies and Markets: The Logic and Limits of Network Forms of Organization*. Oxford: Oxford University Press.

Weaver, R.M. 2001 [1960]. "Conservativism and Libertarianism: The Common Ground." In *In Defense of Tradition: Collected Shorter Writings of Richard M. Weaver, 1929–1963*, edited by T. J. Smith III. Carmel, IN: Liberty Fund.

7 Conservative realism

The managerial class

The American philosopher James Burnham (1905–1987) was one the twentieth century's most incisive critics of managerialism, socialism, communism and social liberalism.[1] His view of these was shaped by his conservative realism. In his 1941 book *The Managerial Revolution*, Burnham looked around him at the ideologies of the time. These appeared to fall principally into two camps: the defenders of capitalism and the defenders of socialism. No, said Burnham. What mattered increasingly was neither capitalism nor socialism but rather managerialism. What he observed was a new kind of society being born: the managerial society. Its partisans stood for planning against enterprise, security against initiative and 'human rights' against 'property rights'.

A new ruling class was emerging: the class of managers. This class was historically distinctive. It was not a pre-modern or early-modern courtier class, patrimonial class or collegial class. Its power did not rest on individual private property rights. It was not a capitalist class. In fact, it existed in direct competition with the capitalist class of owners. It was not an owning class but rather a controlling class. Burnham offered a number of models of this control.

First, there is control achieved through the expansion of the state. This means government control through regulation and regulatory agencies, the expansion of government ownership, the creation of industries that no longer operated at a profit, the financing of social policy through large government deficits and debt and the creation of tax bills designed to secure social ends rather than simply fiscal ends.

Second, there is technocracy. This entails the replacement of ownership direction by management control, the reduction of ownership to drawing dividends and the growth of administrative, technical, expert and bureaucratic staff in the public and private sectors.

Third, there is qualification-based power. This emerged as one of the foci of Burnham's 1964 study *Suicide of the West*. The management class is a knowledge class. It legitimates its control by claims to knowledge and expertise. This explains what Burnham in 1941 rightly described as the 'confidence and aggression' of the managerial class. Not that, in reality, this class is very knowledgeable.

Rather, its power is rooted in a status that is defined by educational qualifications (today, principally, university qualifications).

In the 1940s, the managerial class was on the rise. Other classes, Burnham observed, were filled with doubts, fears, worry and gloom. But the managerial class was self-assured. It thought of itself as being indispensable for modern society. Seven decades later this class was pervasive in business, government, the public sector and the universities. In the course of 70 years it engineered an increasingly bureaucratic society. Its sense of self-importance was undiminished. If anything, it was more certain of itself than ever. Its ideology emphasized controlling economic and social behavior. It adopted a predominately social-liberal view of the world.

This was the opposite of the centuries-long classical view of the world, perhaps best summed up by stoicism. The Stoics pointed out that there were things within the control of human beings and things that were not within their control. Human beings could direct the former but had to adapt to the latter. In his 1943 book *The Machiavellians*, Burnham updated this view. He argued that 'the broad patterns of social change are established by factors beyond deliberate human control'. Development is 'determined by technological change and by other factors quite beyond the likelihood of human control'.[2] For Burnham, the conservative realist, the emphasis was on being rather than becoming, on system rather than process.[3] This paralleled the outlook of the Italian-Swiss economist and sociologist Vilfredo Pareto (1848–1923). Burnham noted that Pareto did not offer any program of social improvement or express an ideal of what a society or government should be.[4] Pareto did not confuse wish and reality.

Burnham observed that in a managerial society the emphasis is almost entirely on 'deliberate' action. Action, it is supposed, is purposeful. It has an end-in-view. Accordingly, it can be planned. Some human actions are like this. They have explicit goals and means of achieving these goals. The carpenter has the end of making a table and the means (the materials and tools) to achieve this. In work and productive activity, logical plans can be conceived in order to best match means and ends. Yet as Pareto argued in his 1919 work *Mind and Society*, a lot of human action is not purposive-rational in nature. Much of it is either pseudo-rational or non-logical.[5] Pseudo-rational behavior is based on what Pareto called 'derivations', namely wishful or fantasy-filled rationalizations of behavior. Logical or goal-rational action plays a key role in work and production and carrying out tasks. But, as Burnham argued, it plays little role in broader social and political life. Whereas ideology, myth-making, dreams, fancies and delusions do.[6]

Pseudo-rationality is commonplace in organizations. They spend a disproportionate amount of their time and resources on what Burnham amusingly called 'verbalisms'. Purposive action, Burnham observed, involves 'consciously understood and deliberately chosen goals'. These are 'real and possible goals', like the making of a table, not ideological and fantasy goals like 'universal peace and plenty and joy'. Pareto also described a class of action that is neither purposive-rational nor non-logical but rather creative and durable. Just like 'derivations', Pareto's word for this class of action, 'residues', is awkward. Burnham talked more usefully about patterns. That is, in addition to purposive and pseudo-rational action, there is pattern action. Firms, factories, organizations are all swept up in larger patterns of social development beyond explicit human control.

Power laws

Liberal interventionism, socialism and a host of other twentieth-century ideologies supposed that purposeful-rational individual action could be replicated on a broad social scale. Society could be planned like a work task. But it couldn't. An investor withdraws money from a field of investment that is drying up in favor of a new and expanding industry.[7] That's logical. But markets, like any other self-organizing system, are not logical. This is not to say they are illogical or anti-logical. Rather they are non-logical. A state using a model of purposive-rational planning to correct a market cycle is doomed to failure because large-scale social systems of all kinds, including markets, are not purposive-rational in the way that task-related activity is.

Pareto did not develop a theory of self-organizing systems. Yet in his early work in the 1890s he did observe the kind of power law that commonly steers autopoietic systems.[8] Power laws are not the laws of legislators. Nor are they the rules and regulations of policy-makers. Instead, power laws mirror relationships between quantities that repeatedly occur in nature, society and art. Pareto observed that 80 percent of Italy's land was owned by 20 percent of the population.[9] When he looked at other countries, he found broadly the same ratio. He further found that this power law applied not just to wealth in the form of land but also to income. This 80:20 income ratio has remained remarkably persistent across time and space. The 1990 to 2007 data on the distribution of world income by population showed that the wealthiest 20 percent of humankind over the period enjoyed 80 percent of the income.[10] In the past 120 years all 'equality' programs have made zero difference to that outcome.

This is unsurprising given that Pareto made the observation of his power law after spotting that 20 percent of the peapods in his garden produced 80 percent of the peas. There is something of a natural arrangement in the 80:20 ratio. Since Pareto, the 80:20 distribution pattern has been observed to apply in a remarkable range of circumstances, across political, social, engineering, natural and art systems. In the case of organizations, 20 percent of variables commonly explain 80 percent of organizational outcomes.[11] Take marketing as an example. Eighty percent of sales frequently come from 20 percent of customers. Conversely, 80 percent of consumer complaints relate to 20 percent of products and to 20 percent of customers. Similarly, 80 percent of a company's revenue will characteristically come from 20 percent of its staff's time. In healthcare, twenty percent of occupational health and safety hazards account for 80 percent of injuries while 20 percent of patients consume 80 percent of resources.

We find golden ratio patterns in stock market support-and-resistance levels and the timing of major stock price movements. Markets of all kinds are structured in non-linear short, medium and long-term waves.[12] Opinions such as market predictions, in contrast, tend to be linear rather than oscillating. Yet the structure of reality is not linear but rather super-positional. Thus, when things are going down there are less visible forces pushing in the opposite direction. The same applies to upward motion. In a stock market, the drive upwards will meet a point of resistance; the drive downward will meet a point of support. Longer-term upward phases incorporate periods of downward movement just as downward phases interpolate upward movements. The overall picture has a fractal-like shape.[13] Micro-periods have the same jagged 'up-down-up-down' pattern as macro-periods. The same pattern repeats at all scales.

Modern technology (industry innovation) has a wave-like character similar to large-scale markets.[14] So do cities and publics.[15] Cyclical motion is one example of the way that patterns meld contrasts (in this case, up–down, growing–shrinking). Pattern behavior is the outcome of the interaction of large-scale countervailing forces, including 'bear and bull' stock markets, 'conservative and liberal' public opinion, 'expanding and declining' cities, 'productivity-driven and protectionist' industries, and so on. The bipolar nature of modern societies is such that every social tendency is met by a counter-tendency. This antithetical social motion creates waves and cycles of collective behavior. This is not crowd or herd behavior.[16] Crowds and herds tend to unanimity. Self-organizing systems instead have a *phi*-like structure. A dominant polarity will rarely rise above a 62 percent support ceiling. A subordinate polarity will rarely fall beneath a 38 percent floor.

That is, self-organizing behavior is fractal or super-positional in nature. It does not rely on the conscious judgement of a single individual or a handful of individuals. Nor on uniform crowd psychology. Rather, it is shaped by the actions of millions of individuals behaving (to a large extent) anonymously. Anonymous contrariety builds in corrections to herd-like behavior, whether of peers or packs. Modern societies are autonomous societies. That is, they are self-organizing to a significant degree. Broad social development in them occurs more or less automatically through self-regulating mechanisms in which not the hundreds or even thousands participate but rather hundreds of thousands and millions of people participate such that their individual actions aggregate to create large-scale social patterns.

Power laws such as the Pareto principle are key in explaining collective social behavior. They frequently override, negate or constrain the laws of legislators. This points to a deep flaw in many theories of modern government. Those theories suppose that social and political action is largely or mainly purposive-rational in nature. That is, it is modelled on the way that carpenters make things. The carpenter decides on a goal (producing a table) and organizes materials and tools and time to do this. Carpenters are also subject to industrial and legal rules that govern their work practices. This model of behavior explains a portion of human activity. But, as Pareto pointed out in *Mind and Society*, purposive-rational or logical action is far from the only kind of human action. The conduct of individuals, Burnham summarized, is logical only under certain conditions. Namely, when actions are motivated by purposes that are (a) deliberately sought, (b) possible to reach, and (c) where the means of reaching the goals are appropriate.

Purposeful-rational action exists, especially in the realm of work. In a logical action, the projected goal and the achieved goal are identical. Yet in reality, many of the projections that people make are either too vague or abstract or else too fanciful and improbable to be goals. When persons start to chase such phantoms they often rely on verbal sleights of hand. These provide seemingly logical justifications for what are non-logical behaviors. For instance, claims, at the height of a stock-market bubble, that the market will 'rise forever'. But no stock market rises forever. When self-deceptive rationalizations eventually collapse, panic and alarm sets in. This also ends up being rationalized.

Human beings have a strong non-logical impulse to make human actions seem logical.[17] Yet the actions set in train by taboos, ideologies and fantasies are not purposive-rational. Many socially decisive actions spring from non-logical roots.[18] Thus, Burnham observed, societies are shaped by rational action only to a relatively small degree.[19] So what does influence them? The verbalisms of magic, myth, organized religion and secular rationalism for one thing. Then there is geography, climate, biological and physical characteristics. The latter are not goals but, rather, givens. They are not the purpose of action but, rather, its context or environment. What about philosophical abstractions like freedom and happiness? These are too vague to be goals. They are subject to too many competing interpretations to steer purposeful action. The quest for constitutional freedom is not like taking logical steps in pursuit of a goal.[20] On the same day, Burnham wryly noted, an Attorney General can speak in favor free speech and arrest individuals for exercising free speech.[21] Legislators routinely praise free enterprise while expanding regulation over it.

Rationalized behavior is widespread. Yet it typically ends in futility. At its core it lacks substance. This does not mean that societies are insubstantial. Rather, it means that their substance is not dependent on verbal rationalizations but rather on what Pareto called 'residues', of which the most important are two classes of non-logical action: firstly, the creative combination of contrary forces that then leads to a second class of action, namely the stable or durable element in social behavior. These two represent substantial permanence and change in society—and perhaps even more importantly the paradoxical super-positioning of the two. Residues are what are left over in social behavior after purposive-logical and verbal-illusory actions are bracketed.

Pattern behavior

Creative combination is prominent in self-organizing systems. It occurs as antipodal forces coalesce to form stable long-term cyclical patterns. These patterns fuse permanence and change. They are dynamic yet in a repeating self-similar continuous, that is to say conservative, manner. In modern self-organizing systems individuals make free decisions. They do so in pursuit of happiness. But they don't produce freedom or happiness in the way that the carpenter produces a table. Rather, such philosophical abstractions are created autopoietically. They are a function of free societies and happy societies that have interpolated large-scale self-organizing systems.

Modern industrial-capitalist societies have distinct repeating patterns. Firstly, they are cyclical. That is, they have short, medium and long-term up and down economic cycles. Secondly, they are industrial. They are propelled by automation. They move through phases dominated by agriculture, manufacturing, services and (now) auto-industrialism. Thirdly, they are urban. Population in them moves from the country to the city to the megacity and these grow in accordance with power laws. Fourthly, advanced modern societies have large publics. These interact with governments yet are separate from them. Publics possess authority where governments have power. Democratic elections represent the intersection of publics and power.

From time to time publics will adopt a rhythm and tone sharply at odds with governments. It is a common belief in modern societies that government decisions, plans and policies can modify or abate negative effects as cycles, phases and shifts occur in these societies. As problems or dramas arise, it is assumed that government can 'fix' things. But, as people eventually discover after the fact, most articulated policy goals of government are never achieved. They may for a time console those negatively affected by the society's cycles, phases and shifts, but soothing action is not the same as effective action. The pursuit of policy goals—whether these happen to be classical-liberal or social-liberal goals—takes place within powerful difficult-to-shake tessellated frameworks.

The same applies to all the major goal-directed organizations in modern societies. Firms, universities, and planners are no match for markets, industries and cities, any more than parties or governments can keep pace with publics. Each modern self-organizing system has an institutional equivalent. The state stands to the public as firms do to markets, hospitals to industries, planners to cities and schools to publics. Each of the former has difficulty keeping up with each of the latter. Local governments decide that a city is not allowed to expand beyond its planned boundaries. In a short time we find that city development has defied the zoned city limits. It is not that cities do not have distinct forms. They do. Many even are millennia old. But these forms are tacit compared with the explicit manner of institutional direction.

In short, modern societies are not nearly as contingent as many of their denizens think. Spending more money or being more activist or interventionist rarely if ever decisively over-determines the tacit patterns of capitalism, industrialism, urbanism and symbolism. These have their own 'natural laws'. Their goods exist tacitly in the background. Organizations, in contrast, foreground explicit goods. Yet their goal-directed intentional actions often fail. These actions have unintended consequences. Syncing policies with the 'natural laws' of modern society is difficult. For example, government industry policy, which seeks to pick company winners in order to subsidize them and thereby give them a leg up, usually ends up backing losers. Rather than making things better for companies by subsidizing them, all that such subsidies do is to disguise the true economic situation of the sponsored firms. This encourages them to continue to take harmful courses of action. This outcome may not have been intended by the state, but often there is a large gap between intention and consequence. The underlying mistake is to think that goal-directed action can outwit the stable taciturn patterns of dynamic modern societies.

The progressive-liberal view is that reality is determined by will. The state mobilized to intervene in society is the greatest agency of human will. What it decides, works. Except that it does not. Big government does not erase economic cycles. Periodic prolonged large downturns like those of the late 1830s and early 1840s, 1890s, 1930s and 2010s—or their smaller-scale fractal cousins in the 1810s, 1860s, 1870s, early 1920s, 1970s and early 1980s—do not respond well to government intervention (Table 2.1). As Joseph Schumpeter long ago pointed out, these cycles are neither caused nor cured by policy but by technology. New technologies like the motor car caused the 1920s to boom. In the 1930s, the same technologies eliminated jobs. When cars replaced horses, the farmers who produced horse-feed went out of business. Industrial mechanization eliminated many other farm occupations. Large waves of technological unemployment cycle around. Farm labor shrank in the 1930s. Expansion of manufacturing replaced these jobs in the 1940s, 1950s and 1960s. Then manufacturing's share of employment declined sharply beginning in the 1970s. Post-industrial office-and-service, education-and-health jobs took their place. In the 2000s and 2010s white-collar and pink-collar jobs started to decline as they began to be automated.

We live in a cyclical world, not a progressive world. Modern economies oscillate. They have a natural rhythm. Governments can't control this rhythm or vary it except in incidental ways. The state cannot bring back the lost worlds of 1870s rural employment or 1970s manufacturing jobs. Technology (industrial automation) replaces labor with machines with an undulating automaticity. Just as it also eventually and less visibly brings new industry sectors and new kinds of occupation into existence. Many governments today face a dilemma. They want to spend more on public goods. Yet they cannot expand the post-industrial health-and-education sectors indefinitely or stop the natural shrinkage of employment as auto-industrialism (the combination of computing, networks, cheap digital sensors and robotics) replaces office-and-service staff.

We see the latter happening today as capital work is growing incrementally in place of salaried office work. Small businesses, micro-businesses, self-employment, partnerships, contract work and household-based occupations are expanding as wage-and-salary office-and-factory work declines (Tables 12.2, 12.3, 12.4 and 12.5).[22] The natural law of industrial society applies to all economic sectors. Eventually, machines replace labor. And in due course alternate types of work are invented. Whatever automation saves consumers is spent elsewhere on alternative kinds of goods. We see a DIY sector is growing as the service sector has reached its natural ceiling. Meanwhile, the taxpayer-funded education-and-health industry struggles with low productivity, high price inflation and declining real outcomes. Governments borrow to keep these sectors afloat. But as fiscal debts mount, the question is raised as to whether taxpayer-funded organizations are really a good option compared with self-organizing systems and their aesthetic-like economic and social orders.

Notes

1 Burnham, 1941, 1943, 1964.
2 Burnham, 1943, 197, 200.
3 The Australian poet A.D. Hope (1974: 151) compared the classical literary tradition of Dryden, Swift and Pope with that of the Romantics. 'The one [Classicism] views man and the universe as he is, the other as he might be; the one we could call the tradition of being, the other the tradition of becoming; the one views the world as a system, the other as a process.'
4 Burnham, 1943, 191.
5 Pareto, 1965 [1917–1919, 1935]. See also Burnham, 1943, 124–163; Parsons, 1949 [1937], 178–203; Aron, 1970 [1965], 119–218.
6 A similar point was made, this time from the political left, by Cornelius Castoriadis, whose social philosophy focused on the self-organizing capacity of societies. Castoriadis (e.g. 1979) emphasized the pseudo rationality of bureaucratic organizations and depicted these as giving rise to arational, afunctional occultation, confusion and mystification, an astute description of many jargon-heavy organizations that set specious goals underscored by extravagant fantasies of omnipotence and 'total control'. Those fantasies rest on the voluntarist fallacy that human will or desire can master all objects and all circumstances (1976).
7 Burnham, 1943, 194.
8 Gabaix, 2016, 2009; Bouchaud, 2001.
9 The observation was made in his *Cours d'économie politique* [*Course in Political Economy*], 1896/1897. For a pen-portrait of Pareto as an economist, see Schumpeter, 1997 [1952], 110–142.
10 Ortiz and Cummins, 2011, 11–12.
11 Craft and Leake, 2002.
12 Elliott, 1938; Schumpeter, 1939.
13 The stock analyst Prechter (1999) developed an industry-analytic social-psychological theory of this stock-price fractal pattern and its parallels with other forms of pattern-based collective social behavior including elections and warfare.
14 Freeman and Louca, 2001.
15 Montgomery, 2007; Stimson, 1999, 2004; Bruscox and Roy, 2015; Schlesinger Sr., 1949; Schlesinger Jr., 1968; Adams, 1986 [1889–1891].
16 In contradistinction to Prechter, 1999.
17 Burnham, 1943, 203.
18 Burnham, 1943, 202.
19 Burnham, 1943, 196.
20 Burnham, 1943, 199.
21 Burnham, 1943, 200.
22 Murphy, 2017.

Bibliography

Adams, H. 1986 [1889–1891]. *History of the United States during the Administrations of James Madison*. New York: Library of America.

Aron, R. 1970 [1965]. *Main Currents in Sociological Thought Volume II: Durkheim, Pareto, Weber*. New York: Doubleday.

Bouchaud, J.P. 2001. "Power Laws in Economics and Finance: Some Ideas from Physics." *Quantitative Finance* 1, no. 1: 105–112.

Bruscox, S. and J. Roy. 2015. "Cycles in Public Opinion and the Dynamics of Stable Party Systems." *Department of Economics Working Papers*. New York: Stony Brook University, October 1.

Burnham, J. 2014 [1964]. *Suicide of the West: An Essay on the Meaning and Destiny of Liberalism.* Foreword, John O'Sullivan; Introduction, Roger Kimball. New York: Encounter Books.

Burnham, J. 1943. *The Machiavellians: Defenders of Freedom.* London: Putnam.

Burnham, J. 1941. *The Managerial Revolution.* New York: John Day.

Castoriadis, C. 1993 [1979]. "Socialism and Autonomous Society." In *Political and Social Writings* Volume III, edited by D.A. Curtis, 314–334. Minneapolis: University of Minnesota Press.

Castoriadis, C. 1991 [1976]. "Reflections on 'Rationality' and 'Development'." In *Philosophy, Politics, Autonomy*, edited by D.A. Curtis, 175–218. New York: Oxford University Press.

Craft, R.C. and C. Leake. 2002. "The Pareto Principle in Organizational Decision Making." *Management Decision* 40, no. 8: 729–733.

Elliott, R.N. 1938. *The Wave Principle.* n.p.: Monetary Research Limited.

Freeman, C. and F. Louca. 2001. *As Time Goes By: From Industrial Revolutions to the Information Revolution.* Oxford: Oxford University Press.

Gabaix, X. 2016. "Power Laws in Economics: An Introduction." *Journal of Economic Perspectives* 30, no. 1: 185–206.

Gabaix, X. 2009. "Power Laws in Economics and Finance." *Annual Review of Economics* 1: 255–293.

Hope, A.D. 1974. *Native Companions: Essays and Comments on Australian Literature, 1936–1966.* Sydney: Angus and Robertson.

Montgomery, J. 2007. *The New Wealth of Cities: City Dynamics and the Fifth Wave.* Farnham, UK: Ashgate.

Murphy, P. 2017. *Auto-Industrialism.* London: Sage.

Ortiz, I. and M. Cummins. 2011. *Global Inequality: Beyond the Bottom Billion, a Rapid Review of Income Distribution in 141 Countries.* New York: UNICEF, April.

Pareto, V. 1965 [1917–1919, 1935]. *Mind and Society: A Treatise on General Sociology.* New York: Dover.

Prechter, R.R. 1999. *The Wave Principle of Human Social Behavior and the New Science of Socionomics.* Gainesville, GA: New Classics Library.

Schumpeter, J. 1997 [1952]. *Ten Great Economists.* London: Routledge.

Schumpeter, J. 1939. *Business Cycles: A Theoretical, Historical and Statistical Analysis of the Capitalist Process.* New York: McGraw-Hill.

Schlesinger, A.M. Jr. 1986. *The Cycles of American History*, Boston, MA: Houghton, Mifflin.

Schlesinger, A.M. Sr. 1949. *Paths to the Present*, New York: Macmillan.

Stimson, J. 1999. *Public Opinion in America: Moods, Cycles, and Swings.* Boulder, CO: Westview.

Stimson, J. 1964. *Tides of Consent: How Public Opinion Shapes American Politics.* New York: Cambridge University Press.

8 Political economy

Government intervention via monetary and budget policy can make relatively minor adjustments to economic cycles. But it cannot eliminate them. Intervention also can exacerbate the extremes of cyclical behavior. Rather than correct, it can magnify depressive or speculative behavior. Between 1990 and 2015 the Japanese government spent a very large amount on public infrastructure. It did so in the hope of growing its stagnant economy. It failed. The economy was unresponsive. Similarly, in 2010 the Obama administration in the United States spent nearly a trillion dollars (in a 17 trillion dollar economy) to stimulate economic activity. The positive effect was practically zero. There is a large cost involved in the quixotic fighting of economic cycles. Underpinning such action is the voluntarist approach to society. Modern societies are self-regulating. Voluntarists wish to reverse this. They do so by treating society as an organization. Governments are comfortable with this because they are organizations. Like all organizations, government has rules, a budget and a plan. Governments tend to project organizational techniques onto the broader society. In doing so, they start to treat society as an organization whose problems can be solved organizationally.

Accordingly, since the 1930s, governments have treated economic downturns as an organizational problem. How do you solve an organizational problem? Firstly, allocate resources from a budget. Governments spend money to stimulate a sluggish economy. But such fiscal measures typically have a short-term stimulus effect only, if that. The second classic organizational strategy is to get one part of an organization to subsidize another part. A way of applying the same technique to society as a whole is for central banks to set interest rates at unnaturally low levels. This transfers wealth from savers to borrowers. Even so, abnormally low interest rates usually do not tempt sound businesses to borrow and invest. Rather, such measures keep unsound businesses afloat for a time, underwriting poor investments that in time will fail. In doing so, governments and central banks do not correct or abate the economic cycle; they just prolong it and its pain. They give false hope that voluntarism can obviate economic automaticity and periodicity. It can't.

So here we have two views of the world. The conservative realist thinks that modern societies combine the 'freedom to choose' with a sense of 'leave-it-alone', *laissez-faire*. The liberal-progressive however cannot stand to leave things alone.

Progressives are natural meddlers. Not for them any Enlightenment-era deist-style laws of nature. The admonition to 'leave things be' means rejecting action for contemplation. Standing back and watching means, for the progressive, a 'complacent' optimism, even a Panglossian sentiment that 'all is for the best' in this 'best of all possible worlds'. At the very least it supposes that society's nature-like processes are in the end 'beneficent'. Worst of all, in the eyes of the progressives, it assumes that modern society has a component that is 'providential'.[1]

Liberal-progressives are annoyed by the notion of limits. To them recurrence and relapse seem tantamount to human misery. This comes out in Jean Charles de Sismondi's objection to Jean-Baptiste Say's view of modern autonomous society. '[Let] us beware of this dangerous theory of equilibrium which is supposed to be automatically established. A certain kind of equilibrium, it is true, is reestablished in the long run, but it is after a frightful amount of suffering.' That anticipates two centuries of liberal-progressive thought. The presupposition is that a 'society without suffering' is possible so long as governments intervene in the economy to fix things so as 'to regulate the progress of wealth'. This desire to 'regulate the progress of wealth' became the most far-reaching ambition of social-liberals in the twentieth century. Nothing was closer to their hearts. Thus, nothing signified the failure of social liberalism more than its profound inability to prevent economic cycles periodically cycling down. Its ambition was not only in vain but positively damaging to economic well-being. Intervention not only did not reverse or abate cyclical economic downturns. In addition to not correcting economic periodicity, government intervention had an additional three key dampening effects on economies: regulation, perverse calculability and wastefulness.

The ambition of social liberalism, in its many varieties, was to treat society as if it was an organization. The rationale for this was that an organization could be planned and controlled. Society then would not be subject to nature-like ups and downs or ideal ratios. Society would not advance in waves, its forward motion entailing backwards motion. Its ups would not instantiate downs. 'Share price to company earnings' ratios would not place an invisible limit on the rise of stock prices. A firm operating successfully would not have to keep prudential ratios of 'debt to equity', 'interest payments to business income', 'current assets to current liabilities', 'operating expenses to total revenue', 'net profit to shareholder equity', 'business revenue to business expenses', and so on. Such judicious ratios equilibrate contrary forces such as assets and liabilities, revenue and expenses. They identify a right relationship between the contraries. They are measures of productive stability amidst constant countervailing change. They don't just take account of change but also the antipodal nature of so much change. It is not just that assets change (up or down) but so do liabilities (lesser or greater). The judgments needed to be made are not simply linear: last quarter, quantity X went up. Rather they are antipodal: quantity X (assets) has gone up while quantity Y (liabilities) has gone down. Is the firm still on an even keel?

Progressive liberalism does not like antipodal reasoning. It violates its sense of progress. In an antipodal world, every motion entails a counter-motion. A social unit cannot be represented in a straight line that in turn represents a goal (assets) and the means (revenues) established by a plan. Antipodal thinking, rather, looks to a positive relationship between 'assets and liabilities', 'revenues and expenses'. Self-regulating societies operate by constantly adjusting the relation between contraries. They do this via markets, industries, cities and publics. These societies have a pendulum-like quality.[2] They equilibrate not just assets and liabilities but also invention and innovation, big metropolises and small towns, majority and minority opinions. Organization tries to circumvent the pendulum-effect.

The state is an organization. It is a large organization, much bigger than firms or companies. Like all organizations, even those reputed to be flat, it ties its members or staff together by a combination of hierarchies, rules and goals. Organizations dislike pendulum or antipodal structures. The state is no exception. In some cases though, a pendulum order is superimposed over the state. The American constitution for example does this. It maintains a pendulum-like 'balance of power' between its executive, legislative and judicial branches. Order over-determines organization. The pendulum-like or swing pattern of this order takes precedence over the purposive model of policy-driven social action. Much lip-service is paid to pendulum orders. But human beings, being who they are, also have deep attachments to organizations. The reasons for this vary. But self-delusion is not least among them. The staff of organizations often think that the goal-driven policies of organizations will over-ride the clockwork-like mechanisms of pendulum order. The visible and voluntary workings of organizations have a powerful superficial appeal in place of the largely invisible and involuntary working of antipodal order. The ambidexterity of the latter—its propensity to pay attention as much to things small as those big, expense as well as revenue—has great subtlety but none of the triumphalism of the former.

In an organization—whether state, firm or charity—purpose rather than pendulum dominates. Goal-achievement rather than pattern-maintenance is key. Purposes are defined by plans and strategies. Once they are defined, purposes are carried into effect via rules and hierarchies. Human beings are attracted to rules and hierarchies. Rules and procedures structure relations between persons who are known to each other. That's one of the attractions of an organization to its members. The members are all known entities. They fit into an organizational grid. Their photos can be pinned up on the wall. They can form cliques, lobbies, factions, networks, webs, groups and connections. This is infinitely interesting to some people. They love the politicking of organizations. Who is in, who is out; strategic games, maneuvers, plays, all fascinate a certain type of personality. So do hierarchies.

We sometimes think of hierarchies as old-fashioned. Pre-modern societies are structured around status hierarchies. Self-organizing societies displace hierarchies. Their principles of ratio, symmetry, antipodes, and the like, reduce the need for hierarchies. But the psychological need for hierarchies persists with many people. They find it satisfied by modern organizational hierarchies. These, like their pre-modern predecessors, are also status hierarchies. Organizational actors acquire increased status by climbing the organizational ladder They are drawn to becoming the 'chief', 'senior', 'head', 'directing' office-holder. For many, being the 'assistant' or 'deputy' to the head or chief is sought after.

The Scottish historian and jurist Henry Maine (1822–1888) famously observed that modern societies tend to replace status with contract. This was evident through the eighteenth and nineteenth centuries. However, once we get to 1930 the trend starts to reverse. This did not mean a reversion to the medieval style of social order structured around status groups that persons typically were born into and largely (though never entirely) stayed in. Pre-modern status implies relatively small amounts of social mobility from one status to another. It is true that the degree of pre-modern social mobility is often underestimated just as the amount of modern social mobility tends to be overestimated. Even with that qualification stated, modern contract-type societies did expand social mobility substantially. Yet in their wake we also saw the re-emergence of the status society, this time based on organizations.

Those involved in self-organizing orders think first about pattern maintenance rather than policy. They spend much less time setting goals and organizing staff through rules and hierarchies to achieve set objectives. They spend a lot more time paying attention to the kinds of antipodal patterns that secure a satisfactory and satisfying balance between society's assets and liabilities, knowledge and intuition, spatial concentration and spread, and so on. The policy model assumes that staff, resourcing, rules and procedures achieve outcomes by setting a group of known persons (staff or members) in pursuit of goals. The pendulum model assumes that society achieves prosperity, peace and happiness by stimulating patterned interactions between strangers.

The term organization 'took off' in the late nineteenth century. Over the next hundred years it grew in use and influence. Social liberalism advanced hand-in-hand with it, both a cause and an effect of the growth of organizations. As various kinds of progressive politics and social liberalisms swelled so did the administrative state. The rise of the administrative state should be distinguished from socialism and communism. They are not the same phenomena. Socialism and communism assumed that one organization, the state, would swallow all other organizations as well as self-organizing society. The state would nationalize the means of production and it would create a command economy where all economic and social behavior would be subject to state direction and instruction. Liberal interventionism works differently. It doesn't aim to reduce society to a single organization, the state. Rather it uses the state to expand the number and scope of organizations in society. Rather than turning society into one giant bureaucratic hierarchy, it multiplies the number of bureaucratic hierarchies in society. It replicates in society more and more organizations like itself.

One of the key ways of doing this is through regulation. Regulation is a kind of administrative law making. It proliferated in the twentieth century. Historically, law was discovered by judges as they decided specific cases. Later on, parliaments created laws through discussion and legislation. In both cases, law was something general in nature. It emerged through the consideration of specific cases or specific issues. Once formulated by court or parliament, the generalities of law were then applicable to particular disputes, complaints and actions. Regulation, in contrast, is specific where law is general. It is composed of microscopic rules. The effect of regulation is to replace pattern-based interaction with tiny rules. The further effect of this is to substitute self-organized interaction between strangers with rule-based organizations. Regulation demands compliance. Compliance requires replacing pendulum-like behavior with step-like methodical linear behaviors governed by procedures and rules. This favors organizations. The larger the organization the more easily it copes with government regulation. It has the staff to report to government, monitor its own compliance with government rules and structure its behavior to mimic the step-like procedures and processes of government. The economic cost of this, though, is large. After a century of the bureaucratic society, upwards of 15 percent of a nation's GDP today is devoted to regulatory compliance.

Rules are the life-blood of modern organizations. Organizations coordinate action through rules, procedures, directives, decrees and the like. Regulation applies the same ambition to society as a whole. It seeks to control social actions by rules. It looks to turn social action into organized action rather than pattern action. Charities, schools, universities, laboratories and hospitals gradually become bureaucracies. The interventionist state does not create one big bureaucracy to swallow society. Rather, it mires society in multiple bureaucracies. Society's focus moves away from productive behavior to procedural behavior. It becomes less important to create value and more important to follow rules. The overt intention lying behind this is to solve social problems. The consequence of it though is to reduce social energy and increase social rigidity.

Perverse and positive paradoxes

Regulation addresses social issues via rules. This assumes that society can be planned or controlled. Regulation lays down specific rules and procedures, often today in thousands of pages of government documentation, to manage some area of public interest, from education to the environment, retirement to health. Regulation assumes that future problems can be anticipated accurately by the state and obviated by rules that prohibit or require certain kinds of action. Regulation supposes omniscience. This intellectual faculty avoids, removes, forestalls and prevents problems by setting out in advance concrete rules that dictate behavior. The promise of these rules is that they will avert or hinder the recurrence of a perceived problem. Each such rule is a tiny plan for the future. Yet so many of these petite plans fail or lapse in practice. This is because neither social problems nor the manner of avoiding of them are predictable. A rule that today appears to address a problem may tomorrow create its own unintended problems. Human foresight is far from omniscient.

In the twentieth century, the liberal-democratic state did two key things. First, it encouraged the growth of organizations in civil society. Second, the state itself grew. The growth of the state undermined the rationality of the state. As the state grew beyond a modest size, perverse paradoxes began to vex it in a number of ways.

The first of these perverse paradoxes is the problem of ignorant expertise. Government administrations were reformed in the nineteenth century. Patronage was replaced by civil service examinations. Later on, the possession of a university degree replaced or supplemented exams. Knowledge and expertise superseded sponsorship by notable persons. This was accompanied by the growth of legal-rationality. The state, like any organization, has to account for its own efficacy. The eighteenth-century state relied on virtue terms like loyalty, fidelity and allegiance to underwrite its own validity. By the twentieth century the ideal type of state was increasingly procedural. Both kinds of state organization were hierarchical. The older form was tied together by threads of loyalty and notions of dependable service. The procedural state emphasized that it followed rules. Its staff members were knowledgeable or expert in the rules as they were in the rules that regulated the wider society. But the skeptical Lord Salisbury thought that this claim amounted in practice to little more than a 'mania for paperwork' and 'endless temptations to pedantry and circumlocution', a judgment that few on reflection would disagree with.[3] The knowledge of rules turns swiftly into the fetishism of rules.

A second perverse paradox followed swiftly upon the first. The modern state as an organization readily identifies itself with the public. It is not the organ of a monarch or an aristocracy but rather more indirectly of the broader populace that chooses governments in democratic elections. Whatever the theory of the modern state, its executive wing claims to represent the public good. It often describes itself as a public service. It funds and regulates a rather larger public sector. But how public is it? State employees may claim to serve the public good. But often their private group interests outweigh their public service. Thus, public and private are paradoxically reversed.

This occurs in a number of ways. When modern states adopted forms of procedural rationality, they offered staff permanency. The trade-off was lower income than their peers in private industry in exchange for job security. A century later though, public employees typically earnt more than their counterparts in the private sector. The growth of government departments is similarly contrary. Organizations like to grow. This is true of public and private organizations alike. Although organizations exist in principle to achieve goals, the number of people an organization employs often has a tangential relation only to its functional needs. Core functions of organizations, including the state, are limited in number. The impulse of organizations, though, is to employ an unlimited number of people. Status grows with size even if functionality often declines with size. So what is functionally necessary and the size of government departments rarely coincide. Their telos is to get bigger and spend more. As they grow beyond functional needs, they spend ever-more time on rule-making and status-driven activities.

Why does this happen? In part because government departments, and public-sector organizations more generally, have poor mechanisms for calculating their proper size. Firms are in a better position to do this. The latter are disciplined by a number of factors. A firm offers a good or service at a price. If customers don't want the good or service, the firm is out of business. It has to ensure the costs of supplying the good do not exceed the price it can sell its product for. Its costs have to allow for a decent profit as well; otherwise, the firm cannot justify investment in the business. To control its costs, the firm ensures its staff numbers are not excessive. A lean firm avoids ploughing resources into unproductive or dysfunctional activities. Successful firms not only economize they also innovate. They apply science, technology and design to automate their operations, reduce production costs and create more interesting products. Government and the public sector are poor innovators. They resist the logic of industrial society which is to mechanize and automate. Preoccupied with rules and procedures, the products of government are frequently awkward and ungainly. The aesthetic shape of the best goods or services is sacrificed by public organizations in the name of finicky, overly methodical and overly detailed activity that echoes the spirit of legal-rationality. This readily turns any good idea into a poor outcome.

Government and the public sector are also bad economizers. In part, this is because there are no direct customers for public goods or else, if there are, these customers are heavily subsidized, making their choices meaningless as a guide to effectiveness. In reality, governments decide on programs—what those programs entail ranges from the necessary and functional to the self-indulgent and ridiculous. Democratic governments respond to voters in designing programs. But voter sentiment constitutes little more than a vague outline. The difference between a voter echoing a politician calling for 'better education' or 'better hospitals' and a consumer choosing a brand of car with known performance characteristics for a specific price is enormous. A public 'better education' program can entail elements that mean that students learn and understand more, but more likely the program will fund additional administration, further status-boosting projects, added useless functions and extra costly procedures. It is not that firms are immune to this. But eventually, if they persist in doing things of this nature, they will go out business. Government cannot go out of business. Worse still, governments in the past century have come to identify the supersizing of administration, status, unworkable functions and procedures with the public good. As social liberalism spread, together with various kinds of socialism and social democracy, and with these big government, the concept of the public good morphed. Bureaucracies grew in size, and as they did, their latent private interest in more administration, higher status, indulgent functions and cumbersome procedures overdetermined the public interest in efficiently providing a limited number of core services.

Public finances

Markets determine the size of companies by virtue of prices set and outputs purchased. Bureaucracies determine their own size subject only to inputs, that is, tax revenue. Accordingly, Cyril Northcote Parkinson in the 1950s observed how the number of employees in Britain's Colonial Office increased even while the country's global empire shrank.[4] Or as Lord Salisbury earlier noted, Whitehall 'will create business for itself as surely as a new railway will create traffic'.[5]

Good governments control and reduce public spending. In the course of the twentieth century, fiscally prudent governments became the exception instead of the rule. Choosing between economic growth and the growth of government, governments chose the growth of government. The growth of government means increasing taxes (Table 8.1). When voter patience with higher taxes is exhausted,

Table 8.1 Taxes: US federal government receipts by source as % of gross domestic product, 1934–2020

Fiscal Year	Individual Income Taxes	Corporation Income Taxes	Social Insurance and Retirement Receipts			Excise Taxes	Other	Total Receipts		
			Total	(On-Budget)	(Off-Budget)*			Total	(On-Budget)	(Off-Budget)
1934	0.7	0.6	*	(*)	....	2.2	1.3	4.8	4.8	....
1935	0.7	0.8	*	(*)	....	2.0	1.5	5.1	5.1	....
1936	0.8	0.9	0.1	0.1	....	2.0	1.1	4.9	4.9	....
1937	1.2	1.2	0.7	0.4	0.3	2.1	0.9	6.1	5.8	0.3
1938	1.4	1.4	1.7	1.3	0.4	2.1	0.9	7.5	7.1	0.4
1939	1.1	1.2	1.8	1.2	0.6	2.1	0.7	7.0	6.4	0.6
1940	0.9	1.2	1.8	1.3	0.6	2.0	0.7	6.7	6.1	0.6
1941	1.1	1.8	1.7	1.1	0.6	2.2	0.7	7.5	6.9	0.6
1942	2.2	3.2	1.7	1.1	0.6	2.3	0.5	9.9	9.3	0.6
1943	3.5	5.2	1.6	1.0	0.6	2.2	0.4	13.0	12.4	0.6
1944	9.2	6.9	1.6	1.0	0.6	2.2	0.5	20.5	19.9	0.6
1945	8.1	7.1	1.5	0.9	0.6	2.8	0.5	19.9	19.4	0.6
1946	7.1	5.2	1.4	0.8	0.5	3.1	0.5	17.2	16.7	0.5
1947	7.5	3.6	1.4	0.8	0.6	3.0	0.6	16.1	15.5	0.6
1948	7.4	3.7	1.4	0.8	0.6	2.8	0.6	15.8	15.2	0.6
1949	5.6	4.0	1.4	0.8	0.6	2.7	0.5	14.2	13.6	0.6
1950	5.6	3.7	1.6	0.8	0.8	2.7	0.5	14.1	13.4	0.8
1951	6.6	4.3	1.7	0.8	1.0	2.6	0.5	15.8	14.8	1.0
1952	7.8	5.9	1.8	0.8	1.0	2.5	0.5	18.5	17.5	1.0
1953	7.8	5.6	1.8	0.7	1.1	2.6	0.5	18.2	17.1	1.1
1954	7.6	5.4	1.9	0.7	1.2	2.6	0.5	18.0	16.8	1.2
1955	7.1	4.4	1.9	0.7	1.2	2.2	0.5	16.1	14.8	1.2

1956	7.3	4.8	2.1	0.7	1.5	2.3	0.5	17.0	15.5	1.5
1957	7.7	4.6	2.2	0.7	1.5	2.3	0.6	17.2	15.8	1.5
1958	7.3	4.2	2.4	0.7	1.7	2.2	0.6	16.8	15.1	1.7
1959	7.3	3.4	2.3	0.7	1.6	2.1	0.6	15.7	14.0	1.6
1960	7.6	4.0	2.7	0.8	2.0	2.2	0.7	17.3	15.3	2.0
1961	7.5	3.8	3.0	0.8	2.2	2.2	0.7	17.2	15.0	2.2
1962	7.8	3.5	2.9	0.8	2.1	2.1	0.7	17.0	14.9	2.1
1963	7.7	3.5	3.2	0.9	2.3	2.1	0.7	17.2	14.9	2.3
1964	7.3	3.5	3.3	0.8	2.5	2.1	0.7	17.0	14.5	2.5
1965	6.9	3.6	3.1	0.8	2.4	2.1	0.8	16.4	14.1	2.4
1966	7.1	3.8	3.3	0.8	2.4	1.7	0.9	16.7	14.3	2.4
1967	7.3	4.1	3.9	1.0	2.9	1.6	0.8	17.8	14.8	2.9
1968	7.6	3.2	3.8	1.0	2.8	1.6	0.8	17.0	14.2	2.8
1969	8.9	3.7	4.0	1.0	2.9	1.5	0.9	19.0	16.1	2.9
1970	8.6	3.1	4.2	1.0	3.2	1.5	0.9	18.4	15.2	3.2
1971	7.7	2.4	4.2	1.0	3.2	1.5	0.9	16.7	13.5	3.2
1972	7.8	2.6	4.3	1.0	3.3	1.3	1.0	17.0	13.7	3.3
1973	7.6	2.7	4.7	1.3	3.4	1.2	0.9	17.0	13.6	3.4
1974	8.0	2.6	5.1	1.4	3.6	1.1	0.9	17.7	14.1	3.6
1975	7.6	2.5	5.2	1.4	3.9	1.0	0.9	17.3	13.5	3.9
1976	7.4	2.3	5.1	1.4	3.7	0.9	1.0	16.6	12.9	3.7
1977	7.8	2.7	5.2	1.5	3.8	0.9	0.9	17.5	13.7	3.8
1978	7.9	2.6	5.3	1.6	3.7	0.8	0.8	17.5	13.8	3.7
1979	8.5	2.6	5.4	1.6	3.8	0.7	0.9	18.0	14.2	3.8
1980	8.7	2.3	5.6	1.6	4.0	0.9	0.9	18.5	14.4	4.0
1981	9.1	1.9	5.8	1.7	4.1	1.3	0.9	19.1	14.9	4.1

1982	9.0	1.5	6.1	1.8	4.3	1.1	1.0	18.6	14.3	4.3
1983	8.2	1.0	5.9	1.7	4.2	1.0	0.9	17.0	12.8	4.2
1984	7.5	1.4	6.1	1.9	4.2	0.9	0.9	16.9	12.7	4.2
1985	7.8	1.4	6.2	1.8	4.4	0.8	0.9	17.2	12.8	4.4
1986	7.7	1.4	6.3	1.8	4.4	0.7	0.9	17.0	12.5	4.4
1987	8.2	1.8	6.3	1.9	4.5	0.7	0.9	17.9	13.4	4.5
1988	7.8	1.8	6.5	1.8	4.7	0.7	0.9	17.6	13.0	4.7
1989	8.0	1.9	6.5	1.7	4.7	0.6	0.9	17.8	13.1	4.7
1990	7.9	1.6	6.4	1.7	4.8	0.6	0.9	17.4	12.7	4.8
1991	7.7	1.6	6.5	1.7	4.8	0.7	0.8	17.3	12.5	4.8
1992	7.4	1.6	6.4	1.7	4.7	0.7	0.9	17.0	12.3	4.7
1993	7.5	1.7	6.3	1.7	4.6	0.7	0.7	17.0	12.4	4.6
1994	7.5	2.0	6.4	1.8	4.7	0.8	0.8	17.5	12.8	4.7
1995	7.8	2.1	6.4	1.8	4.6	0.8	0.8	17.8	13.2	4.6
1996	8.2	2.2	6.4	1.8	4.6	0.7	0.8	18.2	13.6	4.6
1997	8.7	2.1	6.4	1.7	4.6	0.7	0.7	18.6	14.0	4.6
1998	9.3	2.1	6.4	1.7	4.6	0.6	0.8	19.2	14.6	4.6
1999	9.2	1.9	6.4	1.8	4.7	0.7	0.9	19.2	14.5	4.7
2000	9.9	2.0	6.4	1.7	4.7	0.7	0.9	20.0	15.2	4.7
2001	9.4	1.4	6.6	1.8	4.8	0.6	0.8	18.8	14.0	4.8
2002	7.9	1.4	6.4	1.7	4.7	0.6	0.7	17.0	12.3	4.7
2003	7.0	1.2	6.3	1.7	4.6	0.6	0.7	15.7	11.1	4.6
2004	6.7	1.6	6.1	1.6	4.4	0.6	0.6	15.6	11.1	4.4
2005	7.2	2.2	6.2	1.7	4.5	0.6	0.6	16.7	12.2	4.5
2006	7.6	2.6	6.1	1.7	4.4	0.5	0.7	17.6	13.1	4.4
2007	8.1	2.6	6.1	1.6	4.4	0.5	0.7	17.9	13.5	4.4

2008	7.8	2.1	6.1	1.6	4.5	0.5	0.7	17.1	12.6	4.5
2009	6.3	1.0	6.2	1.6	4.5	0.4	0.7	14.6	10.1	4.5
2010	6.1	1.3	5.8	1.6	4.3	0.5	1.0	14.6	10.3	4.3
2011	7.1	1.2	5.3	1.6	3.7	0.5	0.9	15.0	11.3	3.7
2012	7.1	1.5	5.3	1.7	3.6	0.5	0.9	15.3	11.7	3.6
2013	7.9	1.6	5.7	1.7	4.1	0.5	0.9	16.7	12.7	4.1
2014	8.1	1.9	5.9	1.7	4.3	0.5	1.1	17.5	13.3	4.3

Source: https://obamawhitehouse.archives.gov/omb/budget/Historicals Office of Management and Budget, Historical Tables, Table 2.3.

*Payroll receipts that go into the Social Security Trust Fund are considered “off budget” but nonetheless are used as budget revenue.

governments then borrow money. They go into debt to finance spending (Tables 8.2 and 8.3).

Countries borrow money to avoid levying additional taxes when instituting new operations or else to avoid having to cut existing operations to make way for new ones. Sometimes this is done out of necessity, as when countries go to war; often it is done out of expediency. Debt allows governments in democratic states to fund new services while pretending to voters that they don't have to pay higher taxes for more services. This magical thinking only delays the tax burden. In the end, tax money is required to pay down a country's debt. Meanwhile, taxes are extracted from a nation's total productive wealth. If a country's debt-to-GDP ratio is too high, a government will find itself taxing an excessive portion of the country's productive output in order to pay off the public debt. If it does not impose higher taxes, then it will have to either reduce public services or borrow yet more money (creating a larger debt burden).

Table 8.2 US federal debt, 1940–2015

End of Fiscal Year	Gross Federal Debt as % of GDP	End of Fiscal Year	Gross Federal Debt as % of GDP	End of Fiscal Year	Gross Federal Debt as % of GDP	End of Fiscal Year	Gross Federal Debt as % of GDP
1940	51.6	1950	92.1	1960	54.3	1970	36.3
1941	49.5	1951	78.0	1961	53.4	1971	36.5
1942	53.6	1952	72.5	1962	51.6	1972	35.7
1943	77.3	1953	69.5	1963	50.1	1973	34.4
1944	95.5	1954	69.9	1964	47.7	1974	32.6
1945	114.9	1955	67.4	1965	45.4	1975	33.6
1946	118.9	1956	62.1	1966	42.0	1976	35.1
1947	107.6	1957	58.6	1967	40.6	1977	34.8
1948	96.0	1958	59.0	1968	41.0	1978	34.1
1949	91.3	1959	56.9	1969	37.2	1979	32.3
End of Fiscal Year	**Gross Federal Debt as % of GDP**	**End of Fiscal Year**	**Gross Federal Debt as % of GDP**	**End of Fiscal Year**	**Gross Federal Debt as % of GDP**	**End of Fiscal Year**	**Gross Federal Debt as % of GDP**
1980	32.5	1990	54.2	2000	55.5	2010	91.4
1981	31.7	1991	58.9	2001	54.6	2011	96.0
1982	34.3	1992	62.2	2002	57.0	2012	100.1
1983	38.7	1993	64.0	2003	59.7	2013	101.3
1984	39.6	1994	64.5	2004	60.8	2014	103.6
1985	42.6	1995	64.9	2005	61.3	2015	101.8
1986	46.7	1996	64.9	2006	61.8		
1987	49.1	1997	63.3	2007	62.5		
1988	50.5	1998	61.2	2008	67.7		
1989	51.5	1999	58.9	2009	82.4		

Source: https://obamawhitehouse.archives.gov/omb/budget/Historicals

Table 8.3 General government debt as % of GDP, 2014

Country	% of GDP	Country	% of GDP
Estonia	14	Netherlands	81
Chile	22	Germany	83
Luxembourg	29	Hungary	99
Norway	33	Slovenia	99
Turkey	33	Austria	102
Mexico	45	Canada	109
Switzerland	45	United Kingdom	113
Latvia	46	Spain	118
Lithuania	53	France	120
Czech Republic	57	Ireland	122
Denmark	59	United States	124
Slovak Republic	60	Belgium	130
Sweden	64	Portugal	151
Australia	64	Italy	156
Poland	70	Greece	180
Finland	72	Japan	234
Israel	78		

Source: OECD statistics, General Government Debt.

When is a state's debt-to-GDP ratio too high? Often the answer to this depends on the value attributed to every additional unit of government spending. Big-government sympathizers tend to define the debt-level threshold as one where a state cannot effectively borrow further to meet a sovereign risk such as war, financial crash or other similar shock.[6] In such cases, additional borrowing to cushion sovereign risk has become, paradoxically, a sovereign risk. This is because the country will be unable to meet its repayment obligations and will default or else will need other countries to bail it out. As sovereign risk grows, lenders raise interest rates. If a country does not face sovereign risk, the argument goes, then it should reduce its debt-to-GDP ratio through economic growth.[7] Yet, just as arguably, public debt is a drag on long-term economic growth.[8] The negative impact is greatest where the total public debt of a country is greater than 80–90 percent of GDP. In such cases it is estimated that for every ten percent increase in debt there is a reduction in annual real per capita GDP growth of around 0.19 percent per year.[9] A study of 26 national debt histories concluded that countries during periods when debt levels rose above 90 percent had an average growth rate of 2.3 percent compared with 3.5 percent in lower debt eras.[10]

Despite this, public borrowing remains popular with governments. In 2014, 14 of 33 countries in the OECD had total public debts greater than 83 percent of GDP, including France, the United States, Italy, Greece and Japan (Table 8.3). In each case, the sovereign risk of this high debt was different. But the growth-suffocating effect of it was evident. Governments, though, commonly ignore this. They do so because organizations respond to different incentives compared with self-organizing systems. Their 'logic' is purposeful. The result is that governments take the view that a modern economy and society can be approached like a carpenter making a chair. A goal is set. Tools and materials are organized. Purposive-rationality of this kind underpins many kinds of human action. But not large-scale economic and social behavior. Modern societies are more than just purposive-rational in nature. They run not just 'purposively' but also 'automatically' or 'autonomously'. On a macro-scale they are, in effect, autonomous societies.[11] The carpenter-table model has limited application. When applied on the large scale, the results are shoddy.

Notes

1 Dewey, 1958 [1929], 103.
2 'Pendulum' is the term introduced by the social philosopher Agnes Heller (1999: 160, 193) to describe the swing-shift character of modern society.
3 Roberts, chapter 17.
4 Parkinson, 1955.
5 Roberts, chapter 17.
6 Ostry, Ghosh and Espinoza, 2015. The authors argue that paying down public debt is not required as long as 'fiscal space' is ample. This, they say, 'cannot be established through some mechanical rule but will generally require judgments based on stress testing fiscal balance sheets to withstand extreme shocks' (5).
7 Ostry, Ghosh and Espinoza, 2015, 1, 14.
8 Reinhart, Reinhart and Rogoff, 2012; Cecchetti, Mohanty and Zampolli, 2011; Kumar and Woo, 2010.
9 Cecchetti, Mohanty and Zampolli, 2011; Kumar and Woo, 2010.
10 Reinhart, Reinhart and Rogoff, 2012.
11 The 'autonomous society' was the term used by the Greek-French philosopher Cornelius Castoriadis (1997). He modelled the autonomous society not after markets as Hayek did, or after industries as Schumpeter did, but after cities. Castoriadis was a thinker of the political left. Hayek and Schumpeter were of the political center-right. Yet despite the clear divergences, there is a common thread that runs the gamut of these thinkers. Castoriadis' social theory was weakest when he emphasized the idea of society giving laws to itself, and strongest when he stressed the way society that organized itself according to forms.

Bibliography

Castoriadis, C. 1991. *World in Fragments: Writings on Politics, Society, Psychoanalysis and the Imagination*. Stanford, CA: Stanford University Press.

Cecchetti, S.G., M.S. Mohanty and F. Zampolli. 2011. *The Real Effects of Debt*. BIS Working Papers No. 352, September.

Dewey, J. 1958 [1929]. *Experience and Nature*. New York: Dover.

Heller, A. 1999. *A Theory of Modernity*. Oxford: Blackwell.

Kumar, M.S. and J. Woo. 2010. *Public Debt and Growth*, IMF Working Paper, July.

Ostry, J.D., A.R. Ghosh and R. Espinoza. 2015. *When Should Public Debt Be Reduced?* IMF Staff Discussion Note.

Parkinson, C.N. 1955. "Parkinson's Law", *Economist*, November 19.

Reinhart, C.M., V.R. Reinhart and K.S. Rogoff. *Debt Overhangs: Past and Present*. NBER Working Paper, April.

Roberts, A. 2012 [1999]. *Salisbury: Victorian Titan*. London: Faber and Faber.

9 Health 1

Low-productivity post-industrialism

In agricultural and manufacturing industries, over time, product quality has risen and the real prices of goods have declined. That drove remarkable, historically unprecedented, increases in the levels of social wealth and, consequently, in the general standard of living in the early and mid-twentieth century (Table 1.1). After 1970, this process slowed down. The slowdown occurred as the percentage of the workforce in the post-industrial sectors of health and education ballooned (Table 2.1). The nominal advantage of this ballooning was that the post-industrial sectors offered 'lots of jobs'. The disadvantage was that these jobs were, in the main, low-productivity jobs. That being the case, after 1970, the cost of health and education to consumers and taxpayers, employers and employees over time increased more rapidly than the general rate of inflation. The multifactor productivity increases that drove the early and mid-twentieth century increases in general prosperity declined (Table 1.2).

The general explanation of why this happened is that the post-industrial economic sectors were dominated by purposive organizations. Their thinking and behavior was managerial and bureaucratic in spirit. As a result, they tended to waste time, activity and resources. One of the worst instances of this was the healthcare sector. A massive leap in medical science occurred between 1920 and 1970.[1] For the first time in human history, a visit to a doctor or hospital was really worth it. Demand for health services grew accordingly. After 1970 the measurable quality of these services increased but at a decelerating rate while service prices multiplied by a factor of two or three times in real terms. The managerial class—entrenched in governments, hospitals, the insurance industry and professional interest groups—talked sanctimoniously about the value of healthcare. But the sector that they oversaw held down productivity and drove up prices.

The United States illustrates what happened. Between 1990 and 2010 in the US, labor productivity in manufacturing grew 4.7 percent and sector employment declined 2.1 percent.[2] In healthcare, the opposite occurred. Labor productivity declined 0.6 percent and employment grew 2.9 percent. Fifty-six percent of American healthcare costs are wages. The sector is labor-intensive. Yet, in the two decades prior to 2010, it managed negligible labor-shedding productivity growth. Between 1993 and 2013 American hospital labor productivity grew an average of 0.5 percent per annum (Table 9.1). Over the same period, real GDP

Table 9.1 US labor productivity, hospitals and medical laboratories, 1993–2015

2007=100		**1993**	**1994**	**1995**	**1996**	**1997**	**1998**	**1999**	**2000**	**2001**	**2002**	**2003**	**2004**
6215 - Medical and diagnostic laboratories	*Annual % increase/decrease*	n.a.	–0.3	4.1	6.4	18.9	5.6	5.9	2.4	1.9	2.5	0.7	–0.8
	2007 = 100	63.8	63.6	66.2	70.4	83.7	88.5	93.7	95.9	97.8	100.3	100.9	100.1
62151 - Medical and diagnostic laboratories	*Annual % increase/decrease*	n.a.	–0.3	4.1	6.4	18.9	5.6	5.9	2.4	1.9	2.5	0.7	–0.8
	2007 = 100	63.8	63.6	66.2	70.4	83.7	88.5	93.7	95.9	97.8	100.3	100.9	100.1
621511 - Medical laboratories	*Annual % increase/decrease*	n.a.	–0.8	3.7	6.2	17.3	4.3	5.1	0.1	–3.3	3.9	1.7	–3.2
	2007 = 100	69.5	68.9	71.4	75.9	88.9	92.8	97.5	97.6	94.3	98.1	99.7	96.5
621512 - Diagnostic imaging centers	*Annual % increase/decrease*	n.a.	0.5	4.8	6.8	21.5	7.4	7.9	5.8	10.2	–0.7	–2.7	2.8
	2007 = 100	59.0	59.3	62.2	66.4	80.7	86.7	93.6	99.0	109.1	108.3	105.4	108.4
6221,3 - Hospitals, except psychiatric and substance abuse hospitals	*Annual % increase/decrease*	0.4	6.6	2.0	–1.3	0.7	3.8	1.3	0.8	–1.3	–2.3	–0.8	–1.4
	2007 = 100	94.6	100.9	103.0	101.6	102.3	106.1	107.5	108.3	106.9	104.4	103.6	102.1

		2005	**2006**	**2007**	**2008**	**2009**	**2010**	**2011**	**2012**	**2013**	**2014**	**Average 1993–2014**
6215 - Medical and diagnostic laboratories	*Annual % increase/decrease*	2.1	–2.2	8.3	1.6	–5.3	–2.8	–4.6	1.4	0.3	–1.7	**2.1**
	2007 = 100	102.2	100.0	108.3	110.0	104.2	101.3	96.7	98.0	98.3	96.6	
62151 - Medical and diagnostic laboratories	*Annual % increase/decrease*	2.1	–2.2	8.3	1.6	–5.3	–2.8	–4.6	1.4	0.3	–1.7	**2.1**
	2007 = 100	102.2	100.0	108.3	110.0	104.2	101.3	96.7	98.0	98.3	96.6	

621511 - Medical laboratories	*Annual % increase/decrease*	1.3	2.3	9.1	4.8	–6.1	–1.0	–4.5	3.6	–0.6	–1.3	**2.0**
	2007 = 100	97.7	100.0	109.1	114.3	107.3	106.2	101.4	105.1	104.4	103.1	
621512 - Diagnostic imaging centers	*Annual % increase/decrease*	3.3	–10.7	7.8	–3.0	–2.0	–4.4	–4.6	–2.4	3.8	–2.3	**2.4**
	2007 = 100	111.9	100.0	107.8	104.6	102.5	98.0	93.5	91.3	94.8	92.6	
6221,3 - Hospitals, except psychiatric and substance abuse hospitals	*Annual % increase/decrease*	1.2	–3.3	0.1	1.5	0.5	1.3	0.4	0.1	n.a.	n.a.	**0.5**
	2007 = 100	103.4	100.0	100.1	101.7	102.1	103.5	103.9	104.0	n.a.	n.a.	

Source: Bureau of Labor Statistics, Labor Productivity and Costs by Industry Tables, February 9, 2017.

grew 2.5 percent annually. Increased labor productivity across the entire American economy contributed over seventy percent of GDP growth (1.8 percent annually). But not in healthcare. Only in the more machine-focused parts of the health sector—in US medical and diagnostic laboratories—was labor productivity over the period elevated, running at 2.1 percent annually. Between 1987 and 2014, hospitals' multifactor productivity *decreased* by 2 percent; ambulatory health care, by 4 percent. Meanwhile, private nonfarm multifactor productivity as a whole grew by 91 percent (Table 9.2).

The roots of stagnant health labor productivity extends back to the start of the post-industrial era. Between 1967 and 1994, output per employee in medical services in the US grew annually by 0.1 percent while unit labor costs grew by 6.6 percent annually (Table 9.3). The story is the same in education. Between 1968 and 1994, labor productivity in the education sector grew 0.4 percent annually and unit labor costs 5.6 percent (Table 9.4). Without increases in labor productivity, economies flatten and then stagnate. This is what happened to the international economy in the 2010s. The other consequence is escalating costs. Healthcare is a classic example of this. It not only experienced low productivity across multiple decades but at the same time increasing demands on its services—as new and better treatments become available. Increased productivity delivers more outputs and better outputs with fewer inputs. If this does not occur, then costs rise. In the United States, for 31 of the 40 years after 1970—across the span of the post-industrial age—health-cost increases outpaced the growth of the American economy.[3] Had the cost of other basic goods risen as quickly as healthcare, then in 2013 'a dozen eggs [would have cost] $55, a gallon of milk … $48, and a dozen oranges … $134'.[4] Instead, it was healthcare that charged such exorbitant prices.

But, surely, in spite of the low productivity 'the jobs' were worth it? Is not a low-productivity job better than no job at all? Is it not sounder to have ten people generating an annual output worth $60,000 each than six people generating an annual output worth $100,000 per head? If that was true, then the industrial revolution would never have happened. In our example, the $240,000 additional value created by a more productive workforce is not lost to the economy. The people who benefit by sector productivity increases don't stop spending or investing the extra value thereby saved. Rather, they reallocate it to other higher-end consumption and investment. By doing so, the overall standard or quality of living in a society increases—and energetic new industry sectors are able to emerge. The great stagnation of the 2010s is easy enough to explain. Some of it was the result of the long-term business cycle. The 2010s repeated in a milder form the cyclical low-ebb of the 1930s. But interlaced with this downcycle was the structural phenomenon of the low-productivity post-industrial employment sectors.

One of the key contributors to this structural phenomenon was the meagre labor-productivity of the healthcare industry. Some commentators are of the view that low productivity is inevitable in the health sector because the sector is intrinsically labor-intensive. This was the opinion of the Princeton economist William Baumol in 1967. Writing right on the cusp of the post-industrial age, Baumol argued that 'inherent in the technological structure' of 'municipal government,

Table 9.2 Contribution of health multifactor productivity to US private nonfarm business productivity, 1987–2014

Industry	1987–2014	1987–1990	1990–1995	1995–2000	2000–2007	2007–2014	2013–2014
Educational Services	–1.00%	–0.01	0.00	–0.01	0.00	–0.01	0.01
Ambulatory Health Care Services	–4.00%	–0.06	–0.14	0.00	0.00	–0.01	0.00
Hospitals and Nursing and Residential Care Facilities	–2.00%	–0.04	–0.04	–0.03	–0.02	0.00	–0.01
Total Nonmanufacturing Contribution	43.00%	0.45	0.13	0.37	0.69	0.42	0.53
Private Nonfarm Multi-factor Productivity	91.00%	0.66	0.54	1.46	1.38	0.41	0.72

Source: US Bureau of Labor Statistics, Contributions of Nonmanufacturing Industries to private nonfarm business productivity, June 22, 2016.

Table 9.3 US labor productivity medical services, 1967–1994

Year [1987 = 100]	Output per employee year	Output	Employee years	Compensation per employee year	Unit labor costs
1967	92.7	67.2	72.4	25.5	27.5
1968	94.5	70.4	74.5	26.8	28.3
1969	94.8	71.2	75.1	28	29.6
1970	94	70.3	74.7	31.9	33.9
1971	93.4	70.4	75.4	34.8	37.2
1972	88.5	69.5	78.6	38	43
1973	91.3	75.1	82.2	40.3	44.1
1974	91.1	75.8	83.2	43	47.2
1975	92.8	78.4	84.4	46.8	50.4
1976	94.3	81.3	86.2	52.3	55.4
1977	94.2	82	87	54.1	57.4
1978	92.5	82.3	88.9	56.8	61.3
1979	92.7	82.9	89.4	60.4	65.1
1980	94.7	85.3	90.1	65.3	69
1981	95	85.7	90.2	73.9	77.7
1982	96.1	90.6	94.4	79.6	82.8
1983	98	94.2	96.1	83	84.7
1984	97.5	94.7	97.2	86.2	88.5
1985	97.6	95.8	98.2	89.3	91.4
1986	99.4	98.2	98.8	93.8	94.4
1987	100	100	100	100	100
1988	104	102.2	98.3	105.4	101.3
1989	102.8	100.3	97.6	111.1	108
1990	100.6	100.5	99.8	117	116.2
1991	94.3	98.1	104	124.4	131.9
1992	93.9	96.3	102.6	132.5	141.1
1993	95.5	95.6	100.1	139.5	145.9
1994	90.6	95.4	105.4	141.5	156.2
Average annual rates of change					
1967–94	–0.1	1.3	1.4	6.6	6.6
1987–94	–1.4	–0.7	0.8	5.1	6.6
1993–94	–5.2	–0.2	5.2	1.4	7.1

Source: Federal Productivity Measurement Program March 1996, Medical services: Indexes of output per employee year and related data, fiscal years 1967–94 https://www.bls.gov/lpc/medical.txt

education, the performing arts, restaurants and leisure time activity' are 'forces working almost unavoidably for progressive and cumulative increases in the real costs incurred in supplying them'. As a consequence of this, Baumol thought that 'efforts to offset these cost increases, while they may succeed temporarily, in the long run are merely palliatives which can have no significant effect on the underlying trends'.[5]

Table 9.4 US labor productivity education and training, 1968–1994

Year [1987 = 100]	Output per employee year	Output	Employee years	Compensation per employee year	Unit labor costs
1968	84.9	88.2	104	27.8	32.8
1969	84.9	96.6	113.7	30.1	35.5
1970	77.3	97.9	126.6	32.1	41.4
1971	77.9	97.9	125.7	35.1	45.1
1972	80.5	101.3	125.8	40.5	50.3
1973	78.7	98.1	124.7	41.8	53.1
1974	77.5	90	116.2	45.4	58.6
1975	75.1	85.4	113.8	48.4	64.5
1976	82.1	83.8	102.1	51.6	62.9
1977	92.7	89.6	96.6	56.7	61.2
1978	91.5	85.4	93.3	58.7	64.2
1979	97.2	85.5	88	61.7	63.5
1980	97.8	88.8	90.8	67.1	68.7
1981	107.4	90.1	83.9	75.3	70.1
1982	103.7	95.4	92	80.5	77.6
1983	101.3	94	92.8	85.1	84
1984	100.3	95.3	95	89.2	89
1985	100.7	97.6	97	93.2	92.6
1986	101.3	99.4	98.1	98.4	97.2
1987	100	100	100	100	100
1988	102.6	96	93.6	103	100.4
1989	101.6	93	91.6	105.8	104.2
1990	107.9	95.6	88.6	110.9	102.7
1991	93.3	78.8	84.5	115.1	123.4
1992	90.3	75.3	83.4	119.6	132.4
1993	95.7	72.3	75.6	124.1	129.6
1994	95.3	67.7	71.1	130.4	136.8
Average annual rates of change					
1968–94	0.4	–1	–1.5	6.1	5.6
1987–94	–0.7	–5.4	–4.8	3.9	4.6
1993–94	–0.4	–6.4	–6	5	5.5

Source: Federal Productivity Measurement Program March 1996, Education and training: Indexes of output per employee year and related data, fiscal years 1968–94, https://www.bls.gov/lpc/educti1.txt

So what are the 'forces' driving up 'real costs'? The post-industrial industries, Baumol reasoned, rest on 'activities which, by their very nature, permit only sporadic increases in productivity'. This, he argued, was a 'manifestation of the activity's technological structure, which determines quite definitely whether the productivity of its labor inputs will grow slowly or rapidly'. In some industries—manufacturing being a salient example—labor is 'primarily an instrument'. Accordingly, it is a factor that is incidental to the final product. 'When someone purchases an air conditioner he neither knows nor cares how much labor went into it'; in other industries, however, 'for all practical purposes the labor is itself the end product'.[6]

Baumol's example of an industry in which labor is an end in itself was teaching. In education, he suggested, 'quality is judged directly in terms of amount of labor'. For example, class size is often taken as a critical index of quality. That is to say, the smaller the class size, the lower the labor productivity, the better. This was true, Baumol thought, 'despite the invention of teaching machines and the use of closed circuit television and a variety of other innovations'. Even after such technology changes 'there still seem to be fairly firm limits to class size'. Consequently 'we are deeply concerned when elementary school classes grow to 50 pupils and are disquieted by the idea of college lectures attended by 2000 underclassmen'.

It was true in 1967—and it remains true today—that there are some industries that think that their end product is 'labor'. That is a perfect description of the post-1970 health and education sectors. They developed an ideology that conceived low-productivity labor as the corner-stone of the sectors. Sanctimonious descriptions of this low-productivity labor proliferated. Baumol understood that productivity rests on social judgments. Early on, he grasped the kind of judgment that began to crystallize around post-industrial work. He thought that 'without a complete revolution in our approach to teaching' there was no prospect that the sector would 'ever go beyond' its established low levels of productivity. Thus he concluded that there were 'the relatively constant productivity industries' and 'those in which productivity can and does rise'. As an empirical prediction, Baumol was right. Over six subsequent decades, health and education produced little or no productivity growth and correspondingly large increases in real costs.

A persistent view in the post-industrial industries, not least amongst their super-managers, is that *'we are labor-intensive and defiantly disinterested in productivity improvement'*. Reporting on health productivity in 2016, the US Brookings Institution summed up the core anti-productivity view prevalent in the health sector this way: 'because healthcare is a labor intensive occupation, there is little scope for increasing productivity by substituting capital for labor, as is done in other industries'.[7] That view, though, has done nothing to stop the health sector increasing wages and salaries well in advance of its level of productivity. High wages in low-productivity industries, the Brookings' paper suggested, are caused by wage growth in high-productivity sectors. In general, in efficient industries 'when productivity increases, employers can raise wages without raising prices because each worker produces more.' That's a very good mechanism that benefits everyone. Yet low-productivity post-industrial sectors simply pay themselves higher wages—beginning with their super-managers who excuse this by pointing the finger at high-productivity industries. 'When wages in the overall economy rise because labor productivity is increasing, wages also will rise in sectors with low productivity growth so that workers in that industry won't quit their jobs and move into other industries.' The cost of this, though, is stagnant or lower standards of living across entire economies and the capture of resources that would be better allocated to new, more energetic, emergent industries.

So is low productivity inevitable in the big institutionalized managerial-driven post-industrial sector? Some economists say 'no'—on the grounds that hospitals already achieve higher productivity than conventionally measured because they achieve better quality of outcomes (longer life, more successful treatments and treatment of more intensely ill patients) for the same quantity of labor and capital inputs.[8] However, no one would reason this way about manufacturing. To buy a color TV in 1959, an average American worker had to work 127 hours.[9] In 2013, it was 20 hours. Not only was the television in real terms much cheaper but its quality was also much greater. Productivity means increasing quality *and* decreasing real cost simultaneously. This combination eludes the health and education sectors. But, arguably, it does not need to. It is not inevitable.

In the case of healthcare, how is increased productivity possible? In 2013 the American National Academies Institute of Medicine produced a lengthy report, *Best Care at Lower Cost*, which detailed the unnecessary spending in the US health system. Of a total US health expenditure in 2009 of $2500 billion, the report concluded that a third of it—$750 billion—was waste. If you doubt this figure then consider Table 9.5. Hospital costs per capita in the top-performing US state with above-average longevity (Utah) are 74 percent of the national average, that is, $2006 cheaper than the average and with much better outcomes (Table 9.5, 2009 dollars). If that $2006 per capita saving were spread over the whole US population, that's a savings equivalent of $616 billion. Another way of approaching this is to look at the cohort of good-value (low-spending, high-outcome) states in the US (Table 9.5). In 2009 these spent an average of $5606 compared to the state average of $7037. If the $1431 gap per capita between the high-performing cohort and the average state was spread over the entire population, that would represent a saving of $439 billion.

Powerful medical, hospital and insurance lobbies pressure governments to maintain a system that is improvident but whose waste-generation is also lucrative for those institutions. The Institute described the deep, abiding and aggressive productivity-aversion of the American health sector in this way: 'If banking were like healthcare, automated teller machine (ATM) transactions would take not seconds but perhaps days or longer as a result of unavailable or misplaced records ... If shopping were like healthcare, product prices would not be posted, and the price charged would vary widely within the same store, depending on the source of payment.'[10] Recurring systemic problems in healthcare include the overuse of services, operational inefficiency, high administrative costs and non-transparent pricing. Inefficient overtreatment, regulations that slow the adoption of good treatments and overly rapid uptake of medical techniques that have little efficacy are commonplace.

Systemic failure

The wasteful nature of post-industrial healthcare can be sub-divided into six basic categories. Waste is caused by the two kinds of failure. The first is autotelic failure, itself sub-dividable into the failures of labor-substitution, organizational dysfunction

Table 9.5 US states health outcomes, spending and productivity

Significantly above-average performance				Significantly below-average performance					
Rank by spending per capita, 2009	State	Life expectancy at birth, 2010 [state average: 78.62]	Health spending per capita, 2009 [state average: $7,037]	Average employee contribution to group health insurance, 2010 [state average: $2,919]	Average employee health insurance deductible contribution, 2010 [state average: $1,722]	Combined average employee contribution compared to health spending per capita, 2010 [state average: 68%]	Average out-of-pocket household health spending, 2016 [state average: $742]	Health spending percent of Gross State Product, 2009 [state average: 16%]	Politics [Red State, Blue State, Purple State] 2004–2016
1	Utah	80.2	$5,031	$3,029	$1,661	93%	$906	12.5%	R
2	Arizona	79.6	$5,434	$3,292	$2,082	99%	$760	14.6%	R
3	Georgia	77.2	$5,467	$2,975	$1,653	85%	$648	13.7%	R
4	Idaho	79.5	$5,658	$3,103	$2,421	98%	$782	16.3%	R
5	Nevada	78.1	$5,735	$2,595	$1,303	68%	$683	12.2%	B
6	Texas	78.5	$5,924	$3,598	$2,013	95%	$873	13.0%	R
7	Colorado	80	$5,994	$2,862	$1,977	81%	$916	12.3%	B
8	Arkansas	76	$6,167	$3,163	$1,571	77%	N/A	18.0%	R
9	California	80.8	$6,238	$3,011	$1,676	75%	$596	12.6%	B
10	Alabama	75.4	$6,272	$3,033	$1,075	65%	N/A	17.9%	R
11	Virginia	79	$6,286	$3,576	$1,635	83%	N/A	12.2%	B
12	South Carolina	77	$6,323	$2,924	$2,054	79%	N/A	18.4%	R
13	Tennessee	76.3	$6,411	$2,827	$1,791	72%	N/A	16.5%	R
14	North Carolina	77.8	$6,444	$2,850	$1,744	71%	N/A	14.7%	R

15	Oklahoma	75.9	$6,532	$3,054	$1,708	73%	$854	17.1%	R
16	Mississippi	75	$6,571	$3,391	$1,789	79%	N/A	21.0%	R
17	Oregon	79.5	$6,580	$3,017	$1,911	75%	$719	14.7%	B
18	Kentucky	76	$6,596	$2,485	$1,735	64%	$646	18.7%	R
19	Michigan	78.2	$6,618	$2,384	$1,563	60%	$601	18.8%	B
20	Montana	78.5	$6,640	$2,454	$2,023	67%	N/A	18.6%	R
21	New Mexico	78.4	$6,651	$3,225	$1,604	73%	N/A	17.9%	B
22	Indiana	77.6	$6,666	$2,873	$1,623	67%	$719	17.1%	R
23	Illinois	79	$6,756	$3,109	$1,635	70%	$788	14.0%	B
24	Kansas	78.7	$6,782	$2,657	$1,559	62%	N/A	15.7%	R
25	Washington	79.9	$6,782	$2,867	$1,634	66%	$825	13.6%	B
26	Louisiana	75.7	$6,795	$3,315	$1,857	76%	$796	15.1%	R
27	Hawaii	81.3	$6,856	$2,226	$1,302	51%	N/A	13.8%	B
28	Iowa	79.7	$6,921	$3,081	$1,640	68%	N/A	15.6%	P
29	Missouri	77.5	$6,967	$2,680	$1,850	65%	N/A	17.6%	R
30	Wyoming	78.3	$7,040	$2,581	$1,997	65%	N/A	11.2%	R
31	Nebraska	79.8	$7,048	$3,060	$1,718	68%	N/A	14.7%	R
32	South Dakota	79.5	$7,056	$3,088	$1,820	70%	N/A	15.5%	R
33	Ohio	77.8	$7,076	$2,683	$1,834	64%	$652	18.1%	P
34	Florida	79.4	$7,156	$3,611	$1,594	73%	$660	18.2%	P
35	Wisconsin	80	$7,233	$2,754	$2,177	68%	$759	17.3%	B
36	Minnesota	81.1	$7,409	$2,632	$1,903	61%	N/A	15.1%	B
37	Maryland	78.8	$7,492	$2,929	$1,451	58%	N/A	15.0%	B
38	New Jersey	80.3	$7,583	$3,197	$1,858	67%	$750	14.0%	B
39	Vermont	80.5	$7,635	$2,477	$2,408	64%	N/A	19.6%	B
40	West Virginia	75.4	$7,667	$2,578	$1,231	50%	$629	23.4%	R

41	Pennsylvania	78.5	$7,730	$2,433	$1,422	50%	N/A	18.1%	B
42	North Dakota	79.5	$7,749	$2,801	$1,249	52%	N/A	15.6%	R
43	New Hampshire	80.3	$7,839	$3,130	$2,011	66%	N/A	17.6%	B
44	Rhode Island	79.9	$8,309	$2,659	$1,706	53%	N/A	18.4%	B
45	New York	80.5	$8,341	$2,811	$1,458	51%	$620	15.2%	B
46	Delaware	78.4	$8,480	$3,425	$1,687	60%	N/A	12.5%	B
47	Maine	79.2	$8,521	$3,551	$2,014	65%	N/A	22.4%	B
48	Connecticut	80.8	$8,654	$3,135	$2,013	59%	$880	14.2%	B
49	Alaska	78.3	$9,128	$2,474	$1,790	47%	N/A	14.0%	R
50	Massachusetts	80.5	$9,278	$2,792	$1,393	45%	N/A	17.0%	B
51	*District of Columbia*	76.5	$10,349	$2,427	$1,003	33%	N/A		B
Significantly above-average performance				**Significantly below-average performance**					

Rank by spending per capita, 2009	State	Median individual earnings, 2009 [national median earnings: $29,235]	Medical Productivity Index, MPI, 2009 [average 13.6, highest 18.89, lowest 8.69]	Health Savings Accounts per 100,000 pop., 2015 [state average: 4844]	Percentage who exercise regularly, 2016 [state average: 53.9%]	Economic Freedom, 2014 [average state score 7, range 5.7 to 8.3]	Median age, by state, 2015 [US median age, 2015: 37.8 years old]	Medicare Cohort Hospital Inpatient Days per capita, 2014 [national average: 1.24 days]	Per capita state hospital costs as % of national hospital costs, 2009 [national cost: $2,542]
1	Utah	$26,126	15.45	5261	56	7.0	30.5	0.77	74%
2	Arizona	$29,049	12.12	3330	55	7.4	36.9	0.99	84%

3	Georgia	$29,453	12.47	3235	52	7.4	36.1	1.24	78%
4	Idaho	$24,776	16.55	5117	59	7.2	35.9	0.83	85%
5	Nevada	$31,122	12.44	2581	52	7.3	37.4	1.11	76%
6	Texas	$27,344	11.66	5582	54	8.0	34.3	1.28	89%
7	Colorado	$30,853	14.28	6030	62	7.3	36.3	0.88	87%
8	Arkansas	$23,471	13.64	2631	52	6.7	37.8	1.29	90%
9	California	$31,008	11.55	1838	57	5.9	36	1.04	84%
10	Alabama	$26,112	11.83	1340	50	7.0	38.6	1.4	85%
11	Virginia	$32,467	12.71	4968	54	7.8	37.7	1.14	94%
12	South Carolina	$26,247	12.84	2105	52	6.7	38.8	1.22	101%
13	Tennessee	$26,044	11.33	6986	52	7.9	38.6	1.31	85%
14	North Carolina	$26,943	10.81	3903	53	7.3	38.3	1.2	91%
15	Oklahoma	$25,283	13.67	2879	53	7.4	36.2	1.29	97%
16	Mississippi	$24,620	14.28	1381	52	6.4	36.7	1.4	107%
17	Oregon	$27,285	16.43	3213	57	6.3	39.3	0.84	89%
18	Kentucky	$25,861	13.41	4065	48	6.4	38.5	1.56	106%
19	Michigan	$27,125	12.48	2696	52	6.9	39.6	1.44	107%
20	Montana	$24,033	17.52	7936	57	6.9	39.6	0.91	115%
21	New Mexico	$24,495	16.5	1848	61	6.2	37.2	0.97	103%
22	Indiana	$27,677	14.13	7422	50	7.2	37.4	1.27	108%
23	Illinois	$30,964	13.07	9958	51	6.7	37.5	1.29	106%
24	Kansas	$27,690	13.49	4608	52	7.3	36.2	1.16	98%
25	Washington	$31,812	13.84	7548	56	6.9	37.5	0.9	100%
26	Louisiana	$26,357	14.44	4430	51	7.0	36.1	1.34	103%
27	Hawaii	$31,766	14.2	46	62	6.2	38.1	0.89	95%
28	Iowa	$26,857	15.72	5689	52	6.9	38.2	1.06	107%

29	Missouri	$26,801	13.49	4136	53	7.4	38.5	1.3	119%
30	Wyoming	$29,507	18.89	3420	60	7.0	36.6	0.96	119%
31	Nebraska	$26,659	14.58	7049	55	7.4	36.2	1.05	118%
32	South Dakota	$25,717	15.5	5239	52	8.0	36.6	1.03	133%
33	Ohio	$27,805	12.95	7250	50	6.5	39.4	1.31	121%
34	Florida	$27,366	8.62	3547	53	8.1	41.6	1.38	91%
35	Wisconsin	$29,168	13.97	3934	54	6.7	39.2	1.06	111%
36	Minnesota	$31,442	14.99	15203	55	6.3	37.8	0.92	105%
37	Maryland	$37,320	11.47	6453	51	7.2	38.3	1.28	111%
38	New Jersey	$37,707	8.69	4431	50	6.7	39.4	1.45	98%
39	Vermont	$26,627	17.62	8765	64	6.3	42.8	0.91	141%
40	West Virginia	$24,404	15.41	1656	51	6.3	41.9	1.59	128%
41	Pennsylvania	$29,891	12.56	6586	51	7.2	40.7	1.32	110%
42	North Dakota	$26,224	15.67	6737	53	7.4	35.1	1.04	133%
43	New Hampshire	$32,207	15.09	6099	57	8.3	42.5	1.04	124%
44	Rhode Island	$31,179	12.44	1351	50	6.8	39.8	1.29	121%
45	New York	$31,963	10.84	3110	51	5.7	38.2	1.53	120%
46	Delaware	$31,320	12.1	2989	49	6.7	39.6	1.34	120%
47	Maine	$26,120	15.92	8024	55	6.5	44.1	1.08	127%
48	Connecticut	$36,827	10.71	8075	53	7.1	40.5	1.29	106%
49	Alaska	$31,774	18.2	5780	63	6.2	33.3	1.07	150%
50	Massachusetts	$35,533	12.09	3598	55	7.3	39.4	1.24	142%
51	*District of Columbia*	$40,342	12.94	5001		7.0	33.8	1.2	195%

Sources: The Henry J. Kaiser Family Foundation, "State Health Facts"; Centers for Medicare & Medicaid Services, US Department of Health & Human Services, Personal Health Care Expenditures per capita by state for 2009; Ballotpedia, Total healthcare spending by state, 2009 ['percent of GSP']; Social Science Research Council, The Measure of America: American Human Development Index by State, 2013–2014, 2010–2011, 2008–2009 [includes data drawn from the U.S. Census Bureau, American Community Survey 2010 and Population Estimates Program as well as the Centers for Disease Control and Prevention, National Center for Health Statistics]; Stephen T. Parente, Development of a Medical Productivity Index for health insurance beneficiaries, Insurance Markets and Companies: Analyses and Actuarial Computations, Volume 2, Issue 3, 2011, Table 1 MPI State Ranking, 3rd quarter 2009, Traditional Medicare; Gallup, % Exercise frequently State of the States data, 2016; Dean Stansel, José Torra & Fred McMahon, Economic Freedom of North America 2016, Fraser Institute, Figure 1.2b: Summary of US Ratings for Economic Freedom at the Subnational Level, 2014; U.S. Census Bureau's American Community Survey; Sara R. Collins, David C. Radley, Munira Z. Gunja, and Sophie Beutel, The Slowdown in Employer Insurance Cost Growth: Why Many Workers Still Feel the Pinch, Issue Brief, The Commonwealth Fund, October 2016, Table 4. Average Employee Cost: Premium Contribution + Deductible, by State, 2006, 2010, and 2015; Federal Reserve Bank of St Louis, Real Median Personal Income in the United States; OECD Statistics, Health expenditure and financing; JPMorgan, Chase & Co Institute, Paying Out-of-Pocket: The Healthcare Spending of 2 million US familes, September 2017; Centers for Medicare & Medicaid Services, US Department of Health & Human Services, Table 12: Total All Payers Per Capita State Estimates by State of Residence 1991–2014, Hospital Services.

Definitions: Red, blue, purple presidential politics: Red = state voted three or four times in the 2004, 2008, 2012, 2016 elections for the Republican presidential candidate; Blue = state voted three or four times in 2004, 2008, 2012, 2016 for the Democrat presidential candidate; Purple = state voted twice for Democrat and twice for the Republican candidate in 2004, 2008, 2012, 2016; MPI: a combined measure of health outcomes and medical care effort based on a national sample of Medicare 2007–2009 claims data involving 1.875 million beneficiaries. The index measures the cost of physician time and capital relative to patient time, age, gender, health status (level of illness over a 90-day period) and genetic disposition; Exercise: The percentage of state residents who report exercising for at least 30 minutes three or more days per week; Economic Freedom: measures the extent to which the policies of individual states in 2014 supported economic freedom and the ability of individuals to act in the economic sphere free of undue restrictions. The economic freedom score is a measure of government spending, taxation and labor market factors; Total Health Spending: includes spending for all privately and publicly funded personal health care services and products (hospital care, physician services, nursing home care, prescription drugs, etc.) by state of residence. Hospital spending is included and reflects the total net revenue (gross charges less contractual adjustments, bad debts, and charity care); Out of pocket: healthcare paid for directly by consumers excluding insurance and health savings accounts (JPMorgan, Chase & Co Institute, 2017).

and excessive administration. The second is the failure of pseudo-markets, further divisible into the overuse of services, opaque pricing and managerial price-setting.

Autotelic failure

1 *Labor-substitution failure.* In 1970, 200,000 medical research publications were produced. In 2010 it was 750,000.[11] That meant each day in 2010 the results of 2000+ scientific publications, 75 clinical trials and 11 systematic reviews were released. The more that scientific knowledge grows, often the slower it is adopted into common use. It can take 15 years for the findings of a landmark study to be implemented in practice.[12] No human being can read even a tiny percentage of the literature that now records medical research advances and failures. Related to this, clinical decisions and clinical guidelines often lack a clear basis in evidence.[13] This need not be the case. The laborious Promethean task of reading the vast medical literature can be auto-industrialized. It is increasingly possible to use digital decision-support tools that offer treatment suggestions based on current information. Decision support does not replace the health practitioner's judgment or responsibility. But it does expand the up-to-date knowledge base that the practitioner can access with speed.

Industrial societies advance by replacing labor with machines. This displaces labor. In doing so it reduces the costs to consumers. That frees up income for consumers to spend in other ways. When healthcare organizations fail to innovate in an industrial sense, reducing wastage of time and resources, this not only does not reduce costs but it increases them, making consumers less able to spend money in other sectors and in new industry sectors.

Auto-industrialization now and in the near-future offers the prospect of replacing repetitive or poorly coordinated labor. Support tasks in hospitals tend to be labor-intensive and repetitious. Automated fulfillment of hospital pharmacy orders and robotic hospital delivery machines are examples of labor-replacement technology that offer increased reliability and reduce costs. But this is offset by the widespread tacit post-industrial ideology of labor that is happy to employ technology so long as it is not labor-replacing. There is the assumption that tax payers will always underwrite increasing real costs because 'hospitals save lives'.

2 *Organizational failure.* Post-industrialism emphasized the role of organizations. But hospitals are rife with organizational, notably coordination, failures.[14] These are systemic work glitches: failures to coordinate and deliver to frontline staff the correct medications, medical orders, equipment, supplies and staff assistance. It is estimated that nurses experience 'glitches'—ranging from supply- or equipment-related problems to missing information or fruitless waiting, redundant work or co-ordination errors—at a rate of two per hour.[15] Poor coordination—a failure of organization—occurs not just within hospitals but also between hospitals and out-of-hospital care. One-fifth of Medicare patients in the US are re-hospitalized after 30 days, at a huge cost.[16]

The glitch-ridden hospital undermines 'flow', the key characteristic of highly engaged conscientious work.[17] Flow is a generic synonym for work that involves concentration, clarity of thought, feelings of potency, good memory and patient thinking among the workforce. Flow is the opposite of distracted thinking. Flow defines work that is both of high-quality and efficient. So much modern organization causes task-work to be unfocused, sidetracked and inattentive. This is because its design is of poor quality. It creates systemic disruption, distraction and delay. It defeats concentration on the task at hand. Institutions that flow properly are streamlined and lean.[18] Information, equipment, staff, consumables and patients can be structured so as to flow. The converse of flow is waste. Classic command-and-control organizations are afflicted by unnecessary inventory, employee movement, transportation and waiting. They are plagued by over-processing and over-production.

The corrective to waste is lean operating. The lean concept (not the word but the idea) was crystallized by the Japanese industrial engineer Taiichi Ohno (1912–1990). Ohno developed the Toyota Production System. The methodology echoes Japanese aesthetics. The Zen Buddhist concept of *mottainai* encapsulates the pervasive Japanese sense of not-being-wasteful—whether this is with time, thought, money or things. The ethos is mirrored in the Japanese idea of *iki*, that beauty, while subtle, is something simple, stark, straightforward and unself-conscious. That ideal is the opposite of the archetype of most twentieth-century managerial culture in which things are organized so as to be complicated, convoluted, evasive, and pretentious.

Lean organizations of all kinds, including hospitals, eliminate wasted time and unnecessary procedures, equipment and facilities.[19] They respond well to uneven customer demand. They avoid command-economy-style long queues. They eliminate time-consuming walks around institutions that eat into staff time. They cut out redundant activities. They jettison resources and functions that add no value to the core business of the institution. They get rid of endless meetings. They expand the stream, flow, steadiness, smoothness and continuity of enjoyable productive useful work. They utilize visual design to communicate more effectively. They reduce coordination bottlenecks between departments.

Twentieth-century organization was a kind of procedural command-and-control system, a mix of rules and hierarchies. What it lacked was the aesthetic-style coordination typical of self-organizing systems. Flow is the institutional equivalent of self-organizing social aesthetics. Autotelic workplace behavior roughly equates autopoietic behavior, if not on the same scale or with the same anonymous characteristics. It is typically paired with Pareto-style management. That is management that emphasizes ratios rather than rules. Ratio, like flow or stream, is ultimately an aesthetic-style concept. Ratio and proportionality—and related phenomena such as symmetry and equilibrium—are repeatedly found across nature, society and art. The core concept of Pareto management is 80:20 ratios, for example the precept that 80 percent of defects in a process are caused by 20 percent of problems that afflict the process.[20]

Poor hospital organization is a fractal of a larger social syndrome. This is the general failure of organizations in the post-1920 organizational era. Organizations deliver status and careers but not the coordination prowess that their advocates promised. Today, computerization and auto-industrialization of medication delivery, physician order entry, equipment maintenance, supplies and cleaning/housekeeping assistance offers the realistic technological prospect of reducing systemic coordination glitches and failures through the application of artificial intelligence to key hospital support tasks. Yet technology alone cannot solve the failure of organization.

In post-industrial sectors, the way that technology is applied tends perversely to reduce rather than increase productivity. I am referring here to technology that is used for organizational purposes (rather than strictly clinical or treatment purposes). The poor organizational application of technology is ironic. For the large health and education sectors, which only began to develop in the mid-twentieth century, were influenced deeply by the managerial ethos that emerged in the 1930s and 1940s. Managerialism pushed to separate ownership from control in companies. It agitated to elevate the firm above the market. It promised that procedurally focused rule-driven organizations would efficiently deliver goods and services to people who don't purchase them but rather receive them as benefits. Yet the managerial class who gradually assumed control of healthcare and education—pushing out older-style collegiate directors—proved to be terrible at organization and management.

The 'professionalization' of hospital management occurred in the UK in the 1980s.[21] The same happened in Australia in 1980s.[22] In Australia, in the same decade, professors were stripped of collegial authority over universities.[23] Their authority was replaced by the executive power of vice-chancellors who in turn directed growing numbers of professional and academic administrators. This process was supposed to achieve greater efficiency. It resulted in the opposite.

What is it about the managerial class that makes it so poor at organizing things? Simply put, its outlook is not that directed to 'fixing problems' but rather 'making the world better'. The former focuses on streamlining outputs; the latter on increasing inputs. The managerial class does not really organize. Rather, it lobbies governments for funding. Its logic is not one of saving money but spending it. It concentrates on increasing fiscal allocations not on tailoring expenditures. Its ethos is one of distribution rather than production. It conceives its role first and foremost in terms of distributive fairness not productive fecundity.[24] It is interested more in the dissemination of resources than in the achievement of operational results.

3 *Administrative excess*. Modern organizations are coordinated through procedural hierarchies and paperwork. Behavior is "organized" by dividing goal-directed action into steps and codifying the acts and the steps. To check that codes and procedures are adhered to, each part of a process in an organization is then documented. The documentation is often highly detailed, often to the point where the larger picture of the organization is lost in the detail of the documentation. Information technology developed in no small measure as a response to this problem, as a means of managing the volume of documentation. But it could never obviate the underlying propensity of organizations to look in ever-more granular detail where instead breadth of outlook was required.

Healthcare is a sector where the poor application of good technology is rife. In 2013, the British Royal College of Nursing (RCN) surveyed 6,000 nurses. Two-thirds of those surveyed indicated that the use of information technology had increased the amount of time spent on paperwork and administration.[25] One nurse, commenting on the survey results, remarked:[26]

> In my [NHS] trust obs are supposed to be input directly onto the computer via an electronic handset. It is often impossible to get connected to the system and at other times I have had to walk up and down the ward to try and get a signal. In the end I often resort to writing all the obs down in my notebook and then going to input them directly onto the computer, which means that it can be nearly an hour before the first set of obs I did actually gets put onto the system. Even more frustrating are the times when I need to check the patient's latest BP reading before giving meds, and I cannot access the system via the handset, so have to go to the computer terminal, which is often in use by another member of staff, to check the previous obs—again this causes long time delays.

As such organizational incoordination and administrative documentation has grown, the time allocated to direct patient care has declined. On one account, hospital nurses in the US now spend only 30 percent of their time on direct patient care.[27] In another account, the greatest portion of nursing time (35 percent) in American hospitals is spent on documentation.[28] Care coordination—dealing with other staff—takes-up a further 20 percent of time. Direct patient care gets allocated a residual 20 percent of time. A 2001 study of American hospitals concluded that staff had to devote a minimum of 30 minutes paperwork for every hour of patient care. On top of that an additional 25 percent of costs was devoted to generic hospital administration.[29]

The United Kingdom has a single-payer health system, different from America's multi-payer system. But the burden of paperwork is just as evident.[30] In the large 2013 Royal College of Nursing survey, British nurses reported that close to a fifth (17.3 percent) of their hours consisted of paperwork.[31] Conducting a review of Britain's National Health Service (NHS) for the Cameron Government, Lord Rose described the service as 'drowning in bureaucracy'.[32] He argued that there were two reasons for this. One was that the NHS was 'too vertically structured'; secondly, there were 'too many regulatory organizations making too many reporting requests'. He observed that as the NHS had grown more independent from government over the years, the amount of regulatory over-sight had expanded, paradoxically making it more dependent on government. Each new regulatory agency added a further imperious layer of paperwork. Each had 'its own mandate; each issues its own demands for data.' This had 'spawned an industry of data collecting. Requests for data are often made regardless of whether the data has been collected in a different format elsewhere and irrespective of the impact on daily business.' In addition, the data collected focused on 'inputs rather than outputs'.

In 2012 a NHS Institute for Innovation and Improvement (III) study surveyed 2,000 nurses.[33] Seventy-seven percent of those surveyed thought that NHS paperwork was time-consuming and difficult to complete. Sixty-eight percent thought that it added little value to patient care. The key objection to the paperwork was 'duplication', a familiar story in all public-sector administrative systems. Duplication means that the same information is entered time and time again. The NHS III study also sought comment from focus groups. As one respondent put it:

> The lack of interface between the systems means we have to enter the same information multiple times and log in to each individual programme which is so time consuming.

In large organizations, data is collected as much to protect those in charge as it is to do the job effectively. This was also observed by one of the III respondents:

> Most of the data collected is to ensure that the [health trust] is covered in case of a claim of neglect by patient. Reams of documents will be available to show we must have done all the care as the box is ticked. In one unit the care plan tick box is 26 pages … I would rather just write a small paragraph rather than tick 'dentures applicable or not applicable, cleaned, cleaned by client, if not cleaned why.' You cannot tell anyone higher up as they are just happy that boxes are ticked and they are covered. 'Your mother was not left without a drink all day, look the boxes were ticked every hour to say she was offered a drink.'

What follows from this is a lack of common sense. As two other study respondents commented:

> Does a 21-year-old independent man really need a falls risk, a Braden score, a moving and handling chart and a MUST score?
>
> I work in the recovery department and on many occasions the patients stay for a short period of time. Because there is so much paperwork to fill in, many times I do not find time to speak to the patient!

What managerial culture does is to turn clinical occupations into clerical jobs:

> Nurses became nurses to care for patients, not sit at a computer all day ticking boxes while untrained staff are left to provide care for complex patients who need our expertise—if I had wanted to [do] this type of work I would have gone for an office job.

In fact, the logic of managerialism is to turn all work into office work.

The NHS III study reported that what was most pointlessly time-consuming was the data collection and paperwork connected with audits. Regulatory standards, quality targets and financial measures are introduced by governments with the intention of diminishing costs and increasing the number of good outcomes. Governments use audits to collect information to check if its norms and targets are being complied with. These audits have some disciplinary effect on organizations. Yet, perversely, they also consume a lot of employee time. The net effect of them is to increase costs and reduce good outcomes.

Underlying this is the self-defeating attempt of government to implement a bureaucratic solution (the audit) to a bureaucratic problem, namely that work in administrative systems—as opposed to market systems or industrial systems—multiples time-and-effort rather than reducing it.[34] This is why 'cuts' in public-sector organizations after a short time usually end in the expansion of the size of the organization. The operative principle is that more people take longer to produce the same result.[35] Administration measures its success by the size of its staff not by the productivity of its staff. Markets offer profits as a sign of achievement; industries offer innovation; cities offer location. Each of these self-organizing social systems rewards efficiency. Profits are increased by increasing productivity. Industrialization increases productivity by replacing labour with machines. Cities increase efficiency by deepening and intensifying human interaction. Administrations and organizations, however, behave quite differently. They value low productivity not in itself but because the number of staff employed is the measure of administrative and organizational success. An organization fails if staff numbers are cut, even if a reduction in such numbers is a government target. In self-organizing systems, less is more. In organized systems, more is more.

Paperwork is one of the prime means of multiplying administrative work. So it is not surprising that documentation consumes a large portion of contemporary hospital time. This is a fractal of a larger social development. The bureaucratic societies that developed in the twentieth century widely adopted the view that risk was best managed by the following of rules, regulations and procedures—and that such rule-following needs to be intensively documented. The consequence of this is summed-up in this example:

> I work on a 23-bedded orthopedic ward with many immobile, elderly unwell patients and we do not get any pressure ulcers and that is not an easy achievement and will only come with regular and intensive nursing care which is carried by an excellent, thoughtful and conscientious team of nurses who are struggling with the volume of paperwork … I am ordering a new filing cabinet and I need space for 70 forms. Basically I have the training, the qualifications, the ethics, the NMC code, the honesty, my own integrity and trust of my colleagues so why isn't my word good enough? In the past it was enough for nurses to simply evaluate and document the care given to each patient for the period of time that you were caring for them.[36]

In large post-industrial organizations, like hospitals and universities, such documentation is not only pervasive and obsessive but it is also done very inefficiently. The NHS III feedback put it in these terms:

> We need to get rid of the duplication, and get away from the current practice of completing an initial assessment and then a risk assessment document, crisis and contingency and CPA document even though there is no risk of wandering, fire or other.

> Each patient should have a central electronic record that can be accessed/logged onto by healthcare staff. Staff should then be given hand-held devices, e.g. tablets, and then the record could be viewed, all documentation could be recorded at time and place and referrals/prescriptions etc. could all be done from there.

The following description of hospital practice could apply equally to any part of the post-industrial-era public sector:

> …nurses and other care providers often must transfer information between data collection systems, consuming nursing time and contributing to transcription errors. Documentation is often duplicated between departments and disciplines because of the lack of a single patient problem list for all providers. The result is fragmentation of care, duplication of data sets and the inability to quantify the outcome of the care provided. Evolving regulatory and public policy requirements for documentation … may exacerbate these problems.[37]

The possibilities for the auto-industrialization of process documentation is enormous. Yet the resistance to this in the public sector is also enormous. It is remarkable that in 2011, more than two decades after the appearance of the personal computer, only 34 percent of physician offices in the US had access to electronic patient records (and only 18 percent of hospitals did).[38]

From the standpoint of the bureaucratic society, nothing is more valuable than laborious documentation. Those who direct and manage bureaucratic institutions, and who draw their status and income from these organizations, see nothing wrong with healthcare consumers paying for a third of hospital nursing time to be allocated to manual documentation. Automation of this activity is not simply a technological issue. It is also an issue of ethos. For if serious, proficient, error-resistant automation was implemented, as it has been in mega-scale online retailing, it would eliminate the pointless duplication and labor-intensive manual handling of data and provide much better, as well as much larger, operational data sets to analyze and reflect on.

This, though, is a touchy matter. For it also means that a machine promises to do a better job than a century of human 'documentocracies' have. It mocks the inner spirit of the bureaucratic society by saying that the obsessive recording of persons and events was frequently time-wasting, inaccurate, distracting, unnecessarily repetitive, laborious and tedious.

In an organizational society, the drain on time that is caused by documentation has multiple sources. There is governmental regulation, hospital procedure and insurer paperwork. Every society has to deal with risk and fraud. A bureaucratic society does so with entitlement and treatment rules. Underlying such rules is a labor-intensive process of monitoring, checking, reviewing, approving and rejecting. In the US, non-hospital-based primary care and specialist physicians report spending 3 hours a week—that is, 3 weeks a year in total—dealing with patient health plans.[39] Nurses in these practices spend 13 hours a week on the same. In 2009 the estimated total cost of medical practices dealing with insurance plans was $23 to $31 billion per year—one percent of health expenditure. There is an argument that less paperwork frees time for more communication with patients which results in fewer tests and unnecessary referrals.[40]

In a managerial society, what first parties pay for is less front-line service and more bureaucratic process and procedure. These invariably attend both government, social-insurance and private-insurance benefit systems. By their nature, such systems involve substantial administration. Any form of indirect third-party purchase of a good or service does. To avoid fraud, third-party healthcare payers—public and private—rely on eligibility requirements and application screening, in short, paperwork.

Items 1–3 collectively can be described *autotelic failures*. Autotelic is a term used by the American psychologist Mihaly Csikszentmihalyi to describe the best kind of skilled or demanding work that human beings do.[41] Autotelic work occurs when persons at work feel that they are not wasting their time. Their own self (the 'auto' part) can concentrate on goals (the 'telic' part) without being repeatedly interrupted, distracted, obstructed or frustrated by external conditions. Modern organizations, not least hospitals, are often chronically heterotelic, which is to say they systematically waste the time of those they employ. Whether it is excessive walking of corridors, oppressive paperwork, dysfunctional technology or unresponsive departments, the result is the same: a decline in the sense of human autonomy and a decrease in feelings of satisfaction.

Autotelic work is a key aspect of an auto-industrial society. It is a vital component of the 'auto' in auto-industrial. Self-organizing systems tend to have a high degree of autotelic functioning. Take the case of markets. Even the commonest consumer commodity passes through multiple hands and stages to get your table. Its division of labor is complex. Yet on the whole, markets flow smoothly. Occasionally, a drought or flood will disrupt the supply of (say) bananas. Prices will go up for a few months. Consumers will buy alternative fruits and eventually things will return to normal with generally little frustration having occurred. Self-organizing systems make complex divisions of labor work simply. They achieve this paradoxical but very pleasant state by avoiding command-and-control systems of operation. In this they are unlike most organizations. Large-scale self-organizing systems like markets, industries, cities and publics coordinate interactions through media that have an aesthetic-like character, that is, through pattern-order. Declining supply generates increasing prices generates declining demand, a symmetrical, almost geometrical, pattern of behavior.

Compare that with an average organization where there is also a complex division of labor. Unlike markets or other self-organizing systems, organizations do not typically encourage autotelic behavior. In fact, their kind of division of labor routinely causes all manner of time-wasting blockages for those who work for the organization. Time is money. So wasting time is wasting money. Wasting money in large public-sector organizations such as hospitals adds to costs. Mounting costs eventually lead to unsustainable public budgets.

How might this be obviated? By systematically addressing and reducing autotelic blockages. In part this means asking how work can be 'organized' (or better still pattern-ordered) so as to reduce distraction and institutional noise. How do we free time so persons can focus on core work-tasks? Institutions steal time: they divert attention and concentration away from core work-tasks. They create structural or technological disruptions, disturbances and diversions that interfere with flow. Flow is a cognitive and physical state. When we experience flow, we are able to work in a way that is persistent, uninterrupted and not subject to casual interference. That's a good use of time. It leaves human beings with a sense of autonomy and control. It obviates boring spells of kicking one's heels waiting for an order to be filled. It allows for sustained involvement in a task.

The failure of pseudo-markets

Items 4–6 below are not autotelic failures but rather the failures of the pseudo-markets that are common in modern health industries.

4 *Overuse of services.* Whatever is free or heavily subsidized will be overused. Whenever payers pay a third party to pay for their services, the first party is always tempted to overuse services for the sake of extracting more hypothetical value from what has already been paid for via taxation or insurance.

Third-party payers of all kinds—whether single-payers or multiple-payers—distort perceptions of medical needs and wants. A free service or a schedule of benefits invariably will be overused because it is either free (meaning it is paid for by the taxpayer) or it has already been paid for (when an insurance plan was purchased). Users of services don't perceive themselves as taxpayers or as policy-holders but as a beneficiary using a seemingly 'costless' service paid for by 'others' (the government, the employer, the insurer). A 'costless' economy ('they're paying, I'm not') is an illusion, but it is a powerful one. In the end, the cost of free or subsidized services is reflected in national economic performance, government debt, the shrinking of discretionary government expenditure, and so on. These costs seem abstract and distant so users are not bothered. Yet the indirect costs to users are substantial.

In 2017 the Canada Institute for Health Information concluded that many common tests, treatments and procedures are not necessary. It found, for example, in Alberta that 30 percent of patients with lower-back pain without red flags had at least one unnecessary X-ray, CT or MRI; 1-in-10 seniors in Canada uses a benzodiazepine (a sedative-hypnotic) on a regular basis even though this is not recommended by experts. Thirty percent of emergency department patients in Ontario and Alberta with low-risk minor head trauma received a CT head scan, and so on.[42]

5 *Non-transparent pricing.* Third-party-payer systems involve a relative handful of hospital, insurance and government decision-makers 'negotiating' (i.e. setting) prices. This is not a centralized command economy. But it is not a free-market economy either. In a centrally planned economy there is a single price authority. In a managerial third-party-payer system, there is a polyarchy. This plurality of institutional authorities: governments, insurers,

> hospitals, professional associations, staff unions, pharmaceutical and medical-equipment companies set prices (or really a schedule of costs) directly and indirectly through pressuring, bargaining, contracting and lobbying. The process occurs in the shadows outside the public spotlight. Prices are set but they are not revealed or else exist in formats that make price comparisons difficult to do. As Australia's Productivity Commission put it, 'data on individual hospital costs are collected but not published'.[43]

These 'prices' are not intended to signal information (relevant to making a purchase) to the ultimate consumer. This is because in the majority of cases of healthcare consumption, the consumer does not directly purchase the service or good. In the managerial pseudo-market system, near-incomprehensible pseudo-pricing is the norm. The result is the absence of any correlation between price and quality or any way of making an intelligible comparison between insurer rates or provider prices.[44] In the simplest terms, the cost or price of medical procedures are not itemized in any meaningful way on provider invoices or websites. This means that the health market while notionally a market in reality is not a market.[45] Rather, it is a polyarchy. In a polyarchy, decision making occurs not via the actions of millions who participate in free markets but instead through the offices of a relatively small number of competing-cooperating institutional actors who strike institutionally brokered agreements to establish arbitrary and obfuscating cost-and-remuneration schedules couched in aggressively opaque terms.

The polyarchs are not paying for goods or services they consume themselves but rather they are paying for services that other parties (i.e. first parties) consume. The primary interest of the polyarchs is not in the price and quality of the service but rather in the bargains that are struck with other polyarchs. Such bargains at times can be awful. Take the case of Australia's Pharmaceutical Benefits Scheme. The Australian government 'subsidizes' the cost of expensive pharmaceutical drugs. This, ostensibly, is a social good. In doing so it 'negotiates' prices with pharmaceutical manufacturers. In 2011 the result was prices markedly *above* international levels.[46] In 2011 the UK Office of Health Economics compared prices for a basket of the 250 most-prescribed drugs across 13 countries that included Australia. The Australian prices overall were higher than in all countries excepting the US and Germany. That cost the Australian government $1.5 billion dollars of additional government revenue, out of a total health spend of $59.5 billion.[47] Eight of the common generic drugs that were surveyed cost Australians on average ten times the international price.

A 2013 study similarly concluded that Australia was over-paying by $1.3 billion a year or 14 percent of the Pharmaceutical Benefits Scheme.[48] The study observed that 'key decisions are made by a committee inside [Australia's Federal] Department of Health and Ageing that includes among its six members two representatives of drug companies.'[49] Australia's Medicare Benefits Schedule [MBS], which lists government-subsidized medical services, exhibits similar perverse outcomes. Market prices are dynamic. Bureaucratic prices much less so. As one expert observer noted 'once items are on the MBS, as long as they are still being used, they are rarely re-evaluated, and they attract the yearly rise in benefit level'.[50] Take the case of cataract surgery. One Australian health minister tried to reduce ophthalmologists' fees for the surgery by 50 percent. Pricing for the surgery was

> introduced when the procedure was not considered routine, took much longer than today and required an inpatient stay of more than a week. The benefit reflected this. In the nearly 40 years since, technology has moved on and now this surgery can be performed under local anaesthetic as a day-procedure lasting 20 minutes. Private patients are sometimes charged more than $4000 for this procedure. In the end, the Minister was only able to achieve a 12 percent reduction on the MBS fee. The top providers of this item have performed more than 20 procedures in one day, according to Medicare Australia data.

Australia's Medical Services Advisory Committee advises Australia's federal health minister on the safety, clinical effectiveness and price of government-subsidized health technologies and procedures. In 2017 the Committee had 22 members while the MBS handbook had over 900 pages of scheduled fees. Markets have millions of participants and are ever-evolving. Bureaucratic price-setting for medical technologies and procedures faces the same problem that any centralized planned economy does: the price-setters do not have sufficient reliable information or the time to acquire it in order to make good pricing decisions.

In so many ways post-industrial health systems obfuscate prices and costs. This makes it difficult to establish whether a procedure is over-priced or under-priced, too expensive or inexpensive. Consequently, system-wide comparisons of price or efficiency are not easy to make, a boon to the least-effective operators. Relying on confidential data, one Australian study by the Grattan Institute in 2014 found that the median cost in different Australian states to remove a gall bladder (a laparoscopic cholecystectomy) varied from $5,000 to $7,000 across the nation and the median cost of hip replacements varied from less than $17,000 to over $23,000.[51]

In Australia in 2010–2011, state governments spent almost $20 billion on public hospital services. How much of this was 'avoidable' due to factors such as unnecessary delays? The Grattan Institute study made an estimate, by comparing the costs in different hospitals of treating patients with the same health needs. It first looked at the lowest-cost hospital in each state. It then calculated the average level of costs across the state above the low-cost benchmark. It then calculated the manifestly 'avoidable' costs, i.e. those clustered above the average level of costs above the low-cost benchmark. The latter figure, conservatively reached, was $1 billion, one dollar in twenty of state government expenditure on public hospitals.[52] This represented savings estimated on intra-state comparisons only. Interstate comparisons between high-cost and lower-cost states were also revealing. Compared to the lowest-cost state (Victoria) other states' cost-per-hospital admission ranged between $370 and $800 more.[53] Notably in the Australian Capital Territory, where the country's federal government is located, hospital admission cost $1,500 more than the cheapest state—just as America's District of Columbia has the highest health spending per capita in the US (Table 9.5).

6 *Administered pricing*. The underlying driver of both arbitrary prices and high prices in healthcare is the concentration of decision making in the hands of a few institutional actors.

Polyarchs routinely commend themselves for acting in the public interest. What actually results from their behavior, though, is not better value for each dollar spent but rather poorer value. The difference is between millions of anonymous persons (strangers) who interact to produce an optimal economic result and a handful of institutional bargainers who know each other and who negotiate outcomes that are less than optimal yet which are constantly legitimated by a rhetoric of benefits that idealizes and even fantasizes the consequences of such managerially orchestrated arranging of 'who gets what, when and where'. Though they may be economically inept, they are very skilled in symbol-wielding. This class routinely turns practical failure into symbolic success by the artful representation of its superior goodness.

Notes

1 Murphy, 2015, 17–18, 20–23.
2 Kocher and Sahni, 2011, 1371.
3 Smith, Saunders, Stuckhardt and McGinnis, 99.
4 Smith, Saunders, Stuckhardt and McGinnis, 99–100.
5 Baumol, 415.
6 Baumol, 416.
7 Sheiner and Malinovskaya, 2016.
8 Sheiner and Malinovskaya, 2016, 4–6; Romley, Goldman and Sood, 2015.
9 Perry, 2014.
10 Smith, Saunders, Stuckhardt and McGinnis, 5–6.
11 Smith, Saunders, Stuckhardt and McGinnis, 9, 75, 150, 152.
12 Smith, Saunders, Stuckhardt and McGinnis, 21, 75.
13 Smith, Saunders, Stuckhardt and McGinnis, 94.
14 Tucker and Spear, 2006, 650.
15 Wallace and Savitz, 2008, 2.
16 Smith, Saunders, Stuckhardt and McGinnis, 24, 96.
17 Csikszentmihalyi, 2002 [1990].
18 As applied to hospitals, see for example Weber, 2006; Teich and Faddoul, 2013; Arthur, 2016.
19 Black and Miler, 2008.
20 The originator of Pareto-style management theory was the American engineer Joseph Juran, 1951, 1954.
21 Rose, 2016, 33.
22 Graham, 2009.
23 Murphy, 2015, 142 (footnote 30).
24 The classic philosophical formulation of this world-view was John Rawls' 1958 essay 'Justice as Fairness'.
25 Anon, 2013
26 Another commented: 'In Health Visiting, a [Health Visitor] can write a client's name & address 14! times on various documents. So much is duplicated and even triple written/copied. We have a computer system that is not up to the job and is often offline, team assistants who are willing to do more but their bosses say NO! We can spend upwards of 2 hrs a day on client related paperwork and the same again on paperwork the authority insists we complete.' Anon, 2013.

27 Smith, Saunders, Stuckhardt and McGinnis, 11.
28 Hendrich, Chow, Skierczynski, and Lu, 30.
29 PricewaterhouseCoopers, 2001.
30 Cunningham, Kennedy, Nwolisa, Callard and Wike, 2012.
31 Anon, 2013.
32 Rose, 40.
33 Cunningham, Kennedy, Nwolisa, Callard and Wike, 2012.
34 One of Parkinson's Laws: Parkinson, 1955.
35 Parkinson, 1955.
36 Cunningham, Kennedy, Nwolisa, Callard and Wike, 2012.
37 Hendrich, Chow, Skierczynski, and Lu, 32.
38 Smith, Saunders, Stuckhardt and McGinnis, 15, 160.
39 Casalino, Nicholson, Gans, Hammons, Morra, Karrison, and Levinson, W., 2009.
40 Smith, Saunders, Stuckhardt and McGinnis, 23.
41 Csikszentmihalyi, 2002 [1990].
42 Canada Institute for Health Information and Choosing Wisely Canada, 2017.
43 Productivity Commission, 2015, 4.
44 Office of the Attorney General of Massachusetts, 2011, 15–18.
45 One of the consequences of subsidized pricing is over-servicing, that is, persons going needlessly to doctors about trivial matters. This happens so much in the NHS that the Royal College of GPs has taken to recommending the DIY option, Dr Google. 'We're just asking people to stop and think, when you reach for the phone to book a GP appointment think: "Can I do this myself? Do I need some online help? Could a pharmacists help me?"'. Turner, 2017.
46 Clarke, 2013, 37–48.
47 Australian Institute of Health and Welfare, 15.
48 Duckett, 2013.
49 Duckett, 2013, 2.
50 Webber, 18.
51 Duckett and Breadon, 2014, Figures 10 and 12. Based on 2010–2011 data.
52 Duckett and Breadon, 2014, 10, Figure 8.
53 Duckett and Breadon, 2014, Figure 16.

Bibliography

Anon. 2013. "Paperwork Burden Affects Patient Care." *Nursing in Practice*, April 22.

Arthur, J. 2016. *Lean Six Sigma for Hospitals: Improving Patient Safety, Patient Flow and the Bottom Line*, Second Edition. New York: McGraw-Hill.

Australian Institute of Health and Welfare. 2013. *Health Expenditure Australia 2011–12*. Health and Welfare Expenditure Series, no. 50.

Baumol, W. J. 1967. "Macroeconomics of Unbalanced Growth: The Anatomy of Urban Crisis." *The American Economic Review* 57, no. 3: 415–426.

Black, J., D. Miller and J. Sensel. 2016. *The Toyota Way to Healthcare Excellence,* Second Edition. Chicago, IL: Health Administration Press.

Canada Institute for Health Information and Choosing Wisely Canada. 2017. *Unnecessary Care in Canada*, April.

Casalino, L. P., S. Nicholson, D.N. Gans, T. Hammons, D. Morra, T. Karrison and W. Levinson. 2009. "What Does it Cost Physician Practices to Interact with Health Insurance Plans?" *Health Affairs* 28, no. 4: w533–w543.

Clarke, P. 2013. "The Price is Wrong: Pharmaceutical Expenditure in Australia over the Last Decade and Options for Reform." In *Healthcare: Reform or Ration*, edited by Committee for Economic Development of Australia. Melbourne, April.

Csikszentmihalyi, M. 02 [1990]. *Flow*. London: Rider.

Cunningham, L., J. Kennedy, F. Nwolisa, L. Callard and C. Wike. 2012. *Patients Not Paperwork: Bureaucracy Affecting Nurses in the NHS*. NHS Institute for Innovation and Improvement.

Duckett, S. 2013. *Australia's Bad Drug Deal: High Pharmaceutical Prices*. Melbourne: Grattan Institute.

Duckett, S. and P. Breadon. 2014. *Controlling Costly Care: a Billion Dollar Hospital Opportunity*. Melbourne: Grattan Institute.

Graham, G.R. 2009. *The Past is the Future for Public Hospitals: An Insider's Perspective on Hospital* Administration. Sydney: The Centre for Independent Studies.

Hendrich, A., M.P. Chow, B.A. Skierczynski and Z. Lu. 2008. "A 36-Hospital Time and Motion Study: How Do Medical-Surgical Nurses Spend Their Time?" *The Permanente Journal* 12, no. 3: 25–34.

Juran, J.M. 1954. "Universals in Management Planning and Control." *Management Review* 43, no. 11, 748–761.

Juran, J.M. 1951. *Quality Control Handbook*. New York: McGraw-Hill.

Kocher, R. and N.R. Sahni. 2011. "Rethinking Health Care Labor." *New England Journal of Medicine* 365: 1370–1372.

Murphy, P. 2015. *Universities and Innovation Economies*. Farnham, UK: Ashgate.

Office of the Attorney General of Massachusetts. 2011. *Examination of Healthcare Cost Trends and Cost Drivers*. June.

Parkinson, C.N. 1955. "Parkinson's Law." *The Economist*, November 19.

PricewaterhouseCoopers. 2001. *Patients or Paperwork? The Regulatory Burden Facing America's Hos*pitals. Chicago: American Hospital Association.

Productivity Commission, 2015. *Efficiency in Health*. Canberra: Australian Government, April.

Rawls, J. 1958. "Justice as Fairness." *The Philosophical R*eview 67, no. 2: 164–194.

Romley, J., D.P. Goldman and N. Sood. 2015. "US Hospitals Experienced Substantial Productivity Growth During 2002–11." *Health Affairs* 34, no. 3.

Rose, Lord. *Better Leadership for Tomorrow: NHS Leadership Review*. UK Department of Health, June 2016.

Sheiner, L. and A. Malinovskaya. 2016. *Productivity in the Healthcare Sector*. Washington, DC: The Brookings Institution.

Smith, M., R. Saunders, L. Stuckhardt and J.M. McGinnis, eds. 2013. *Best Care at Lower Cost: The Path to Continuously Learning Healthcare in America*. Washington, DC: The National Academies Press.

Teich, S.T. and F.F. Faddoul. 2013. "Lean Management—The Journey from Toyota to Healthcare." *Rambam Maimonides Medical Journal* 4, no. 2.

Tucker, A. L. and S.J. Spear. 2006. "Operational Failures and Interruptions in Hospital Nursing Part 1." *Health Services Research* 41, no. 3: 643–662.

Turner, C. 2017. "Royal College of GPs Recommends Dr Google for the First Time in Bid to Ease Pressure on Surgeries." *The Telegraph*, December 29.

Wallace C.J. and L. Savitz. 2008. "Estimating Waste in Frontline Healthcare Worker Activities." *Journal of Evaluation in Clinical Practice* 14, no. 1: 178–180.

Webber, T. 2012. "What is Wrong with Medicare?" *The Medical Journal of Australia* 196, no. 1: 18–19.

Weber, D. 2006. "Toyota-Style Management Drives Virginia Mason." *The Physician Executive* 32, no. 1: 12–17.

10 Health 2

High-cost low-quality outcomes

Healthcare in the major economies is financed in part by government and in part by private sources of funding. The hybrid public–private systems of paying for healthcare that developed after the Second World War in advanced economies have produced on the whole—with a number of interesting exceptions—poor value for money. These systems mix private insurance, social insurance, out-of-pocket spending by individuals and direct government payment for health services (Table 10.1). An optimal healthcare system delivers consumers good health outcomes (measurable by longevity) for a moderate price. Few contemporary nations do this. A small number do—and how they manage to do so is instructive.

In most advanced economies since the 1960s, overall spending and government spending on healthcare as a percentage of GDP have grown dramatically (Table 10.2). Government spending on health since 1960 has ballooned much more than any other kind of government expenditure (Table 10.4 and 10.5). In spite of this, the health outcomes of such distended spending have been mediocre. Among the major economies, longevity in countries with high per capita spending on health is typically lower than countries with mid-range per capita spending. Hong Kong spends 5.7 percent of its GDP on healthcare; life expectancy at birth is 83.5 years (Table 10.3). The United States spends 17 percent of its GDP on health; life expectancy at birth is 78.8 years. Out of 30 top-performing economies in the world, the United States' health outcome is 29th in rank. The Czech Republic performs better than the United States and only the Slovak Republic does worse. Both the Czech and Slovakian nations were Communist states until 1989 and were subject to four decades of aggressive under-development as a result.

If we look at the advanced economies as a whole, there are a handful of countries where the growth of expenditure on health, both public and private, has been more restrained and yet health outcomes are better than in high-spending states. In short, a handful of countries manage to deliver good value for money (Table 10.6). But these are the exceptions, not the rule. Looking at how and why they achieve good health outcomes with restrained spending helps us understand what it is that otherwise has caused health delivery costs to rise exorbitantly in the major economies.[1]

Table 10.1 Percentage of health expenditure by source of expenditure, 2013. (Unless otherwise noted)

	Country	**First-party payer**	**Third-party payer**					
	Ranked by health expenditure per capita, 2015 constant dollars, highest to lowest	Household out-of-pocket expenditure	General government	Private (individual) insurance	Compulsory social insurance	Non-compulsory group insurance	Other third-party payers	Ratio of employee: employer contribution
1	United States [2010]	12%	25%	2%	20%	31%	10%	1:1 + 1:2.75*
2	Luxembourg	12%	9%	5%	74%			1:1
3	Switzerland	26%	19%	7%	47%		1%	1:1
4	Norway	15%	74%		11%			1:1.75
5	Netherlands	5%	7%	6%	80%		1%	0:1
6	Germany	14%	7%	9%	70%		1%	1:1
7	Sweden	15%	84%	1%				
8	Ireland	17%	67%	13%	0%		2%	
9	Austria	17%	31%	5%	45%		2%	1:1.2
10	Denmark	14%	84%	2%				
11	Belgium	18%	11%	4%	66%			1:2.6
12	Canada	14%	69%	13%	2%		2%	
13	Australia	20%	68%	9%			4%	
14	France	7%	4%	14%	75%			1:4
15	Singapore	61%	39%					
16	Japan	14%	10%	2%	73%		1%	1:1
17	Iceland	18%	53%	2%	28%			0:1
18	United Kingdom	10%	83%	3%			4%	
19	Finland	19%	61%	2%	14%		4%	0:1
20	New Zealand	13%	72%	5%	8%		3%	

21	Italy	22%	77%	1%				
22	Spain	24%	67%	4%	5%			
23	Hong Kong [2011–2012]	35%	48%	7%		8%	1%	
24	Slovenia	13%	3%	15%	68%		1%	0.96:1
25	Portugal	27%	65%	5%	1%		1%	
26	Israel	23%	16%	11%	47%		3%	1:0
27	Korea, South	37%	11%	6%	45%		1%	1:1
28	Czech Republic	15%	6%	1%	78%			1:2
29	Greece	33%	25%	3%	40%			1:1.5
30	Slovak Republic	23%	7%		68%		3%	1:1.5

Source: OECD, Health expenditure and financing, Household out-of-pocket payment, 2000–2015; OECD, Expenditure on health by type of financing, 2013 (or nearest year); Kaiser Family Foundation, Percent Distribution of National Health Expenditures, by Source of Funds, 1960–2010 based on Centers for Medicaid and Medicare Services, National Health Expenditures by type of service and source of funds, CY 1960–2010; NIHCM Foundation, Spending for Private Health Insurance in the United States, January 2013; Singapore Ministry of Health Statistics Government Health Expenditure and Healthcare Financing FY 2014; Thomson Reuters Practical Law, Rates of tax on employment income, 1 November 2016; KPMG, Insights, Other taxes and levies, January 2017; Slovenia Business Point, Social security and the insurance of employees in Slovenia, January 2017.

Note: *= Medicare + group health insurance. *Definition*: OECD Statistics defines household out-of-pocket expenditure on health as comprising 'cost-sharing, self-medication and other expenditure paid directly by private households, irrespective of whether the contact with the health care system was established on referral or on the patient's own initiative'.

Table 10.2 Total health expenditure per capita in constant 2015 dollars (PPP), 1930–2015

	Country	**2015***	**2010**	**2000**	**1990**	**1980**	**1970**	**1960**	**1950**	**1940**	**1930**
1	United States	9,451	8,619	6,126	4,714	2,086	1,397	918	674	502	356
2	Luxembourg	7,765	6,959	5,008	2,542						
3	Switzerland	6,935	5,839	4,723	2,974						
4	Norway	6,567	5,696	4,352	2,163						
5	Netherlands	5,343	5,077	3,147	2,332						
6	Germany	5,267	4,738	3,844	2,760	1,366	751	625			
7	Sweden	5,228	3,852	2,887	2,638						
8	Ireland	5,131	4,984	2,476	1,356						
9	Austria	5,016	4,605	3,775	2,507						
10	Denmark	4,943	4,751	3,574	1,905						
11	Belgium	4,611	4,241	3,073	2,252						
12	Canada	4,608	4,611	3,324	3,284	1,356	1,022	688			
13	Australia	4,420	3,921	3,008	2,375						
14	France	4,407	4,195	4,378	2,700	855	459	292			
15	Singapore	4,264	2,940	1,200							
16	Japan	4,150	3,484	2,534	2,130	1,043	584	187			
17	Iceland	4,012	3,702	3,281	2,500						
18	United Kingdom	4,003	3,300	2,222	1,791	625	438	333			
19	Finland	3,984	3,699	3,281	2,341						
20	New Zealand	3,590	3,283	2,184	1,795						
21	Italy	3,272	3,379	2,887	2,350	459	250	187			
22	Spain	3,153	3,172	2,228	1,403						
23	Hong Kong	2,291	1,998	1,800	928						
24	Slovenia	2,644	2,569	1,930							

25	Portugal	2,631	2,876	2,341	1,004			
26	Israel	2,533	2,202	1,883				
27	Korea, South	2,488	2,121	904				
28	Czech Republic	2,464	2,043	1,261				
29	Greece	2,245	3,104	1,973	725			
30	Slovak Republic	2,064	2,215	831				

* Hong Kong, 2014.

US health expenditure per capita compared with out-of-pocket spending

	2015	2010	2000	1990	1980	1970	1960
United States out-of-pocket spending as % of total health spending	11%	12%	15%	19%	23%	33%	48%
United States decrease of out-of-pocket spending by decade	8%	20%	21%	17%	30%	31%	
United States increase in health spending by decade (2015 constant dollars)	110%	141%	130%	226%	149%	152%	

Sources: OECD, Health expenditure and financing; World Health Organization, Health expenditure per capita; Government of the Hong Kong Special Administrative Region Food and Health Bureau, Health Statistics; International Monetary Fund World Economic Outlook, April 2015; George J. Schieber, Health expenditures in major industrialized countries, 1960–87; Tin, Tsoi, Lee, Chong, Lam, Yeung, Ma & Maw, Hong Kong domestic health spending: financial years 1989/90 to 2011/12, Hong Kong Medical Journal, June 2015; 2015 Taiwan Health and Welfare Report; Manfred Huber and Eva Orosz, Health Expenditure Trends in OECD Countries, 1990–2001, Health Care Financing Review, Fall 2003, Volume 25, Number 1, Table 1, Total Health Care Expenditures as a Percent of Gross Domestic Product, by Country: 1970-2001; Richard Taylor and Glenn Salkeld, Health care expenditure and life expectancy in Australia: how well do we perform? Australian and New Zealand Journal of Public Health 1996 20:3, Table 4; US Department of Health and Human Services, Centers for Medicare & Medicaid Services, National health expenditures by type of service and source of funds: calendar years 1960 to 2016.

Table 10.3 Heath spending vs. health outcomes

An above-average outcome for an average or below-average expenditure					
Country		Total health expenditure per capita in 2015 US dollars (PPP), 2015*	Total health expenditure as percentage of GDP, 2014	Life expectancy at birth, 2014	Healthy life expectancy (HALE) at birth, 2015
Average for all nations		***$4,316***	***9.5%***	***81.7***	***71.8***
1	United States	$9,451	17%	78.8	69.1
2	Luxembourg	$7,765	6.9%	82.3	71.8
3	Switzerland	$6,935	11.6%	83.3	73.1
4	Norway	$6,567	9.2%	82.2	72
5	Netherlands	$5,343	11.6%	81.8	72.2
6	Germany	$5,267	11.2%	81.2	71.3
7	Sweden	$5,228	11.9%	82.3	72
8	Ireland	$5,131	7.7%	81.4	71.5
9	Austria	$5,016	11.2%	81.6	72
10	Denmark	$4,943	10.8%	80.8	71.2
11	Belgium	$4,611	10.5%	81.4	71.1
12	Canada	$4,608	10.4%	81.5	72.3
13	Australia	$4,420	9.4%	82.4	71.9
14	France	$4,407	11.5%	82.8	72.6
15	Singapore	$4,264	4.9%	82.6	73.9
16	Japan	$4,150	10.2%	83.7	74.9
17	Iceland	$4,012	8.8%	82.9	72.7
18	United Kingdom	$4,003	9.1%	81.4	71.4
19	Finland	$3,984	9.6%	81.3	71
20	New Zealand	$3,590	11.3%	81.6	71.6
21	Italy	$3,272	9.2%	83.2	72.8

22	Spain	$3,153	9.0%	83.3	72.4
23	Hong Kong	$2,291	5.7%	83.5	N/A
24	Slovenia	$2,644	9.2%	81.2	71.1
25	Portugal	$2,631	9.5%	81.2	71.4
26	Israel	$2,533	7.5%	82.2	72.8
27	Korea, South	$2,488	7.3%	82.2	73.2
28	Czech Republic	$2,464	7.4%	78.9	69.4
29	Greece	$2,245	8.0%	81.5	71.9
30	Slovak Republic	$2,064	8.0%	76.9	68.1

* Hong Kong, 2014.

Sources: OECD, Health expenditure and financing 2015; World Health Organization, Health expenditure per capita; Government of the Hong Kong Special Administrative Region Food and Health Bureau, Health Statistics; International Monetary Fund World Economic Outlook April 2015; George J. Schieber, Health expenditures in major industrialized countries, 1960–87; Tin, Tsoi, Lee, Chong, Lam, Yeung, Ma & Maw, Hong Kong domestic health spending: financial years 1989/90 to 2011/12, Hong Kong Medical Journal, June 2015; 2015 Taiwan Health and Welfare Report; Manfred Huber and Eva Orosz, Health Expenditure Trends in OECD Countries, 1990–2001, Health Care Financing Review, Fall 2003, Volume 25, Number 1, Table 1, Total Health Care Expenditures as a Percent of Gross Domestic Product, by Country: 1970–2001; Richard Taylor and Glenn Salkeld, Health care expenditure and life expectancy in Australia: how well do we perform? Australian and New Zealand Journal of Public Health 1996 20:3, Table 4; World Health Organization Global Health Expenditure database; World Bank, Health expenditure, total (% of GDP); Aaron C. Catlin and Cathy A. Cowan, History of Health Spending in the United States, 1960–2013, November 19, 2015; Peter Yuen and Mary Armitage, Compendium of Health Statistics 2005–2006, Table 2.4 Total Health Care Expenditure as percent of GDP in OECD and EU countries, 1960–2004 , based on WHO, World Bank and OECD data; Israel Central Bureau of Statistics, National Expenditure on Health, By Type of Expenditure and Service, 2016; Hong Kong Food and Health Bureau, Hong Kong's Domestic Health Accounts (DHA), 1989/90–2013/14, Table 1.1; OECD, Health at a Glance 2013: OECD Indicators Total expenditure on health, percentage of GDP, 1980 to 2011; Eva Liuand and S.Y. Yue, Health Care Expenditure and Financing in Singapore, Legislative Council Secretariat, 9 July 1999; Barbara S. Copper, Nancy Worthington and Paula A. Piro, National Health Expenditures, 1929–73, Social Security Bulletin, March 1974, Table 1.

Table 10.4 Increase in government expenditure as a percentage of GDP, 1960–2000

Nations	**Pensions***	**Health**	**Other**
G-7	2.4	5.4	1.8
Canada	1.8	4.9	1.9
France	7.2	6.4	2.9
Germany	0.8	4.9	3.1
Italy	8.7	4	2.9
Japan	7.8	4.8	1.3
UK	2.6	3.6	0.6
US	0.3	6.2	2.6

*Government pensions do not include government-mandated payroll-based retirement income schemes. Adapted from: Carlo Cottarelli and Andrea Schaechter, Long-Term Trends in Public Finances in the G-7 Economies, IMF, 2010, Figure 5. Sources: OECD, European Commission, United States Congressional Budget Office, Tanzi and Schuknecht (2000), IMF World Economic Outlook, and IMF staff estimates.

Comment from Cottarelli and Schaechter: "The bulk of the increase in public spending (over 80 percent) is due to two items: health care and pensions (Figure 5). In particular, health care spending has surged in many G-7 countries. In the United States, it has accounted for more than two thirds of the increase in the primary spending ratio and more than half in Canada, Germany, and the United Kingdom. Other current spending items increased, partly using the space created by a decline in public investment (on average from 3 percent of potential GDP in 1960 to 2½ percent of potential GDP in 2007) and military spending, which dropped by some 3 percentage points of potential GDP between 1960–2007 on average for the G-7 countries. Nevertheless, it is clear that health and pension spending had the lion's share of the increase in primary public spending."

What applies to nations also applies at the sub-national level. It turns out that health spending—whether modest or excessive—is a fractal phenomenon. Among advanced economies there is a wide range of health spending patterns. Some represent decent value for money; others do not. The same, in turn, applies at sub-national levels. It is obvious that American spending on healthcare—public and private—represents very poor value for money. Yet when we drill down to the sub-national level in the United States, we find that there are a handful of good-value states in the US just as there is a number of these scattered across the globe (Table 9.5 and 10.7).

How is it that some states deliver good value for money—and most do not? In answering that riddle we can begin to unpick the conundrum of out-of-control health spending that has seen it rise from an average of five percent of GDP among major economies in 1970 to ten percent in 2015 (Table 10.5). Two common reasons are given to explain spiraling health spending. One is aging populations. The second is technology. Let's consider each of these in turn.

It is true that populations in advanced economies have grown older since 1970 (Table 10.7). People are living longer. Advances in medical science have increased longevity. The older that persons get, the more expensive are their health costs (Table 10.8). In the United States in 2009 the average lifetime health cost per person was $352,000. Forty percent of this cost was concentrated in the over-65 age-bracket. On the surface this suggests that for every year longer the average person lives beyond 65 substantial costs are added to a person's lifetime health cost. But in fact the larger portion of over-65 health spending is concentrated in the

Table 10.5 Total health expenditure as percentage of GDP

	Country	2014	2010	2000	1990	1980	1970	1960	1950	1940	1930
1	United States	17%	17%	13%	11.9%	8.7%	6.8%	5.0%	4.6%	4.1%	3.6%
2	Luxembourg	6.9%	7.6%	5.5%	6.1%	6.0%	3.6%				
3	Switzerland	11.6%	11.0%	10.4%	8.3%	7.4%	5.5%	4.9%			
4	Norway	9.2%	9.2%	7.7%	7.7%	7.0%	4.4%	2.9%			
5	Netherlands	11.6%	11.0%	8.3%	8.0%	7.5%	5.7%	3.7%			
6	Germany	11.2%	11.2%	10.6%	8.5%	8.7%	6.2%	4.7%			
7	Sweden	11.9%	9.4%	8.4%	8.4%	9.1%	6.9%	4.4%			
8	Ireland	7.7%	8.7%	6.0%	6.1%	8.4%	5.1%	3.7%			
9	Austria	11.2%	11.1%	7.6%	7.0%	7.4%	5.1%	4.5%			
10	Denmark	10.8%	11.0%	8.4%	8.5%	9.1%	5.9%	3.6%			
11	Belgium	10.5%	10.1%	8.6%	7.4%	6.4%	4.0%	3.4%			
12	Canada	10.4%	11.2%	8.9%	9.0%	7.1%	7.0%	5.4%			
13	Australia	9.4%	9.0%	9.0%	7.8%	7.0%	4.2%	4.1%			
14	France	11.5%	11.1%	9.3%	8.6%	7.1%	5.4%	3.8%			
15	Singapore	4.9%	3.9%	2.7%	3.0%	2.5%	3.4%	3.9%			
16	Japan	10.2%	9.5%	7.5%	5.9%	6.5%	4.5%	3.0%			
17	Iceland	8.8%	8.8%	9.2%	8.0%	6.2%	4.8%	3.0%			
18	United Kingdom	9.1%	9.5%	7.1%	5.7%	5.3%	5.4%	3.9%			
19	Finland	9.6%	9.0%	7.2%	7.8%	6.4%	5.6%	3.8%			
20	New Zealand	11.3%	11.1%	7.8%	6.9%	5.9%	5.1%	4.3%			
21	Italy	9.2%	9.4%	7.9%	7.9%	7.0%	5.1%	3.6%			
22	Spain	9.0%	9.5%	7.4%	6.7%	5.4%	3.6%	1.5%			
23	Hong Kong	5.7%	5.1%	5.1%	3.8%						
24	Slovenia	9.2%	9.0%	8.7%							

25	Portugal	9.5%	9.0%	9.2%	6.2%	5.6%	2.7%				
26	Israel *[1991, 1972]*	7.5%	7.4%	7.2%	6.9%	7.9%	7.0%				
27	Korea, South	7.3%	6.7%	4.2%	4.5%	3.6%	2.2%				
28	Czech Republic	7.4%	7.4%	6.6%	4.7%						
29	Greece	8.0%	9.1%	9.9%	7.4%	6.6%	6.1%	3.6%			
30	Slovak Republic	8.0%	8.5%	5.5%							
Total health expenditure (as percentage of GDP) current decade compared to previous decade											
1	United States	100%	130%	110%	137%	128%	136%	109%	112%	114%	
2	Luxembourg	91%	138%	90%	102%	167%					
3	Switzerland	105%	106%	125%	112%	135%	112%				
4	Norway	100%	119%	100%	110%	159%	152%				
5	Netherlands	105%	133%	104%	107%	132%	154%				
6	Germany	100%	106%	125%	98%	140%	132%				
7	Sweden	127%	112%	100%	92%	132%	157%				
8	Ireland	89%	145%	98%	73%	165%	138%				
9	Austria	101%	146%	109%	95%	145%	113%				
10	Denmark	98%	131%	99%	93%	154%	164%				
11	Belgium	104%	117%	116%	116%	160%	118%				
12	Canada	93%	126%	99%	127%	101%	130%				
13	Australia	104%	100%	115%	111%	167%	102%				
14	France	104%	119%	108%	121%	131%	142%				
15	Singapore	126%	144%	90%	120%	74%	87%				
16	Japan	107%	127%	127%	91%	144%	150%				
17	Iceland	100%	96%	115%	129%	129%	160%				
18	United Kingdom	96%	134%	125%	108%	98%	138%				
19	Finland	107%	125%	92%	122%	114%	147%				

20	New Zealand	102%	142%	113%	117%	116%	119%				
21	Italy	98%	119%	100%	113%	137%	142%				
22	Spain	95%	128%	110%	124%	150%	240%				
23	Hong Kong	112%	100%	134%							
24	Slovenia	102%	103%								
25	Portugal	106%	98%	148%	111%	207%					
26	Israel *[1991, 1972]*	101%	103%	104%	87%	113%					
27	Korea, South	109%	160%	93%	125%	164%					
28	Czech Republic	100%	112%	140%							
29	Greece	88%	92%	134%	112%	108%	169%				
30	Slovak Republic	94%	155%								

Sources: OECD, Health expenditure and financing, Financing of health care, 2015; World Health Organization Global Health Expenditure database; World Bank, Health expenditure, total (% of GDP), Government of the Hong Kong Special Administrative Region Food and Health Bureau, Health Statistics; 2015 Taiwan Health and Welfare Report; Aaron C. Catlin and Cathy A. Cowan, History of Health Spending in the United States, 1960–2013, November 19, 2015; Peter Yuen and Mary Armitage, Compendium of Health Statistics 2005–2006, Table 2.4 Total Health Care Expenditure as percentage of GDP in OECD and EU countries, 1960–2004 , based on WHO, World Bank and OECD data; Israel Central Bureau of Statistics, National Expenditure on Health, By Type of Expenditure and Service, 2016; Hong Kong Food and Health Bureau, Hong Kong's Domestic Health Accounts (DHA), 1989/90–2013/14, Table 1.1; OECD, Health at a Glance 2013: OECD Indicators Total expenditure on health, percentage of GDP, 1980 to 2011; Eva Liuand and S.Y. Yue, Health Care Expenditure and Financing in Singapore, Legislative Council Secretariat, 9 July 1999; Barbara S. Copper, Nancy Worthington and Paula A. Piro, National Health Expenditures, 1929-73, Social Security Bulletin, March 1974, Table 1.

Table 10.6 Good value countries

Countries with Below-Average Health Expenditure and High Health Outcomes					
Country	**Total health spending per capita in 2015 US dollars (PPP), 2015 [OECD median: $3999]**	**Total health spending as percentage of GDP, 2014 [OECD average: 12%]**	**Life expectancy at birth, 2014 [OECD average: 80.9 years]**	**Healthy life expectancy (HALE) at birth, 2015 [WHO global HALE average, 2015: 63.1 years]**	**Percentage of first-party (out-of-pocket) spending [OECD average: 13.6%]**
Hong Kong	$2,291	5.7%	83.5	N/A	35%
Korea, South	$2,488	7.3%	82.2	73.2	37%
Israel	$2,533	7.8%	82.2	72.8	23%
Italy	$3,272	9.2%	83.2	72.8	22%
Iceland	$4,012	8.8%	82.9	72.7	19%
Singapore	$4,264	4.9%	82.6	73.9	61%
Australia	$4,420	9.4%	82.4	71.9	20%
	Percentage of population 65 and older, 2014 [OECD average: 15.3%]	**GDP per capita in 2015 US dollars (PPP), 2015 [2015 IMF average for top 50 GDP per capita countries: $48,670]**	**Health spending per capita as % of GDP per capita, 2015**	**Total government spending as % of GDP, 2015-2016**	**Global Rank on the Index of Economic Freedom, 2017**
Hong Kong	15%	$56,878	4.0%	17.6%	1
Korea, South	12%	$36,612	6.8%	32.9%	23
Israel	11%	$34,054	7.4%	40.3%	36
Italy	22%	$35,781	9.1%	50.4%	73
Iceland	13%	$45,666	8.8%	43.6%	22
Singapore	11%	$85,382	5.0%	20.3%	2
Australia	15%	$47,644	9.3%	37.2%	5

Sources: OECD, Health at a Glance: Europe 2016: State of Health in the EU Cycle Life expectancy at birth, 1990 and 2014; OECD Data Health Spending 2014; International Monetary Fund, World Economic Outlook Database, October 2016; WHO, HALE, 2015; United Nations, World Population Prospects 2015 Revision; Heritage Index of Economic Freedom, 2017; OECD Demography data, 2014; World Bank, population ages 65 and above (% of total), 2014.

often-expensive last-year-of-life. Notably for those with multiple chronic health conditions, hospitalization or care in the terminal year of life typically turns out to be very costly. However, each additional post-65 year of life does not entail this level of cost. A person only dies once. Thus, while aging populations represent a component of the escalating costs over the period after 1960, this component cannot in itself explain the extent of the rising tide of costs. Thirteen percent of the American population in 2015 was over 65. Eleven percent of Israel's population was over 65 (Table 10.7). The United States in 2014 spent 17 percent of its GDP on health; Israel spent 7.5 percent. Life expectancy at birth in Israel was 82.2 years in 2014; in the United States it was 78.9 years.

The second common explanation for rising health costs is technology. Medicine is an applied science. It improves longevity by advancing pharmaceutical chemistry and clinical tools. Those tools, as they improve, drive up costs, it is supposed. But two things count against this explanation of cost increases. First, new medical technologies have only a modest impact on costs. A recent study of over 6,000 innovations compared with incumbent medical technologies concluded that on

Table 10.7 Over 65-year-olds, percentage of population

Country	2015	2010	2000	1990	1980	1970	1960	1950
United States	15%	13%	12%	13%	11%	10%	9%	8%
Germany	21%	21%	16%	15%	16%	14%	12%	10%
Sweden	20%	17%	18%	18%	17%	15%	12%	10%
Canada	16%	14%	13%	11%	9%	8%	8%	8%
Australia	15%	13%	12%	11%	10%	8%	9%	8%
Iceland	14%	12%	12%	11%	10%	9%	8%	8%
Singapore	12%	9%	7%	6%	5%	3%	2%	2%
Italy	22%	20%	18%	15%	13%	11%	9%	8%
Israel	11%	10%	10%	9%	9%	6%	5%	4%

Source: United Nations, World Population Prospects 2015 Revision, Volume 1 Comprehensive Tables, Table A.9, Table A.9. Total population at mid-year by major area, region and country.

Table 10.8 Age distribution of US average healthcare spending per person, 2009

Age (in years)	**Average spending per person (2009)**	**Cost by age cohort (2009 dollars)**	**% of cumulative cost by age spans**
<5	$2,468	$9,872	2.8%
5–17	$1,695	$22,035	6.2%
18–24	$1,834	$12,838	3.6%
25–44	$2,739	$54,780	15.5%
45–64	$5,511	$110,220	31.2%
65 and Older*	$9,744	$143,236	40.6%
Average life-time healthcare costs per person, 2009 dollars		**$352,981**	**100.0%**

*2009 US average life expectancy: 78.7 years.
Source: Kaiser Family Foundation, Health Care Costs: A Primer, 2012, Figure 6.

average the new technology cost eight percent more than the old technology or four percent more in quality-adjusted terms (where the price increases but so does the performance of the technology).[2] The authors of the study also note that, in a conventional economic setting, a price increase should be matched by an equivalent price decrease in the time that it takes a technology to move from being an innovation to being an incumbent tool. However, given 'conditions particular to the healthcare industry'—that is, managerial price control, bureaucratic regulatory approval processes and the predominance of third-party payers—what occurs are less rapid declines in price or even increases in quality-adjusted prices over the long run.[3] The problem is not technology in itself but rather administered price-setting and rule-creation.

The historic impact of technology in most non-medical domains over time has been to reduce costs, often dramatically. The most important question to be asked about medical technology is not its impact on rising costs but why hasn't it reduced these costs? The logic of an industrial society is such that technology reduces costs by making labor more productive. This, in turn, is part of a wider syndrome of industry innovation. By altering the organization of production along with the tools of production, industries become increasingly productive. Each unit of land, labor or capital creates more. As this happens the rewards to land, labor and capital increase. Societies as a whole grow wealthier.

So why is it, in a lot of countries, the healthcare sector—now reaching 10–17 percent of GDP in many cases—has failed to follow the normal pathway of an industrial society? To answer this question, the answer to yet another question is first required. Why is it that some states have gone against the tide and have been able to keep health spending—as a percentage of GDP and as a per capita cost—under control? Why are some states with good health outcomes able to keep health spending below 10 percent of GDP, in the 5–9 percent range? What do these low-cost high-outcome states have in common?

Good-value countries

First, let's consider what does not explain low-cost high-outcome performance. The most hackneyed explanation applied to health systems is that 'single-payer' financing of health costs explains such outcomes. It does not. Single-payer financing occurs when governments directly pay for healthcare out of tax-payer funds. Not that far removed from the single-payer model is where government orchestrates a system of compulsory social insurance with health benefits funded by obligatory employer and employee contributions (Table 10.1). Many countries where single-payer financing is a major component of health financing have high costs and less-than-optimal health outcomes. After the United States, the most expensive countries are Luxemburg, Switzerland, Norway, Netherlands, Germany, Sweden and Ireland. The largest portion of their health spending is financed respectively by either compulsory social insurance [Luxemburg, Switzerland, Netherlands and Germany] or by taxpayer funding [Norway, Sweden and Ireland] (Table 10.1).

To understand what works in healthcare financing, we need to consider the factor or factors shared by modest-cost, high-outcome states. The primary common factor among good-value countries is that in each of them the out-of-pocket component of health financing is relatively high.

In 2015 Hong Kong, South Korea, Israel, Italy, Iceland, Singapore and Australia all represented good-value measured in terms of 2015 PPP (purchasing power parity) dollar spending on healthcare (Table 10.6). They had excellent health outcomes, ranging from 82.2 to 83.7 years of life expectancy at birth compared to the OECD average of 80.9 years. Their per capita spending on health was below 50 percent of that of the United States (Table 10.2 and 10.3). Each was lower than the per capita expenditure of the lowest spending American state, Utah (Table 9.5). The lowest, Hong Kong, was half of the level of spending per capita in Utah. The highest of the good-value states, Australia, was 87 percent of the Utah per capita expenditure.

On first sight, the best-value countries constitute a motley group of states. Some of them are low-taxing, others high-taxing states. In some, the total level of government spending as a portion of GDP is quite high; in others it is low. Some of the good-value states exhibit overall high levels of economic freedom. In others, the general level of economic freedom is considerably lower. Notwithstanding all of these factors, the good-value states do have one thing in common: in each of them, out-of-pocket expenses as a percentage of total health financing is relatively high. The average level of out-of-pocket paying for healthcare in the OECD is 13.6 percent. In the good-value states, the portion of out-of-pocket spending ranges from 19 percent in Iceland to 60 percent in Singapore. In Hong Kong SAR, the best-value state, it is 35 percent. In the others it is 37 percent (South Korea), 23 percent (Israel), 22 percent (Italy) and 20 percent (Australia). With one instructive exception (Switzerland) the top 10 most expensive countries all have rates of out-of-pocket spending on health below the OECD average. All of the good-value countries have a life expectancy at birth of over 82 years. The same is true of only four of the top ten spenders (Table 10.3).

There are several ways of financing healthcare spending. Governments can do it directly out of taxpayer revenue. Governments can also create systems of social insurance that require employers and employees to contribute a percentage of payroll to fund healthcare, or else they can provide tax incentives for company-based health insurance. Individuals or employers can also buy private health insurance. Alternatively, individuals can pay for expenses as they arise directly out of their own pocket. Every country has a different mix of government, social insurance, group insurance, personal insurance and out-of-pocket funding (Table 10.1). Out-of-pocket financing is routinely viewed negatively by researchers and commentators. Commonly when they talk about high out-of-pocket expenses, the word 'burden' is used. Health expenses, it is argued, on occasions can be very high. What follows from this are nightmare scenarios of persons ruined financially by having to reach into their own pocket to pay for health services.

However, simply because an expense is paid out-of-pocket tells us nothing about how funds accumulate in that pocket. Take the average person's pocket that is filled with a wage or salary. Context here matters a lot. Does the state take 30 or 40 percent of a person's income in taxation or alternatively 15 to 20 percent? If it is the former, then income that might otherwise pay directly for healthcare is recycled from the taxpayer into government consolidated revenue then to health ministries and finally to hospitals and health practices via subsidies, rebates or direct funding. That is to say, the health dollar goes through multiple third-party hands. In government-mandated or tax-incentivized social-insurance schemes, payrolls are taxed. A percentage of payroll (i.e. employee income and employer out-goings) is siphoned off into a government-regulated or tax-abated revenue pool in order to pay for health services. In both payroll-based and taxation-based systems, third parties loom large in the financing system. As they do in the case of company group-insurance—the American system where employers purchase health insurance on behalf of employees as a tax-reduced partial-wage-substitute or salary-related benefit. This portion of a company's payroll is disposed of by a third-party (the employer) who purchases group health coverage from a fourth-party (an insurer).

In short, how much of a person's earned income remains in their own pocket is contingent. It depends on a state's tax model or the way that a country conceptualizes the nature of a wage-benefit. Is the state high-taxing or low-taxing? Does the employer pay a wage-benefit directly to the employee or instead acts as a third-party agent who purchases the wage-benefit (in this case health insurance) on behalf of all employees? Thus, what portion of individual earnings goes directly into an individual's pocket varies enormously from country to country. So then does the capacity of individuals to pay for costs out of their own pockets. And so does the relative weight of first and third parties in healthcare decision-making and payments.

But even a low-tax state will have a percentage of very low-income persons. In advanced economies these cases are the exception not the rule. But they exist. What then happens if a person's income is so low that there is insufficient in their pocket for health spending? Such spending includes both direct payment for regular everyday costs and insurance against insurable high-cost unpredictable health expenditures. In such cases government can provide negative tax rebates, redistributing income through the tax system. A government can also, in these limited number of cases, act as a third-party provider of health services. But the exception should not be confused with the norm.

The Singapore model

A number of fallacies surround third-party payer models (taxpayer-funded services, social insurance, group insurance, private insurance models). The principal fallacy is that services provided to low-income or modest-income persons are inexpensive compared with first-party payer systems. This has a superficial plausibility. If someone else pays, it does sound like the first-party will get a good deal. But is this so? Take the comparative example of the United States and Singapore. Both are wealthy nations with polar opposite patterns of health spending and outcomes. In 2015 (and measured in US 2015 PPP dollars) Singapore's GDP per capita was $85,382 and America's was $55,836. Yet the richer country, Singapore, had by far the better and cheaper health system. This is because in 1983 Singapore pivoted. Prior to that time it had a third-party payer health system modelled after Britain's single-payer, government-delivered National Health System (NHS). Singapore concluded that third-party single-payer systems of health finance were neither affordable nor did they deliver excellent outcomes.

Singapore moved to a carefully structured mix of first-party payer health savings accounts supplemented by third-party payer government funding of infrastructure as well as services for very-low-income citizens.[4] At the root of this arrangement was Singapore's Central Provident Fund (CPF), created in 1955 during the British colonial era. It was originally designed to provide a system of retirement savings. Mandatory contributions by employees and employers were deposited into individual CPF savings accounts. In 1968 this system was extended by the Singapore government. Employers and employees were obliged to contribute to savings accounts for housing. In 1983 the system was extended again, this time to fund health savings accounts (Medisave accounts) to pay for hospitalization and health insurance. Currently employers are required to contribute 17 percent of the wages of employees below the age of 55; employees compulsorily contribute 20 percent of their wage to the CPF.

The CPF system has a philosophically grounded emphasis on saving. Like a bank account, these savings accounts earn interest. Crucially, they are the taxpayer's own money to save or spend on health. The money is neither the government's nor the employer's. At death, a positive balance in a Medisave account becomes part of a person's estate. The obverse of savings is personal prudence. Money is to be spent but carefully. There is no point in wasting it. The Singapore system militates against careless spending. The total level of CPF health savings is capped. So is the amount of such savings that can be spent per-day on a hospital admission. These measures necessitate that consumers make co-payments from personal savings for expensive services that add little or no value. Such constraints act as incentives for persons not to over-spend on health services. In any health system, any person who over-spends drives up the cost for other consumers.

Singaporeans pay for their hospitalization and day surgery out of their CPF health savings accounts. The health savings accounts can also be used to pay for government-subsidized insurance (Medishield) against large medical costs that are the result of a prolonged or major hospitalization. Singapore has a philosophy-based rather than program-based approach to healthcare. This means that accompanying any government-subsidized or mandated scheme, including savings, is a philosophy of individual responsibility. Consequently, payment from funds is typically accompanied by individual co-payments. For example, taxpayers can purchase private health insurance out of their health savings accounts. But on the proviso that such private insurance also includes a co-payment component. The system implies an inherent skepticism about third parties—of all kinds, even very personalized government provident funds—paying for health services.

The underlying problem is that the instinct of the first-party payer to question costs and prices disappears when third-party payers appear. When this happens, costs and prices rise. Co-payments discourage the over-use of services. They also reduce any false sense that a government benefit is 'free' when it is paid for compulsorily by taxpayers or out of payrolls.[5] Getting the user or the consumer to pay discourages such illusions.

For very-low-income citizens in Singapore, there is a government-funded Medifund, which was established in 1993. It is an endowment fund. It is for persons who—in spite of provident fund savings, insurance and private savings—still cannot pay their medical bills. In such cases, the Singapore government is the payer-of-last-resort. The government also funds 80 percent of hospital infrastructure (buildings and technology) though steps back from running hospitals. In the 1980s Singapore's public hospitals were corporatized. This meant they could make autonomous decisions about key matters such as staffing. The government continued to exercise residual controls over the price of subsidized public beds and charges for private Medisave patients above government reimbursement levels. Otherwise, hospitals were freed-up to compete with each other on quality and price. In primary care, 80 percent of medical and dental services are provided by private practitioners while voluntary welfare organizations dominate the aged long-term care sector.

In 2015 Singapore spent $4,264 per capita on health; America spent $9,451. Singapore's total health expenditure was 4.9 percent of GDP; America's was 17 percent. What difference explains the difference? Simply put: health savings accounts. The original sin of America's poor-value health system was its decision in 1943 to begin to encourage large numbers of employers to offer group health insurance for employees. During the Second World War, American employers were subject to war-time wage controls. To attract scarce employees they wanted to pay higher wages. But legally they could not. So instead they opted to pay an employee fringe benefit—health insurance—that was not subject to war-time controls.[6] As it evolved, this fringe benefit was exempted from taxation. This made employer health benefits very attractive for company employees. Meanwhile, health spending in the non-employer individual health market was given no tax exemption until the George W. Bush administration in 2003 created a modest system of health savings accounts. These HSAs permitted tax-free saving for out-of-pocket medical spending so long as a person bought a high-deductible individual health insurance policy with personal after-tax dollars.[7]

Group health insurance means that decisions about health expenditure are made by employers and insurers rather than those who are directly affected by the outcome of health payment choices. In effect, efficient choice is translated into inefficient benefits on a large scale. This is partially obviated in those US states where employee health insurance contributions and deductible payments are high compared to state health spending per capita (Table 9.5). This appears to act as a surrogate for classic out-of-pocket payments that the US over time has virtually eliminated (Table 10.2). Economic sense asserts itself, it seems, even in a swamp of irrationality. In 2015, 46 percent of Americans covered by health

Table 10.9 US coverage numbers and rates by type of health insurance, 2015

Coverage Plan Type	Numbers covered, thousands	Percent of total
Private Plans		
Employment-based	177,540	46%
Direct-purchase	52,057	13%
Public Plans		
Medicare	51,865	13%
Medicaid	62,384	16%
Military Health	14,849	4%
No Plan		
Uninsured	28,966	7%
Total	**387,661**	**100%**

Source: United States Census Bureau, Health Insurance Coverage in the United States: 2015, Table 1, Coverage Numbers and Rates by Type of Health Insurance: 2013 to 2015.

insurance were in group (employment-based) plans (Table 10.9). This was by far the largest health plan type in the US. It was much larger than either the individual health-insurance market or America's various public single-payer-style schemes, principally the social-insurance-type Medicare scheme. As the largest healthcare financer, employer-based group insurance has the greatest effect on the operation of American healthcare. Of all the systems, it is the one that is most responsible for the poor value of the American health system. Yet it also lends itself to fixing the high-cost, low-outcome American system. If group health insurance benefits were required by law to be paid into mandated individual savings accounts (after all, these are fringe wage-and-salary benefits), transforming the lethargic third- and fourth-party payer arrangement into a first-party payer payment model, competition and innovation in American healthcare would increase substantially.[8]

In 2016 the average annual premium of an employment-based US health plan was $6,435 for single-person coverage and $18,142 for family coverage.[9] Of the total cost, employees contributed 18 percent of single coverage and 30 percent of family coverage. The average US wage for a person 24–54 years old in 2017 was $46,644.[10] That average person paid $11,950 in local, state and federal income taxes plus a further $1,158 toward payroll-based employer-insurance coverage. The total tax and payroll out-going for the average American wage-earner with group coverage was $13,108. Let's then compare that with Singapore. Singapore's average wage in 2016 was US$40,375 of which just over $550 of that was payable in tax (1.25 percent of the total). A further 17 percent ($6,863) was sequestered in provident fund savings accounts. The total tax-or-mandated-saving outgoing for the average Singapore wage-earner was $7,413.

Why then does the average Singaporean have $5,695 less mandated out-goings than the average American? A key reason is that Singapore has a much cheaper health system that still delivers better health outcomes than the American system. Why is that? Because Singapore pays for healthcare via personal health savings accounts. But why does that work? Because health savings accounts are built on a philosophy of personal responsibility for healthcare. Personal responsibility lowers costs. It does so for two reasons. First, it hands much of health purchasing over to those who care most about paying less (in price) for more (in quality): first-party payers. Second, in any health system there are many first-party payers while there are relatively few third-party payers—the managers of insurance companies, hospitals and departments of health mainly. The latter are a small handful compared with literally the millions who will visit a doctor, a dentist or be admitted to hospital. Among the millions there will be at least a significant percentage who make good or very good choices and some who are prepared to be adventurous with their health dollar and try innovative ways of health delivery or treatment. The latter fuel innovation, the life-blood of industrial societies. Innovation drives the development of less time, less energy and less money spent for more and better quality and achievement. The short-hand way of saying this is that innovation drives productivity, both technological and organizational, which drives down prices and drives up quality.

Payers and productivity

Singapore is a small city-state. Its population is 5.5 million. The United States is a large continental republic. Its population is 321 million. Given both its size and its federal structure—its subdivision into states—the US is like a fractal of the world. The health expenditure performance of American states varies widely. In 2009, at the state level, spending per capita in the US varied from $5,301 to $9,278 (Table 9.5). At the low-end of this spectrum, a number of lower-cost but high-outcome US states—all in the $5,000 to $6,000 per capita range—performed much like the upper division of European state spenders, Netherlands, Norway and Switzerland. That is considerably better than the US average but nothing as efficient or effective as Singapore.

There are four unambiguous good-value US states: Utah, Arizona, Idaho and Colorado (Table 9.5). What does this cohort have in common? They have well-above-average life-expectancy at birth. Their health spending per capita is low by US standards, between $5,000 and $6,000 per capita. Typically in these states, medical productivity is above the national average, health spending as a percentage of gross state product is below the national average, the number of health savings accounts (tax-free savings accounts for health spending tied to high-deductible health plans) are above the national average, the amount of out-of-pocket spending is above the national average as are individual contributions to group insurance plans. Typically, levels of economic freedom are above average, the number of inpatient days per capita for Medicare enrollees is below average as is the cost per capita of hospitals while the percentage of the population that exercise regularly (i.e. who self-manage their own health) is above average. Out of these eleven criteria, each of the four good-value states performs above-average on at least nine of the eleven criteria.

Below the surface of this health data lies politics. Utah, Arizona, Idaho and Colorado are regionally specific. They are four Mountain States. Since 1968, in US Presidential elections they have mainly voted for the country's center-right

Republican Party. The exceptions to this were Colorado in 1992, Arizona in 1996, and Colorado (again) in 2008, 2012 and 2016. Something deeper again underlies this voting pattern. It is not that there are no poor performing Republican-leaning states in the US. Though it is also notable that of the 16 highest health-spending states, 14 of them are Democrat-leaning states. More significantly still, the ethos of the high-performing Mountain States comes closest to the distilled essence of the Republican voter. In the half century since 1964, Republican and Democrat-identifying voters have exhibited strong opposing and incommensurable views about the nature of politics.[11] Republicans look to abstract principles or values (to a philosophical politics). Democrat voters think in terms of group benefits.[12] When asked what matters to them politically, the larger majority of Republicans respond by talking about limited government and people being personally responsible for their own lives. Democrats talk about advancing or protecting group interests. Republican voters want people to be able to help themselves. Democrats want government programs to help 'the middle class', 'the working class' or 'the poor'. Both sides say this repeatedly, election after election.

The key difference can be summed up as the difference between the politics of group identity and the politics of abstract values. More than anything else, Republican voters look to the principle of limited government and the kind of 'traditional' image of society and social mores (hard work, self-reliance, personal prudence, literate behavior) that underpins that.[13] Democrats look not to the philosophical abstraction of limited government but to the programs of big government that help 'less advantaged' social groups, however these might be defined. Democrats are primarily group-benefit voters. They are not very interested in philosophical abstractions. 'Philosophical' here is not a synonym for abstruse or difficult to understand concepts. Rather, it is a way of thinking about a world that stretches back to Ralph Waldo Emerson's vision of self-reliance and before that to the American Founders' classic, Christian, deist, Stoic, Lockean and Enlightenment sense of a small, limited, non-despotic role for government. The corollary of this political-philosophical vision is a cluster of do-it-yourself individual virtues—those of self-discipline, prudence, and so on—that make such a thing possible. What Republican voters in the past half-century have repeatedly said that they most dislike about Democrats is that the latter favor 'big government' or 'too much government'.

The Democrat group-benefit model emerged in the 1920s and 1930s as the politics of pressure groups took off.[14] From the beginning, group lobbying formed a key part of the emerging managerial society.[15] Conversely, in the early 1930s there was a sharp turn in Democratic Party politics. The small-government Bourbon Democrat Al Smith campaigned to be the party's presidential nominee in 1932. He was famously defeated by Franklin Roosevelt. What followed was the group-benefit politics of Roosevelt's New Deal. The opposition between group-specific programs and the abstract philosophy of limited government has been at the core of American politics for the past ninety years.

The best value healthcare systems in the world are premised on a paradox. The more individuals pay for healthcare, the less that healthcare costs them. Globally, the greater the portion of costs paid out-of-pocket by users, the lower the costs and the higher the outcome (Table 10.6). Among American states, the more users contribute to group insurance costs typically the lower the state-based cost of healthcare (Table 9.5). Conversely, over time as out-of-pocket spending has fallen in the US, the real cost of healthcare per person has risen dramatically. Between 1960 and 2015, out-of-pocket spending fell from 48 percent to 11 percent of total health spending while spending per capita in real terms multiplied a staggering ten times (Table 10.2). In short, the more that users pay the less they pay. But in order for this paradox to work, the users who pay a greater share of health costs have to be able to able to exercise in aggregate a greater influence on health delivery through their spending choices.

In healthcare, limited government means pivoting health financing on personal savings in a low-tax environment. Saving-to-pay motivates a payer to be judicious, thoughtful and ready to ask questions. It encourages the payer not to waste money on unnecessary things. It also encourages the payer to consider the direct purchase of different, more efficient, more ingenious and less costly ways of doing things. But high-contribution or out-of-pocket spending without the individual choice factor can have desultory outcomes. Take the case of Switzerland. The country has a fairly sizable out-of-pocket health financing component but also a high level of health spending per capita. The reason for this is instructive. The Swiss government requires all citizens to purchase health insurance. But in doing so it also heavily regulates the insurance market, requiring insurers to offer the same standard list of benefits. Each health expense typically has a co-payment attached to it. That is reflected in the country's nominally high out-of-pocket tally. Co-payment is designed to force down costs. But because out-of-pocket paying follows insurance plans that are prescribed by the government, the downward effect on costs is weak. Managerial third-parties—governments, ministries, insurers, hospitals and health lobbies—continue to have the greatest influence on healthcare pricing and efficiency.

First-party payers are not experts. They do not have the professional knowledge of a doctor or engineer or the expertise of the technocrat who knows the (invariably complex) rules of an authority-based directive-and-allocative system. In contrast to expert knowledge concentrated in a few persons, there is another kind of knowledge that is dispersed across millions of first-party payers. This is each person's knowledge of their particular circumstances, purposes, needs, desires and preferences.[16] No one possesses perfect transparent knowledge of themselves, but everyone possesses a greater knowledge of this than does any third-party payer. First-party purchasers not only possess the irreducibly diverse personal knowledge of what they want and how and when they want it but they also possess diverse capacities to bargain with second-party providers, try new things, bear risks and be early adopters of technology. Amongst millions, a relative handful of consumers will enter into innovative bargains, experiments, risk-reward trade-offs and technology try-outs. Not all of these will be motivated by price. Sometimes the motivation is curiosity, a readiness to test things or a heightened risk-reward appetite. These are idiosyncratic traits, but if the innovations struck between adventurous first parties and inventive second parties work, as they sometimes will, then millions of less adventurous consumers will eventually benefit. Given the small number of third-party decision makers (the handful of policy-makers, departmental heads, corporation chiefs, industry lobbyists and sector experts), third parties are poor at delivering productivity increases.

As the classic-liberal economist Milton Friedman observed 'nobody spends somebody else's money as wisely or as frugally as he spends his own'.[17] Consequently, first-party payers 'are likely to do a better job of monitoring medical care providers—because it is in their own interest' than third parties. The more that first-party payers directly pay for services, the more that second-party providers (medical practices and hospitals) are in a position to reduce costly overheads by reducing claims processes and disputes. That is, laborious bureaucratic procedures of submitting, processing, checking, reviewing and contesting payments shrink if third-party insurance payment is scaled back to its proper role of protecting insured parties against unpredictable ruinous expenses. Historically, insurance was developed in order to cover those random rare high-cost events that are economically catastrophic for individuals unlucky to be affected by them. When third parties pay for routine and predictable everyday health costs, a less-interested, less-frugal payer enters the picture. It is true that consumers sometimes are not frugal. However, given that there are millions of consumers, it only requires some of those first-party payers to be prudent in order to control costs. If ten percent of millions of consumers walk away from unduly expensive providers and patronize lean efficient services, 100 percent of consumers eventually benefit as the underperforming providers are obliged to either change their behavior or eventually go out of business.

Third-party payers contribute to low productivity. Millions may consume health services but a handful of decision-makers—governments, health insurers and professional lobbies—who behave a lot like central planners determine the prices of services and taxpayer subsidization of services. Consumers may make choices about who insures them for healthcare and the kind of insurance policy they prefer but they do not pay directly out of their own pockets (or only marginally so) for services received. They don't purchase healthcare like they purchase an automobile. Individual automobile buyers may from time to time make bad choices, but overall, in a net sense, millions make good choices, prompting the manufacturers and retailers of cars to improve productivity in order to compete for customers on the basis of price and quality. Little of the same is evident in healthcare.

As a general social phenomenon, third-party paying expanded dramatically in the twentieth century. It followed closely the rise of the managerial society. In the 1940s, James Burnham predicted the coming of a new ruling class of managers.[18] He was prescient. This new class would eventually dominate not only government but the post-industrial private sector as well. From the mid-twentieth century onwards, health and education sectors expanded radically. Agriculture and manufacturing—motivated by the search for increased productivity—mechanized and automated. The growing health and education sectors did the opposite. They side-stepped pressures to improve the productivity of labor, capital and land. They reveled in the fact that these sectors were 'labor intensive', as if that was a badge of pride.

From the ranks of managers rose a class of super-managers. Most saw themselves as benevolent social engineers. Among their functions was to set prices in healthcare. The super-managers developed as a small institutionally powerful high-remuneration non-entrepreneurial non-ownership class. The United Kingdom's single-payer single-delivery National Health System (NHS) has 1.4 million employees. In 2017, 600 of that number earned salaries over £100,000 (US$130,000) per annum. This compared with the average UK salary of £27,000 and the average salary of £36,320 in health and medicine.[19] In principle, a key role of such super-managers is to control costs while improving outcomes. This they do poorly. Government spending on healthcare in the UK rose from 6.5 percent of GDP in 2003–2004 to 7.9 percent in 2011–2012.[20] Over the same period, the increase in public-sector healthcare productivity averaged a meagre 0.7 percent annually.[21]

In its first year of operation in 1948, the NHS spent (in 2016 dollars) £15 billion. Adjusting for the 28 percent growth in population since, that was the equivalent (in 2016 inflation-adjusted terms) of spending £19.2 billion. What the NHS actually spent in 2016 was £116 billion—six times the 1948 figure in real terms. Even then it found itself 'in crisis' with large budget short-falls.[22] One explanation sometimes offered for its poor fiscal performance is the employment of too many non-clinical staff.[23] The ratio of clinical to non-clinical staff in the NHS has remained pretty constant since 1951 (Table 10.10). There have been changes, but these have been mainly the employment of more doctors in place of nurses and the employment of more professionals, technicians and administrators in place of healthcare assistants and maintenance staff. So, yes, 'administration' in the broadest sense has increased from 10 percent to 36 percent of the NHS workforce. The non-clinical professional and technical class has grown from 3 percent of the workforce to 13 percent. Meanwhile, non-clinical ancillary staff numbers have fallen from 40 percent to 16 percent of the NHS workforce. Yet despite all the additional managerialism that has come with this, the single-payer single-provider service has been unable to adapt to increased health-service demand with greater productivity. Why? The answer, simply put, is that the managerial class is ill-suited to doing what is required. It is not skilled at improving hospital organizational coordination or decreasing the system-wide paperwork burden. In short, the managerial class is not very good at managing.

The deeper reason for this is historical. The rise of the super-manager class to power was dressed up in benign-sounding rhetoric. A medical revolution occurred between 1920 and 1970. For the first time in human history it was really worth going to the doctor or being admitted to hospital. Demand for healthcare accordingly grew across all social classes and groups. As demand grew, it was claimed that first-party payers—those who paid for healthcare out of their savings—were inherently 'burdened'. Relief was promised in the form of third-party systems of payment. That meant a mix of tax-payer, social-insurance and group-insurance

Table 10.10 Number of full-time equivalent staff employed in NHS hospitals and community services by category, UK, 1951–2011

Year	Medical & dental	% of total	Nursing & midwifery	% of total	Clinical % of total	Professional & technical	% of total	Admin & clerical*	% of total	Domestic ancillary#	% of total	Support % of total	Total
1951	15,102	4%	188,580	46%	**50%**	14,110	3%	29,021	7%	163,666	40%	**50%**	410,479
1955	16,870	4%	206,567	48%	**51%**	19,404	4%	33,421	8%	157,917	36%	**49%**	434,179
1960	20,651	4%	242,164	46%	**50%**	24,002	5%	38,450	7%	202,968	38%	**50%**	528,235
1965	23,860	4%	290,338	47%	**51%**	32,720	5%	47,872	8%	218,191	36%	**49%**	612,981
1970	28,511	4%	343,664	49%	**53%**	41,696	6%	56,877	8%	229,313	33%	**47%**	700,061
1975	35,899	4%	440,981	50%	**54%**	57,011	6%	110,429	13%	235,209	27%	**46%**	879,529
1980	41,760	4%	467,500	48%	**53%**	74,558	8%	126,124	13%	258,368	27%	**47%**	968,310
1985	47,308	5%	504,000	50%	**55%**	91,471	9%	137,982	14%	221,334	22%	**45%**	1,002,095
1990	55,838	6%	507,100	51%	**57%**	103,097	10%	164,370	17%	156,995	16%	**43%**	987,400
1995	64,466	7%	421,983	46%	**53%**	118,415	13%	193,210	21%	123,289	13%	**47%**	921,362
1996	67,093	7%	421,521	45%	**53%**	121,933	13%	191,615	21%	127,451	14%	**47%**	929,613
1997	71,180	8%	419,124	45%	**53%**	124,008	13%	191,652	21%	123,571	13%	**47%**	929,535
1998	73,056	8%	420,903	45%	**53%**	127,604	14%	193,396	21%	123,758	13%	**47%**	938,717
1999	74,580	8%	427,994	45%	**52%**	132,344	14%	199,184	21%	123,372	13%	**48%**	957,474
2000	76,591	8%	436,539	45%	**52%**	136,344	14%	206,375	21%	123,529	13%	**48%**	979,378
2001	78,932	8%	430,153	43%	**51%**	142,917	14%	218,318	22%	128,722	13%	**49%**	999,043
2002	84,137	8%	446,462	43%	**51%**	151,667	14%	234,319	22%	132,851	13%	**49%**	1,049,435
2003	88,574	8%	460,843	42%	**50%**	160,625	15%	251,969	23%	136,059	12%	**50%**	1,098,070
2004	95,801	8%	471,056	41%	**50%**	169,971	15%	267,385	23%	139,103	12%	**50%**	1,143,316
2005	100,357	8%	480,860	41%	**49%**	177,104	15%	280,505	24%	144,396	12%	**51%**	1,183,222
2006	105,293	9%	478,529	41%	**50%**	180,062	15%	274,390	23%	139,645	12%	**50%**	1,177,918
2007	107,292	9%	471,365	40%	**50%**	176,125	15%	265,310	23%	146,084	13%	**50%**	1,166,174

2008	111,936	9%	474,601	40%	**49%**	181,388	15%	275,259	23%	153,958	13%	**51%**	1,197,142
2009	117,596	9%	481,573	38%	**48%**	190,313	15%	302,100	24%	161,705	13%	**52%**	1,253,286
2010	118,262	9%	475,940	38%	**47%**	158,726	13%	299,760	24%	199,220	16%	**53%**	1,251,909
2011	120,723	10%	466,772	38%	**48%**	159,097	13%	284,767	23%	197,682	16%	**52%**	1,229,040

includes healthcare assistants, support staff and estates and maintainance staff.

* includes general and senior managers.

Source: Emma Hawe and Lesley Cockcroft, OHE Guide to UK Health and Health Care Statistics, Second Edition, 2013, Table 3.1.

systems. Super-managers emerged to run these third-party payer systems. But rather than the 'burden' of first-party payers being reduced over time, it increased. The super-managers oversaw a sector whose productivity was chronically low—and remained so. While consumers got more in the way of quality in the form of successful medical procedures, prices ballooned rather than shrank.

Positive and perverse paradoxes

Health care is a parable for the entire public sector. Spending ever-more taxpayer dollars or mandated payroll dollars on it does not reap better health outcomes as a consequence. Beyond a moderate and prudential level of expenditure, further spending correlates with no better or even worse health outcomes. This happens because health markets today, in most of the major economies, are pseudo-markets. It is the combined actions of millions of first-party payers that creates real markets. As the more adventurous consumers try different options, real markets generate demand for unpretentious innovation. When this happens, the demand of first-party payers for simultaneous price-reducing and quality-increasing innovation causes producers to focus on productivity rather than rules. Pseudo-markets in contrast are populated by subsidized first-party payers. These are inauthentic first-party payers. If a good is subsidized by 40 percent or 60 percent directly or indirectly by the state, then there is no longer an incentive or a reason for a buyer to 'shop around'. The same applies to employer subsidies that eliminate the consumer's responsibility to size-up optimal outcomes.

When the state makes goods 'affordable', often it creates the perverse paradox that the real underlying price or cost of the goods becomes unaffordable. In some cases this simply means transferring the high cost of a good from the consumer to the taxpayer or employer. The paradox begins with a defined, organized and concentrated group of consumers who pay a visible high cost for a good. They lobby government. The lobbying yields a 'popular' political measure that legislators are eager to create. What results is that the cost of the good (or part of it) is picked by the state. This means that a diffuse and unorganized group—taxpayers—end up paying for costs that otherwise would be incurred by a small but organized lobby.[24] Concentrated benefits are sought by well-organized pressure groups. Few lobbies argue on behalf of reducing diffuse costs. But while the costs may be picked up by the state, they are not eliminated or reduced. Rather, they are simply dispersed among many taxpayers. So the cost, previously visible, becomes largely invisible. Yet it doesn't go away. The result of this often is perverse.

The intent of the political act of 'picking up the cost' is that the cost of the good to the individual consumer is lowered. Yet what happens incrementally over time is that the cost of the good rises above the rate of inflation and the rate of GDP per capita growth. This is not just in spite of but rather because of state subsidization. Thus, what starts out as a modestly costly good purchased by the consumer eventually ends up being a very costly good for consumers. This is so even after factoring in government subsidization and cost-sharing. Even after subsidies, the good ends being more expensive in real terms than it was to begin with. Meanwhile, for the diffuse class of taxpayers, who are called on to subsidize the beneficiaries of state spending, the effect of state-subsidized goods is to drive-up levels of taxation or government borrowing and the cost of interest payments on that debt. The consumer-taxpayers were promised that they would be better off. But as a result of the state's action they ultimately end-up worse off.

Notes

1 Markets [=first-party payers] alone cannot fix the problems of mercantilist-Cameralist-Keynesian states. Free markets have to be matched by innovative industries. That is, for every Hayekian solution there has to be a corresponding Schumpeterian one. Industry innovation addresses the cost side of the economic equation ('Can I find a way of producing a good so that the good is both cheaper and better?'; markets address the subjective value-judgments of consumers, namely 'Do I value a good that is on sale more than the price I have to pay for it?')
2 Hult, Jaffe and Philipson, 2016.
3 '[The] prices negotiated between insurers and providers [are] not designed to encourage or reward provider efficiency.' Office of Massachusetts Attorney-General, 2011, 1.
4 Singapore Ministry of Health, 2017; Haseltine, 2013; Liu & Yue, 1999.
5 As Singapore's founder, Lee Kuan Yew (2000: 100) observed about the differences in behavior when a person pays for something and when they get it for zero price: 'The ideal of free medical services collided against the reality of human behaviour, certainly in Singapore. My first lesson came from government clinics and hospitals. When doctors prescribed free antibiotics, patients took their tablet or capsules for two days, did not feel better, and threw away the balance. They then consulted private doctors, paid for their antibiotics, completed the course, and recovered.'
6 Buchmueller and Monheit, 2009.
7 Cannon, 2005. The HSAs were created under the 2003 Medicare Prescription Drug Improvement and Modernization Act. The 2003 US federal legislative initiative built on 20 state-level Medical Savings Accounts schemes and a related federal pilot program from the mid-1990s. By 2016 it was estimated that 20–22 million Americans—6 percent—were covered by HSAs. Four out of five of these had been opened since the beginning of 2011. See National Conference of State Legislatures, 2017. In 2009 in the United States the average life-time health cost per person was $360,000. Assuming the maximum annual contribution of $3,300 for individual coverage and $6,550 for family coverage, Fronstin, 2014, estimated—given that assets in HSAs can earn interest and can build up over time tax free—'a person contributing for 40 years to an HSA could save up to $360,000 if the rate of return was 2.5 percent, $600,000 if the rate of return was 5 percent, and nearly $1.1 million if the rate of return was 7.5 percent, and if there were no withdrawals'. A. Damodaran, New York University, calculates the average annual return of S&P 500 stocks (including dividends) from 1928 to 2013 was 11.53 percent, and 10-year Treasury Bonds was 4.88 percent. http://people.stern.nyu.edu/adamodar/pc/datasets/histretSP.xls
8 On the potential of health savings accounts for the United States, see Cannon, 2005.
9 Kaiser Family Foundation, 2016 Employer Health Benefits Survey.
10 Bureau of Labor Statistics, Usual Weekly Earnings of Wage and Salary Workers, First Quarter 2017.
11 Grossman and Hopkins, 2006, see especially pp. 32–43.
12 Murphy, 2017.
13 For an account of these mores, see Sasse, 2017.
14 As did the term 'pressure group', see Google N-gram.

15 Intellectual models of 'group-identity, group-benefit, group-pressure' politics developed from Harold Laswell's *Politics: Who Gets What, When, How* (1936) through V.O. Key's *Politics, Parties, and Pressure Groups* (1942) and John Kenneth Galbraith's *American Capitalism: The Concept of Countervailing Power* (1952) to Robert Dahl's *A Preface to Democratic Theory* (1956) and Elmer Schattschneider's *The Semisovereign People* (1960). It is notable that American conservatives—who by the 1960s were a distinct minority among American social science and humanities academics, indeed a minority among the entire, predominantly left-liberal academy—tended to view the world in classic philosophical rather than social group terms. Works such as James Burnham's *The Machiavellians* (1943), Robert Nisbet's *The Quest for Community* (1952), Eric Voegelin's *The New Science of Politics* (1952), Leo Strauss' *Natural Right and History* (1953), and Burnham's *Suicide of the West* (1964) set the tone for this. It is not that American conservatives did not produce social-science public policy. They did. Just one example of this was the thread of conservative social science that extended from Edward C. Banfield to James Q. Wilson and Thomas Sowell. It produced major works including Banfield's *Unheavenly City* (1970), Wilson's *Bureaucracy* (1989) and Sowell's *A Conflict of Visions* (1987). But the premise of these works is captured in Sowell's distinction between the (conservative) 'constrained vision' and the (liberal) 'unconstrained vision'. Limited government is a perfect example of 'constrained vision' at work. The perpetual search by organized lobbies to find yet-another identity-group on whom benefits can be bestowed is a classic example of the 'unconstrained vision' at work.
16 Hayek, 1945.
17 Friedman, 2001.
18 Burnham, 1941.
19 Donnelly, 2017. The French economist Thomas Piketty, 2014, identifies the social class of super-managers but focuses only on their presence in corporations. However, they are commonplace in the public sector as well. They are a sub-set of the 11 percent of the population who constitute the well-remunerated post-industrial-era class of graduate-degree holders. Murphy, 2015, 115, 197, 224.
20 Charlesworth, 2013.
21 UK Office for National Statistics, 2017, Reference table 4: Growth rates and indices for public service healthcare inputs, quality adjusted output and productivity, 1995 to 2014. With a change of government in 2010, from Labour to Conservative coalition, annual public-sector health productivity increased significantly (to 2.9 percent and 2.3 in 2013 and 2014).
22 'Across the NHS the overall surplus fell from £2.1 billion in 2012-13 to £722 million in 2013-14. The percentage of NHS Trusts and Foundation Trusts in deficit increased from 1 in 10 to 1 in four over the same period.' Cawston, 2015.
23 Heffer, 2016.
24 Mancur Olson, 1965, 1982.

Bibliography

Banfield, E. 1970. *The Unheavenly City: The Natural and Future of Our Urban Crisis*. Boston, MA: Little, Brown.

Baumol, W. J. 1967. "Macroeconomics of Unbalanced Growth: The Anatomy of Urban Crisis." *The American Economic Review* 57, no. 3: 415–426.

Burnham, J. 2014 [1964]. *Suicide of the West: An Essay on the Meaning and Destiny of Liberalism*. Foreword, John O'Sullivan; Introduction, Roger Kimball. New York: Encounter Books.

Burnham, J. 1943. *The Machiavellians: Defenders of Freedom*. London: Putnam.

Burnham, J. 1941. *The Managerial Revolution*. New York: John Day.

Buchmueller, T. C. and A.C. Monheit. 2009. *Employer-Sponsored Health Insurance and the Promise of Health Insurance Reform*. NBER Working Paper No. 14839. Cambridge, MA: National Bureau of Economic Research.

Cannon, M. 2005. "Combining Tax Reform and Healthcare Reform with Large HSAs." *Tax and Budget Bulletin* No. 23. Washington, DC: Cato Institute.

Cawston, T. 2015. "Can the NHS get off the cost escalator?" *Policy Exchange*, February 5.

Charlesworth, A. 2013. *Trends in Health Spending and Productivity*. Nuffield Trust, March 5.

Dahl, R.A. 1956. *A Preface to Democratic Theory*. Chicago, IL: University of Chicago Press.

Donnelly, L. 2017. "More than 600 health quango chiefs on six figure salaries amid cash crisis." *Daily Telegraph*, March 5.

Friedman, M. 2012 [2001]. "How to Cure Health Care." In *The Indispensable Milton Friedman: Essays on Politics and Economics*, edited by L. Ebenstein, 81–102. Washington, DC: Regnery, 2012.

Fronstin, P. 2014. "Lifetime Accumulations and Tax Savings from HAS Contributions." *Notes* 35, no. 7: –28. Washington, DC: Employee Benefit Research Institute.

Galbraith, J.K. 1952. *American Capitalism: The Concept of Countervailing Power*. Boston, MA: Houghton Mifflin.

Grossman, M. and D.A. Hopkins. 2016. *Asymmetric Politics: Ideological Republicans and Group Interest Democrats*. New York: Oxford University Press.

Hayek, F.A. 1945. "The Use of Knowledge in Society." *American Economic Review*, XXXV, No. 4: 519–530.

Heffer, S. 2016. "The NHS will Simply Collapse unless Politicians have the Courage to Reform it." *The Daily Telegraph*, August 27.

Hult, K.J., S. Jaffe and T.J. Philipson. 2016. *Quality-Adjusted Prices in Healthcare? Systematic Evidence from Thousands of Innovations*. Becker Friedman Institute for Research in Economics, University of Chicago, December 21.

Key, V.O. 1942. *Politics, Parties and Pressure Groups*. New York: Thomas Y. Crowell.

Laswell, H. 1936. *Politics: Who Gets What, When, How*. New York: McGraw-Hill.

Lee, K.Y. 2000. *From Third World to First: The Singapore Story, 1965–2000*. Singapore: Times Media.

Liu, E. and S.Y. Yue. 1999. *Healthcare Expenditure and Financing in Singapore*. Research and Library Services Division Legislative Council Secretariat, July 9.

Murphy, P. 2017. "The Two Incommensurable Americas." *Quadrant*, October.

Murphy, P. 2015. *Universities and Innovation Economies*. Farnham: Ashgate.

National Conference of State Legislatures. 2017. *State Actions on Health Savings Accounts (HSA) and Consumer-Directed Health Plans, 2004–2017*, April.

Nisbet, R. 1952. *The Quest for Community: A Study in the Ethics of Order and Freedom*. New York: Oxford University Press.

Office of the Attorney General of Massachusetts. 2011. *Examination of Healthcare Cost Trends and Cost Drivers*. June.

Olson, M. 1982. *The Rise and Decline of Nations*. New Haven: Yale University Press.

Olson, M. 1965. *The Logic of Collective Action: Public Goods and the Theory of Groups*. Cambridge, MA: Harvard University Press.

Piketty, T. 2014. *Capital in the Twenty-First Century*. Cambridge, MA: Harvard University Press.

Sasse, B. 2017. *The Vanishing American Adult: Our Coming-of-Age Crisis—and How to Rebuild a Culture of Self-Reliance*. New York: St. Martin's Press.

Schattschneider, E.E. 1960. *The Semisovereign People: A Realist's View of Democracy in America*. New York: Holt, Rinehart and Winston.
Singapore Ministry of Health. 2017. *Schemes & Subsidies*.
Sowell, T. 1987. *A Conflict of Visions: Ideological Origins of Political Struggles*. New York, W. Morrow.
Strauss, L. 1953. *Natural Right and History*. Chicago, IL: University of Chicago Press.
Voegelin, E. 1952. *The New Science of Politics*. Chicago, IL: University of Chicago Press.
Wilson, J.Q. 1989. *Bureaucracy: what government agencies do and why they do it*. New York: Basic Books.

11 Education

Public spending and educational achievement

Education is the third largest component of contemporary public spending after income-support and health. Like the two biggest spending items, education suffers from perverse paradoxes. Simply put: the more that governments spend on education, the less is achieved. Take the case of the United States. Between 1970 and 2010, real spending on primary and secondary schools in the United States tripled. Student performance in reading, writing and mathematics remained static over the period. Total US spending per capita on public schools (in constant 2013–2014 dollars) was $673 in 1960 and $2,137 in 2010. The average NAEP (National Assessment of Educational Progress) 17-year-old reading score in 1971 was 285.[1] In 2008 it was 286. America overspent and under-achieved (Table 11.1).

As US spending on public schools has gone up, the number of public school students as a percentage of the population has gone down. In 1960, it was 20 percent; in 2010, 16 percent. Over the same period the number of public school teachers per capita rose from 7.8 per thousand to 13.4 and the number of public school teachers per 100 students grew from 3.9 to 8.3. At the same time performance scores flatlined. The NAEP average 17-year-old mathematics score in 1973 was 304; in 2010, it was 306. The 23 percent of students who studied calculus or pre-calculus subjects had the highest average score (334) in NAEP mathematics in 2012.[2] Yet while the number of students studying in calculus classes grew from 6 percent to 23 percent between 1978 and 2012, the average math performance of 17-year-olds remained virtually constant over time. This indicates deep systemic problems in education (Table 11.1). Lower-performing American 17-year-olds in 2012 NAEP tests were unable to do many fundamental reading and calculation tasks (Table 11.2).

The mismatch between spending and achievement over the long run is also reflected over the shorter run. At regular intervals since 2000, the OECD's Programme for International Assessment (PISA) assessed 15-year-old student reading, science and mathematics performance across OECD and non-OECD countries. The PISA reading assessment tests student grasp of narrative, exposition and argument; the science assessment, student understanding of concepts of force, motion and change; and in mathematics, student comprehension of quantity,

Table 11.1 US primary and secondary education performance

	1960	**1970**	**1980**	**1990**	**2000**	**2010**
Total US population	177,830,000	201,385,000	225,005,000	246,819,000	279,040,000	306,772,000
US GDP in constant 2014 dollars billions	$4,270	$6,565	$8,225	$10,831	$14,139	$16,241
Total spending on public schools (constant 2013–14 dollars, billions)	$119.60	$254.00	$297.40	$391.40	$524.90	$655.70
Public school expenditure as percentage of GDP constant 2013-14 dollars billions	2.80%	3.87%	3.62%	3.61%	3.71%	4.04%
Total federal, state, local government spending on education as percent of GDP	3.75%	5.79%	5.80%	5.49%	5.72%	6.76%
Public school student numbers	36,087,000	45,550,000	41,651,000	40,534,000	46,857,000	49,361,000
Private school student numbers	5,900,000	5,363,000	5,331,000	5,648,000	6,169,000	5,398,000
Public school student numbers as percent of population	20%	23%	19%	16%	17%	16%
Total students as percent of population	24%	25%	21%	19%	19%	18%
Public school spending per capita (constant 2013–2014 dollars)	$673	$1,261	$1,322	$1,586	$1,881	$2,137
Public school spending per student (constant 2013–2014 dollars)	$3,314	$5,576	$7,140	$9,656	$11,202	$13,284
Number of public teachers, aides, librarians, counselors	1,393,000	2,195,000	2,300,000	2,860,000	3,682,000	4,111,000
Number of private teachers	192,000	233,000	301,000	361,000	424,000	428,000
Number of public teachers, aides, librarians, counselors per capita thousand	7.8	10.9	10.2	11.6	13.2	13.4
Number of private teachers per capita thousand	1.1	1.2	1.3	1.5	1.5	1.4
Public teachers per 100 public students	3.9	4.8	5.5	7.1	7.9	8.3
Private teachers per 100 private students	3.3	4.3	5.6	6.4	6.9	7.9
Administration as a percentage of public school spending	3.4%	3.9%	4.4%	7.7%	6.6%	6.4%
Instruction as a percentage of public school spending	53.5%	52.7%	55.5%	53.4%	52.4%	52.9%

Percentage of high school students not graduating [1972, 2006]		6.1%	6.1%	4.0%	4.8%	3.9%
Percent of 17-year olds 1–2 hours homework [1984, 1996]			27%	24%		
Percent of 17-year olds in homes with adults who read daily [1984, 1996]			42%	39%		
Education Outcomes						
NAEP 17-year old average reading score [1971, 1999, 2008 score]		285	285	290	288	286
NAEP 16-year old average writing score [1984, 1990, 1996 scores]			290	287	283	
NAEP 17-year old average writing score [1998, 2007 scores]					150	153
NAEP 17-year old average math score [1973, 1982, 1998, 2008 score]		304	299	305	308	306
NAEP 17-year old average science score [1969, 1982, 1990 score]		305	283	290		

Sources: US Digest of Education Statistics, Enrollment, number of teachers, pupil/teacher ratio, and expenditures in public elementary and secondary schools: 1960–1961 through 2013–2014; US Digest of Education Statistics, Expenditures of educational institutions related to the gross domestic product, by level of institution: Selected years, 1929–1930 through 2014–2015; US Digest of Educational Statistics, Expenditures of educational institutions, by level and control of institution: Selected years, 1899–1900 through 2014–2015; NCES, Average reading scale scores on the long-term trend National Assessment of Educational Progress (NAEP), by age: Selected years, 1971 through 2012; NCES, Average mathematics scale scores on the long-term trend National Assessment of Educational Progress (NAEP), by age: Selected years, 1973 through 2012; NCES, Long-Term Trends in Student Science Performance, Vol. 3, No. 3, September 1998; NAEP Data Explorer; NAEP The Nations Report Card Writing 2002; NAEP 1996 Trends in Academic Progress; NCES, Historical summary of public elementary and secondary school statistics: Selected years, 1869–1870 through 2010–2011; NCES, Public and private elementary and secondary teachers, enrollment, and pupil/teacher ratios: Selected years, fall 1955 through fall 2020; NCES, Total and current expenditures per pupil in public elementary and secondary schools: Selected years, 1919–1920 through 2011–2012, constant 2013–2014 dollars; National Conference of State Legislatures, Elementary & Secondary Education Revenue and Expenditures, Figure 1 Sources of Revenue School Years 1919–1920 to 2013–2014; http://www.usgovernmentspending.com/education_spending; NCES, Summary of expenditures for public elementary and secondary education and other related programs, by purpose: Selected years, 1919–1920 through 2013–2014; NCES, Percentage of elementary and secondary school students who do homework outside of school, whose parents check that homework is done, and whose parents help with homework, by frequency and selected student and school characteristics: 2003 and 2007; NCES, Average student proficiency in reading, by age and selected characteristics of students: 1971 to 1996 (NAEP data); NCES, Student proficiency in reading, by age, amount of time spent on homework and reading habits: 1984, 1994 and 1996 (NAEP data).

Table 11.2 Reading and calculation tasks not successfully performed by students in US NAEP testing

NAEP 17-year-old students in 2012 with scores under 300 were likely not to be able to:
1. Extend the information in a short historical passage to provide comparisons;
2. Provide a text-based description of the key steps in a process;
3. Make an inference to recognize a non-explicit cause in an expository passage;
4. Provide a description that includes the key aspects of a passage topic;
5. Infer and provide a moral based on a short tale;
6. Provide an example of language and explain its effect on the reader;
7. Provide relevant information about the subject of a biographical sketch and explain why it is important;
8. Recognize a supporting detail from a scientific description;
9. Provide an example to illustrate the author's device for creating a mood;
10. Read a highly detailed schedule to locate specific information.
NAEP 17-year-old students with scores lower than 306 had quite a low probability that they could:
1. Identify a construction using a compass
2. Rewrite an expression involving exponents and radicals
3. Read and interpret data from tables, charts, and graphs
4. Determine a logical result from a statement
5. Compute the area of a circle
6. Analyze a proportional relationship
7. Identify an inequality from its graph
8. Find the median
9. Determine the percent given the part and the whole
10. Estimate a square root
11. Compute the area of a square given its perimeter
12. Add two fractions with unlike denominators
13. Convert between units of weight

Source: NAEP 2012, Trends in Academic Progress, Reading 1971–2012 Mathematics 1973–2012, pp. 13 and 35.

shape, space and relations of change.[3] In 2000, US 15-year-olds scored 504 on the PISA reading scale; in 2015, 497. In mathematics, performance dropped from 493 to 470; in science, from 499 to 496 (Table 11.3). Meanwhile, from 2000 to 2010 real spending on public education in the US (measured in constant 2013-2014 dollars) rose from $524 billion to $655 billion, that is, from 3.71 percent of GDP to 4.01 percent. Per capita spending on public schools grew from $1,881 to $2,137. Spending per public school student grew $11,202 to $13,284 (Table 11.1).

The pattern of scores going down and spending going up was repeated in Australia. That country's PISA reading score dropped from 528 to 503 between 2000 and 2015. Its mathematics score fell from 533 to 494; its science score from 528 to 510 (Table 11.3).[4] At the same time, in constant 2014–2015 dollars Australia's total spending on its primary and secondary schools grew from

Table 11.3 PISA, Programme for International Student Assessment, OECD, 15-year-olds

Country/Scale	**2000**	**2003**	**2006**	**2009**	**2012**	**2015**
Reading scale						
Australia	528	525		515	512	503
Canada	534	528		542	523	527
Finland	546	543		536	524	526
Hong Kong	525	510		533	545	527
Japan	522	498		520	538	516
Korea	525	534		539	536	517
Sweden	516	514		497	483	500
United Kingdom	523			494	499	498
United States	504	495		500	498	497
Shanghai				556	570	
Beijing, Shanghai, Jiangsu and Guangdong						494
Singapore				526	542	535
Taiwan				495	523	497
Mathematical scale						
Australia	533	524		514	504	494
Canada	533	532		527	518	516
Finland	536	544		541	519	511
Hong Kong	560	550		555	573	548
Japan	557	534		529	536	532
Korea	547	542		546	554	524
Sweden	510	509		494	478	494
United Kingdom	529			492	494	492
United States	493	483		487	481	470
Shanghai				600	613	
Beijing, Shanghai, Jiangsu and Guangdong						531
Singapore				562	573	564
Taiwan				543	560	542
Scientific scale						
Australia	528	525	527	527	521	510
Canada	529	519	534	529	525	528
Finland	538	548	563	554	545	531
Hong Kong	541	539	542	549	555	523
Japan	550	548	531	539	547	538
Korea	552	538	522	538	538	516
Sweden	512	506	503	495	485	493
United Kingdom	532		515	514	514	509
United States	499	491	498	502	497	496
Shanghai				575	580	
Beijing, Shanghai, Jiangsu and Guangdong						518
Singapore				542	551	565
Taiwan				520	523	532

Sources: OECD, Knowledge and Skills for Life, First Results from the OECD Programme for International Student Assessment (PISA) 2000; OECD, Learning for Tomorrow's World First Results from PISA 2003; OECD, PISA 2006 Volume 2: Data; OECD, PISA 2009 Results: What Students Know and Can Do, Student Performance in Reading, Mathematics and Science, Volume 1; OECD, PISA 2012 Results in Focus: What 15-year-olds know and what they can do with what they know; OECD, PISA 2015 Results in Focus.

$28 billion to $43 billion and its spending per student increased from $8,700 to $11,536 between 2000–2001 and 2014–2015. Government spending over the period grew 152 percent, student numbers 115 percent and spending per student 131 percent (Table 11.4). A third more spending per student yielded performance drops of 4, 5 and 7 percent in PISA assessments.

The paradox of industrial societies is that economic sectors over time reduce costs and increase quality. That was the history of agriculture and manufacturing in the industrial age. Costs are reduced by increasing productivity. This is achieved by replacing labor with machines. Quality is increased by innovation that reduces time-wasting and pointless activity. The education sector resists both cost reduction and quality improvement. Its primary organization form—the classroom—defies productivity increases and increased quality outcomes. We can see this at a glance when we look at the long-term trend in education productivity. In the United States, the productivity of employees in the education services sector grew 0.19 percent in the years between 1987 and 1995, and 0.95 percent between 1995 and 2001.[5] By comparison, the productivity of the wholesale trade sector in the same years grew 3.43 percent and 4.19 percent respectively. In Australia in 2013, the value added per employee in education and training was $60,264; in manufacturing it was $109,358 (Table 11.5).[6]

The post-industrial education industry has contributed almost nothing in productivity gains over multiple decades (Table 9.4). Meanwhile, other sectors have increased productivity substantially. One then might have expected the salary levels of education employees to fall compared with employees in better performing industries. Yet this did not happen. Teacher salaries in 1950 were 101 percent of median US household income salary; in 2010, 104 percent.[7] In the United States, the increase of multifactor productivity in the private nonfarm economy between 1987 and 2014 was 91 percent. In education it was -1 percent.[8] Education made the American economy less productive. The obvious objection to this is that, surely, it is a terrible thing to talk about education in terms of productivity. Education is inherently labor-intensive, hands-on. To mention productivity is to promise the ruin of children's learning. Or is it? The first thing to be observed is that low-productivity, labor-focused teaching does not work. We can spend twice or three times in real terms on it, with no improvement in outcomes. This is irrational. It also suggests that labor-focused learning may be intrinsically counter-productive.

Reading and student achievement

Is this then an argument to replace educational labor with machines? Does the criticism of educational productivity imply the automation of the classroom? Before answering that question it is worth first asking: what contributes most to student learning? What is most strongly correlated with student achievement?

In 2000 the OECD's Programme for International Assessment (PISA) undertook an international study on student performance in 32 countries, 28 of them OECD countries. In this large-scale study, tens of thousands of students were sampled. Using regression analysis, PISA analyzed 32 separate factors that might

Table 11.4 Government spending on primary and secondary schools, Australia, 1999–2016

		1999–2000	2000–2001	2001–2002	2002–2003	2003–2004	2004–2005	2005–2006	2006–2007
Educational Spending									
Government expenditure on primary and secondary schools in constant 2014–2015 $million (incl. 2015–16)		$28,396	$28,288	$30,057	$31,871	$31,735	$34,267	$34,777	$35,222
Year-on-year percentage growth in expenditure on primary and secondary schools			99.62%	106.25%	106.04%	99.57%	107.98%	101.49%	101.28%
Number of fulltime students [2000–2015, All Schools]			3,247,425					3,373,212	3,392,566
Spending per student, constant 2014–2015 dollars			$8,711					$10,310	$10,382
Spending per student, constant 2014–2015 dollars, compared with prior year									101%
Spending per student, constant 2014–2015 dollars, compared with 2000–2001									119%
Increase/decrease in fulltime student population, year on year									19354
Percentage increase/decrease in fulltime student population, year on year									0.57%

Educational Outcomes									
PISA Scores, Reading Scale			528			525			
PISA Scores, Mathematics Scale			533			524			
PISA Scores, Science Scale			528			525			527
	2007–2008	**2008–2009**	**2009–2010**	**2010–2011**	**2011–2012**	**2012–2013**	**2013–2014**	**2014–2015**	**2015–2016**
Educational Spending									
Government expenditure on primary and secondary schools in constant 2014–2015 $million (incl. 2015–16)	$36,324	$38,309	$40,249	$43,888	$41,391	$42,442	$42,501	$43,270	$44,620
Year-on-year percentage growth in expenditure on primary and secondary schools	103.13%	105.46%	105.06%	109.04%	94.31%	102.54%	100.14%	101.81%	103.12%
Number of fulltime students [2000–2015, All Schools]	3,441,026	3,434,291	3,484,700	3,510,875	3,541,809	3,589,986	3,645,519	3,730,694	3,798,226
Spending per student, constant 2014–2015 dollars	$10,556	$11,155	$11,550	$12,501	$11,686	$11,822	$11,658	$11,598	$11,748
Spending per student, constant 2014–2015 dollars, compared with prior year	102%	106%	104%	108%	93%	101%	99%	99%	101%
Spending per student, constant 2014–2015 dollars, compared with 2000–2001	121%	128%	133%	144%	134%	136%	134%	133%	135%
Increase/decrease in fulltime student population, year on year	48460	–6735	50409	26175	30934	48177	55533	85175	67532

Percentage increase/decrease in fulltime student population, year on year	1.43%	–0.20%	1.47%	0.75%	0.88%	1.36%	1.55%	2.34%	1.81%
Educational Outcomes									
PISA Scores, Reading Scale			515			512			503
PISA Scores, Mathematics Scale			514			504			494
PISA Scores, Science Scale			527			521			510

Sources: Australian Bureau of Statistics, Government Expenditure on Education in Australia 2006–2007 to 2015-16; Australian Bureau of Statistics, Government Finance Statistics, Australia, 2009–2010, 2008–2009, 2007–2008; Australian Bureau of Statistics, Government Finance Statistics, Education, Australia, 2006–2007; Australian Bureau of Statistics, Schools Australia; OECD, Knowledge and Skills for Life, First Results from the OECD Programme for International Student Assessment (PISA) 2000; OECD, Learning for Tomorrow's World First Results from PISA 2003; OECD, PISA 2006 Volume 2: Data; OECD, PISA 2009 Results: What Students Know and Can Do, Student Performance in Reading, Mathematics and Science, Volume 1; OECD, PISA 2012 Results in Focus: What 15-year-olds know and what they can do with what they know; OECD, PISA 2015 Results in Focus.

Table 11.5 Australian labor productivity, 2013

	Value added per worker
Health care and social assistance	$64,522
Education and training	$60,264
Public administration and safety	$63,444
Electricity, gas, water and waste services	$366,414
Rental, hiring and real estate services	$155,296
Manufacturing	$109,358

Source: D. Richardson, Productivity in the construction industry, The Australia Institute, August 2014, Table 3.

explain the variance, up and down, in the performance of 15-year-old students.[9] The single largest factor by far was 'engagement in reading'. Most of the other big factors were related to reading, including 'interest in reading', 'classical culture in the home' and 'activities related to classical culture in the home'. Though less significant, 'homework' was a further intellectual correlate. In some of the countries surveyed 'parental occupational status' was also a significant factor linked to achievement. Yet it was nowhere near as significant as 'reading, classical culture and homework' were. Again, in some countries 'elaboration' and 'control' strategies also played a significant role. Both are do-it-yourself self-regulated styles of learning. Elaboration explores 'how the material relates to things one has learned in other contexts, or asking how the information might be applied in other situations'. Control involves 'students who reported beginning the learning process by figuring out what they needed to learn, who ensured that they understood what they read, tried to figure out which concepts they had not fully grasped, attempted to remember the most important points in a text and sought additional clarifying information when they did not understand something they had read'.[10]

It is notable that the huge array of institutional factors PISA analyzed—including school resources, teaching morale, school autonomy, school selectivity, teacher autonomy, teacher support, teacher shortage and school infrastructure—made little or no difference to learning. Family wealth and home educational resources—like a desk, a quiet study place, dictionaries and textbooks—also made little difference. Reading combined with 'classical culture' (literature, books of poetry and works of art in the home, visiting a museum or art gallery; attending opera, ballet or classical symphony concerts; or watching live theatre) and 'homework' accounted for 41 percent of the variance in student performance across the OECD and as much as 54 percent in Australia. Let us call this model 1. Another model (model 2) epitomized by Korea relies little on 'classical culture' but replaces it with 'elaboration' and 'control' strategies (self-regulated learning) and 'social communication' (the frequency parents talk with children about culture).[11] In Korea, the combination of control, elaboration, classical culture, engagement and interest in reading, 'social communication' (talking with parents) and homework accounted for 62 percent of correlated explanatory factors.[12] In both model 1 and model 2, other factors analyzed mostly explained only tiny percentages of the differences in student achievement.

Two studies in 2007 revaluated the original PISA 2000 data.[13] They analyzed positive and negative coefficients of student scores. Chiu examined science scores. From the strongest to weakest the following positive coefficients were identified: the number of books at home, socio-economic status, cultural communication at home, birth order and cultural possessions. From most potent to least potent negative coefficients, Chiu identified: living with no parents, first-generation immigrant, foreign language spoken at home, grandparents in household and multiple siblings in household. In the same vein, Fuchs and Wößmann examined reading, science and math scores. In the case of positive coefficients for reading scores, the researchers identified the following ranging from the strongest to the weakest: books at home, a city center of a million-plus, at least one parent working full-time, a parent with a white-collar job, the autonomous choice of textbooks and the presence of instructional material. In Fuchs and Wößmann's study the negative coefficients for reading scores (from the most potent to least potent) were: external exams, public schooling, teacher salaries, autonomy in course content, government funding, standardized tests, educational expenditure per students, hiring teachers and budget allocations. In short, scores increase principally with reading at home. At least one parent working full-time in a white-collar job, or similar parental-status factor, also increases scores. So does cultural communication between parents and children. Books at home, though, provide the outstanding boost for learning scores. Nothing else approaches the power of reading.

Among PISA 2000 students, no books at home were reported by 2 percent; 1–10 books (13 percent), 11–50 books (23 percent); 51–100 books (21 percent); 101–250 books (18 percent); 251–500 books (13 percent); and over 500 books (10 percent).[14] Even 1–10 books at home has a strong influence on reading scores; likewise, 11–50 books at home has a strong influence on science and mathematics scores.[15] The 2003 PISA study examined the impact of cultural possessions in the home on mathematical performance. Students in Australia, Korea, Finland, Japan, Sweden and the United States had mean scores in mathematics respectively of 521, 552, 539, 553, 498 and 472.[16] The cohort of students from these countries who came from the top quarter of homes with cultural possessions had mean scores of 556, 574, 564, 563, 545 and 523, improvements of 6 percent, 4 percent, 2 percent, 1.8 percent, 9 percent, and 10 percent on a 600-point scale.[17]

The 2009 PISA exercise concluded that on average across all OECD countries 18 percent of the student variation in reading performance could be 'explained' by how much students reported enjoying reading.[18] In many countries the figure was higher. 'Enjoying reading' statistically accounted for the variation in student reading scores by as much as 27 percent in Finland, 26 percent in Australia and 22 percent in Sweden, Taiwan and the United Kingdom. In Korea, the figure was 18 percent; in Singapore 17 percent. Pleasure in reading counted for less in Japan (15 percent), Hong Kong (14 percent) and Shanghai (12 percent).[19] Even so, when students who 'read 30 minutes a day for enjoyment' and those who 'don't read for enjoyment' are compared, the score-point difference between the two cohorts was 66 points out of the 600-point PISA reading scale in Shanghai, 55 points in Taiwan and Australia, 44 in Japan and Singapore and 34 in Hong Kong.

The OECD average was 44 points.[20] On average across OECD countries, the PISA report concluded, a difference of one unit on 'the index of enjoyment of reading' corresponded to 40 points on PISA's 600-point reading scale or the equivalent of an average school year's progress.[21] In addition to this, reading more—30–60 minutes a day or one-to-two hours or even more a day—further increases performance. Reading one-to-two hours represents an *additional* positive score difference of 45 points in Australia, 45 points in the UK, 30 points in Switzerland, 25 points in Taiwan, 22 points in the US and Korea, 15 points in Japan and Hong Kong, 20 points in Iceland and Singapore and a negligible difference in Shanghai.[22] In short, the child that reads one-to-two hours a day gains the equivalent of a-half-to-one-year's progress at school.

The most common reading styles vary between the top-reading countries. Of the top seven nations or cities, the most common reading style in descending order of performance was: Shanghai (deep and wide readers), Korea (deep and highly restricted readers), Finland (deep and narrow readers), Hong Kong (deep and wide readers), Canada (deep and highly restricted readers), Singapore (deep and wide readers), Japan (split between deep and wide and deep and narrow readers) and Australia (deep and highly restricted readers).[23] Translating the PISA terminology, 'deep' means having a conscious approach to learning. 'Wide' means reading all sorts of materials including fiction and non-fiction books. 'Narrow' readers read principally newspapers and magazines. 'Highly restricted' readers mainly read newspapers. It is not surprising that today the most successful cities in the world—Shanghai, Hong Kong and Singapore—are producing the most intellectually serious readers, the 'deep and wide' readers. These are book readers.

A 2010 home library meta-study provides further evidence that 'books at home' is the most important single reason that explains educational achievement. The study, drawing on data from surveys across 31 countries, concluded that the size of a family's home library is as important a predictor of a child's educational success as the parent's level of education.[24] A family having 500 books at home compared to one book represents a mean gain for a child of 3.2 years of education. That's the same gain as when parents have 15 years of education compared with 3 years. The effects of all other factors, including a father's occupation or the GDP of the home country when the child was young, pale in comparison. The estimated gain in educational years by having a 500-book home library in 1999 varied internationally from 6.6 years in rural China to 1.6 years in Canada. In the mid-range, the gain in Australia was 2.7 years, Sweden 3.6 years and the Philippines 4.0.[25]

Ten percent of survey respondents aggregated in the home library meta-study grew up with no books at home. Twenty-three percent had around 10 books, 16 percent about 25 books, 33 percent around 75 books, and 18 percent grew up with hundreds of books. The average number was 112 books.[26] The conclusions of this meta-study are echoed in the second volume of the PISA 2009 reports. The OECD assessment identifies a series of stand-alone home-based factors that explain the variance in student performance, including parental occupational and education status, cultural possessions and number of books at home, home educational resources, wealth, single-parent family, immigrant status and language spoken at home. Across the OECD, 'books and cultural possessions at home' explained 45 percent of the effect of home-based factors taken by themselves. The other principal, though lesser, factor of 'parental occupation and education' explained 27 percent of home-based effects.[27]

The attrition of reading

If reading matters, then how much reading do students do? Let's consider this in an historical context. A US study from 1931 reported on the numbers of books at home.[28] The research was conducted with care. The researchers went into homes and counted the books in situ. The sample of participants—50 homes in Morris, Illinois—was chosen to closely mirror the social composition of the town. The range of fathers' occupations broke down into: 32 percent unskilled labourers, 18 percent skilled labourers, 32 percent in business and 18 percent in the professions. Twenty-four percent had graduated from high school; 18 percent from college. The average number of newspapers was two subscriptions per family. The average number of magazine subscriptions was five per family. Households subscribed to an average of one child's magazine. The average number of books found in the homes was 150. That included an average of 22 children's books per family, close to the same found in Carsley's 1957 Merseyside study.[29]

Contrast 1931 with 70 years later. The US General Social Survey 2000 survey data included responses to the question 'About how many books were there around your family's house when you were 16 years old?' 1,199 persons answered the question. The average number of books per respondent was 108. That's down a third from the 1931 level. The same applies to other forms of high literacy. Total daily newspaper paid circulation as percentage of households in the USA in 1950 was 123 percent (more than one newspaper per household); in 2010, 38 percent.[30] In Britain in 1950 it was 150 percent; in 2010, 40 percent. Similarly, Canada dropped from 101 percent to 30 percent. Australian households spent $10.50 on 'literature' per week in 1984 and $9.38 in 2009 (in constant 2009 dollars).[31]

As to borrowing books from public libraries, Galbi's 2007 study reports that from 1856 to 1978, library users borrowed about 15 books per user per year from US public libraries. From 1978 to 2004, as the post-industrial era set in, book circulation per user declined by about 50 percent.[32] The 'knowledge society' exhibited a declining social interest in knowledge—at least of the systematically organized kind of knowledge that is found in books, the kind that requires cognitive concentration and persistence. Galbi reports that book borrowing per user in US public libraries reached its peak in 1868, with 19 books borrowed per user per year. Circulation in 1856 was 14 per user; in 1978, 16 per user. Juvenile library-users borrowed 20.5 books per head in 1938 and 18.5 in 1955.[33] Then an abyssal drop occurs. By 2004, library circulation had fallen to 9 items per user.[34] In 2014, it was 7.5 items per capita.[35] Juvenile circulation by 2014 had plummeted to 2.7 items per capita. Between 1978 and 2014 in the US, the number of libraries grew, the number of users grew, the volumes in libraries grew yet borrowing per user declined. In Australia, as with household spending on 'literature', the long-term trend of borrowing by library-users has been more steady-state. In 1996–1997, registered library users in Australia borrowed 16.8 items per user or 8.9 items for every person in Australia. In 2014–2015, circulation was 17.9 items per users (an increase) but 7 items per capita (a decrease).[36] As library loans per capita dropped from 8.1 in 2010–2011 to 7 in 2014–2015, spending on Australian libraries in real terms (2014–2015 dollars) increased from $46.57 per capita to $48.00. Over the same period Australia's population grew from 22.03 million to 23.46 million while the total volume of loan issues decreased from 182.7 million to 166.7 million.

Sharon McKool notes the many studies that show a strong relationship between the amount of out-of-school reading a student does and success in reading at school.[37] Reading out-of-school accelerates 'vocabulary development, fluency, comprehension and general intellectual development'.[38] Yet fewer and fewer students today do this kind of reading. 'Most children do very little reading out-of-school and only a small number read for extended periods of time.'[39] Take the example of Anderson, Wilson, Fielding's 1988 US survey of 155 Illinois 5th-grade students (10–11 year-olds).[40] This study found that the median time these students spent reading books out-of-school was 4.6 minutes a day; the mean time was 10.1 minutes.[41] The mean time for voluntary reading in its totality (books, comics, mail, and magazines) was 18.4 minutes. There was a vast spectrum of reading habits. At the top 98-percentile, students read 4.35 million book-words a year (around 85 books); at the 90-percentile point, 1.82 million book-words (around 35 books). The bottom 2-percentile, on the other hand, read 0 words. At the 50-percentile mark, 282,000 words were read in a year (about 6 books). McKool's 2007 survey of 199 fifth-graders found that they spent an average of 17 minutes a day in voluntary text reading (not homework) outside school. This was a decrease on Anderson, Wilson, Fielding's 1988 finding of 18.4 minutes a day spent on *all* kinds of reading, book and non-book (separate from homework). McKool reported that avid readers spent as much as 46 minutes a day on average engaged in voluntary reading. Reluctant readers spent three minutes on average.[42]

Compare these results with Carsley's 1957 UK Merseyside study, also of 10–11-year-old's reading habits. This study identified significant reading-at-home.[43] The data was broken down by locality, into (1) owner-occupier, (2) higher artisan, (3) lower artisan and (4) housing estate homes, and by gender. The number of books boys read at home per month was: (1) 3.8, (2) 2.5, (3) 1.4 and (4) 2.6. The number of books girls read at home per month was: (1) 4.2, (2) 3.8, (3) 2.6 and (4) 3.4. In short, Merseyside children in 1955 were averaging about over 2 books a month, or 25 a year, at least three times their American peers in the late 1980s. Today, grade-5 (10–11-year-old) American students read on average only 25 books *in total*, for classroom, homework and leisure combined—and after grade 6 the number of books and words read declines markedly.[44] This data is consistent with the hypothesis that there was a general collapse in book reading from the late 1960s as the post-industrial era began. Allan Bloom observed that by the time the students of the 1980s arrived at university they had 'lost the practice of and the taste for reading', a trend he thought had begun in the 1960s.[45]

In the 1957 Merseyside study around 20 percent of the books were sourced from a public library; 10 percent were borrowed. The rest were from various home sources. The size of home libraries ranged from 0–400. The median number of books belonging to boys were: (1) 45, (2) 21, (3) 9 and (4) 21; for girls: (1) 47, (2) 27, (3) 12 and (4) 21.

Both boys and girls ranked adventure stories and mystery stories as their first and second reading preference. Encyclopaedias, the top-positioned non-fiction category, ranked fourth for boys and fifth for girls. Children preferred home reading to school reading because of the following factors: at home there was less distraction of attention by noise and movement, less likelihood of interruption, longer spells could be spent with a book, and there was greater comfort and a more complete feeling of relaxation.[46] As McKool notes, interruption and distraction, which are habitual in school classrooms, are the opposite of what the American psychologist Mihaly Csikszentmihalyi calls the 'flow experience'. 'Flow' is when someone is fully engaged in an activity such that action and awareness coalesce.[47] Anyone who reads or writes or calculates for a living will recognize immediately how important 'flow' is to what they do. Flow is also an index of personality traits that are key to all kinds of human achievement: persistence, attentiveness, tenacity, determination, diligence, resolution and tirelessness. Classrooms destroy flow (offices do much the same). They are implacably hostile to it. McKool describes the flow of reading this way: One student reported that when he was reading an interesting book he didn't realize how much time had passed. His parents often had to interrupt his reading so that he would go to bed. Another student described his voluntary reading as a time when he frequently 'got lost in a book'.[48]

If by 1988 the taste for reading had abated in the case of most school students, for a minority, if anything, it had increased. What made the difference? One factor McKool singled out (using qualitative data: interviews with 5th-grade students) was what PISA calls 'social communication', parents at home talking with children about books. That is, big readers tend to be children who have parents who 'read aloud to them', who model 'reading themselves for recreational purposes', recommend good books and discuss at home books 'that they and their children were reading'.[49] McKool also concludes that self-direction in reading is a further key. This is where students have 'opportunities to read self-selected materials' and 'access to materials [they are] personally interested in reading'.[50] Reluctant reading at home is not, McKool argues, a function of socio-economic status but rather the home educational environment and the value placed on reading at home.

Readucation

There is a strong case to be made that institutional teaching contributes much less to student learning than does reading and related activities. This also suggests why labor-fixated teaching is not effective. It focuses on institutional factors (resources and staffing) rather than on intellectual factors (reading and writing). It is from this vantage-point then that the question about the productivity of the education sector can be answered. In classic industries, including mining, agriculture and manufacturing, productivity has been improved by replacing labor with machines. In education, the parallel would be to replace classroom time with silent-reading time.[51] The term 'classroom' has not always been a key-word. It takes-off around 1905 and escalates in use across the subsequent century. John Dewey was its intellectual pioneer.[52] In 1890, grade-school children in the United States attended classes 99 days in the year.[53] As the push by progressives for more classroom time proceeded, class-time ballooned to 113 days in 1900, 121 in 1920, 143 in 1930, 151 in 1940, 157 in 1950 and 160 in 1960. Did verbal, writing and calculation competencies rise as class-time rose? No. What did rise was public-sector spending, institutionalization, industry lobbies and trade-union power.

In a 2007 study Nie, Golde and Butler looked at evidence of communicative ability. They examined data from the US General Social Survey's (GSS's) vocabulary recognition test and the National Assessment of Adult Literacy (NAAL)'s tests of document and prose literacy.[54] The GSS asks test-takers to match, from a list, a word that is closest in meaning to a test word. The NAAL measures three types of literacy—prose, document and quantitative literacy. Nie and his associates concluded that, in spite of the massive expansion of education in the United States in the twentieth century, there was no parallel increase in the verbal abilities and skills of Americans. The level of educational attainment in America rose from an average of 10 years in 1910 to 14 years in 1974. Yet the massive additional spending on education in real terms over six decades produced no general improvement in the communicative competence of the general population.[55]

It is also evident that not only has there been no general improvement in word capacity over time but that high-level prose comprehension has declined dramatically. In the period 1980 to 2000, spending per school student in the United States in constant 2013–2014 dollar terms rose 60 percent (from $7,140 to $11,202). Yet the society's literate outcomes moved in the opposite direction (Table 11.1, 11.2 and 11.3). Most troubling was that in step with spending increases were decreases in the higher levels of communicative ability. Between the 1992 and 2003 NAAL test rounds, the percentage of American adults with a proficient level of prose and document literacy dropped (Table 11.6).[56] Slight improvements in the mid-literacy range were accompanied by drops in the higher range. The same pattern is reflected even more dramatically in GSS WORDSUM vocabulary scores. Adults surveyed are asked to define ten words. Each word has five multiple choice answer options. Breaking the GSS data by age cohort and percentage of each cohort who correctly define 9 or 10 words reveals a disturbing long-term trend (Table 11.7). Seventeen percent of the cohort born from 1880 to 1929 correctly defined 9 or 10 words. Seventeen percent is society's classic college-ready professional-managerial cohort-in-the-making, the elite who run a modern society.[57] Relative high scores were maintained by the 30s and 40s birth group. Then the fall begins. Fourteen percent of the 50s cohort got 9 or 10 words right; 7 percent of the 70s cohort and 2 percent of the 90s cohort. This signals a serious decline of the intellectual competency of society's professional-managerial strata.

Table 11.6 US literacy

National Assessment of Adult Literacy				
Year/Literacy Type	**Percent of adults: below basic literacy**	**Percent of adults: basic literacy**	**Percent of adults: intermediate literacy**	**Percent of adults: proficient literacy**
1993 Prose	14	28	43	15
2003 Prose	14	29	44	13
1993 Document	14	22	49	15
2003 Document	12	22	53	13
1993 Quantitative	26	32	30	13
2003 Quantitative	22	33	33	13

Source: US National Center for Education Statistics, National Assessment of Adult Literacy (NAAL), 1992 and 2003.

The counter to this is the proposition that the problem is not student comprehension but the GSS word test. The GSS emphasizes constancy over time, and so comparability of data. Consequently it doesn't alter the test words (and asks researchers not to publicize them). But the incidence of word-usage changes over time. So, critics claim, the test has got harder because the appearance in print publication of the most difficult words in the test has declined over time. As the incidence of some published words declines so does the exposure of the population to those words. One study measured the incidence of GSS test words relative to all words in the searchable Google book database.[58] In a person's first 15 years, vocabulary acquisition is the most intense. So the study used a 15-year forward-moving average to calculate print word frequency. The conclusion was that all of the decline in word comprehension could be explained by the decreasing use in publication of the most difficult four words in the 10-word test. The problem with this explanation is that while a level of repeated exposure to words is important in understanding words, such exposure is not a function of author usage but rather of extensive reading (or lack of it).[59] The Google database measures what authors do, not what readers do. Best-selling books like *Lord of the Rings* and the Harry Potter series, read millions of times, each count for one item in the database. Meanwhile, science publishing has ballooned over time. Little-read citation papers have transformed author word-use patterns. But this is not a measure of the volume of child or adult reading that leads to word acquisition.

On the other hand, the most common books today that American high school students read in grades 9–12 are suited to a 5.3 grade reader.[60] In contrast, college-ready-level books range from *Don Quixote* (13.2) to *Pride and Prejudice* (12), *Billy Budd* (10.6), *The Canterbury Tales* (8.1) and *A Farwell to Arms* (6).[61] Grade-level reading is measured by a book's average word length and sentence length, the level of word difficulty and the total number of words in the book. All of these factors feed directly or indirectly into word comprehension.

Table 11.7 US general social survey WORDSUM vocabulary test, by decade of birth

		General Social Survey (GSS) Year										
		1974	1974	1984	1984	1994	1994	2004	2004	2014	2014	
Birth Cohort	**Number of correct answers out of 10 multiple-choice questions**	**Number of respondents**	**Percentage of respondents**	**Number of respondents**	**Percentage of respondents**	**Number of respondents**	**Percentage of respondents**	**Number of respondents**	**Percentage of respondents**	**Number of respondents**	**Percentage of respondents**	**1974–2014: Median percentage of 9s and 10s correctly answered, by birth cohort, excluding samples <100**
1885–1929	0	5	1%	5	1%	0	0%	0	0%	0		
	1	9	1%	10	2%	7	2%	0	0%	0		
	2	33	5%	17	4%	11	4%	1	2%	0		
	3	49	8%	27	7%	24	9%	1	2%	2		
	4	73	11%	44	11%	32	11%	7	12%	0		
	5	112	18%	59	14%	40	14%	8	14%	12		
	6	107	17%	67	16%	46	16%	16	27%	2		
	7	82	13%	61	15%	45	16%	9	15%	1		
	8	64	10%	47	11%	36	13%	5	8%	3		
	9	50	8%	38	9%	31	11%	8	14%	2		
	10	54	8%	36	9%	10	4%	4	7%	0		
		638	100%	411	100%	282	100%	59	100%	22		17%
1930–1939	0	4	2%	0	0%	0	0%	0	0%	0		
	1	4	2%	4	2%	4	2%	2	2%	1		
	2	5	2%	6	3%	7	3%	0	0%	1		
	3	8	3%	13	7%	8	4%	6	6%	5		
	4	27	10%	26	13%	15	7%	7	7%	16		

	5	43	17%	24	12%	28	14%	11	10%	12		
	6	59	23%	27	14%	53	26%	28	26%	25		
	7	41	16%	32	16%	31	15%	14	13%	15		
	8	32	12%	42	21%	26	13%	16	15%	11		
	9	21	8%	10	5%	21	10%	13	12%	9		
	10	16	6%	16	8%	10	5%	9	8%	2		
		260	100%	200	100%	203	100%	106	100%	97	0%	**15%**
1940–1949	0	0	0%	2	1%	4	1%	1	0%	0	0%	
	1	1	0%	2	1%	7	2%	0	0%	1	1%	
	2	10	3%	11	4%	6	2%	4	2%	1	1%	
	3	15	5%	17	6%	19	5%	9	4%	11	8%	
	4	26	8%	21	7%	30	8%	18	8%	12	8%	
	5	50	16%	41	14%	47	13%	33	15%	18	12%	
	6	70	23%	53	18%	86	23%	40	18%	31	21%	
	7	54	18%	47	16%	64	17%	52	23%	21	14%	
	8	33	11%	39	13%	44	12%	28	13%	27	18%	
	9	20	7%	38	13%	35	9%	17	8%	13	9%	
	10	27	9%	21	7%	28	8%	21	9%	11	8%	
		306	100%	292	100%	370	100%	223	100%	146	100%	**17%**
1950–1959	0	3	1%	1	0%	1	0%	8	3%	2	1%	
	1	5	2%	3	1%	8	2%	4	1%	5	2%	
	2	6	3%	15	5%	8	2%	9	3%	12	4%	
	3	15	7%	23	7%	14	3%	7	2%	13	4%	
	4	35	15%	34	10%	39	10%	22	7%	32	10%	
	5	60	26%	59	18%	71	17%	54	18%	34	11%	

	6	45	20%	74	22%	90	22%	54	18%	77	24%	
	7	23	10%	53	16%	69	17%	55	18%	62	20%	
	8	18	8%	26	8%	38	9%	44	15%	35	11%	
	9	8	4%	25	8%	30	7%	30	10%	28	9%	
	10	10	4%	16	5%	42	10%	15	5%	16	5%	
		228	100%	329	100%	410	100%	302	100%	316	100%	**14%**
		General Social Survey (GSS) Year										
		1974	**1974**	**1984**	**1984**	**1994**	**1994**	**2004**	**2004**	**2014**	**2014**	
1960–1969	0	0		2	1%	3	1%	4	1%	1	0%	
	1	0		5	2%	4	1%	3	1%	7	2%	
	2	0		12	5%	10	2%	1	0%	5	2%	
	3	0		8	3%	22	5%	20	7%	16	6%	
	4	0		38	16%	45	11%	17	6%	24	8%	
	5	0		59	25%	86	20%	41	15%	58	20%	
	6	0		45	19%	104	24%	63	23%	77	27%	
	7	0		33	14%	77	18%	72	26%	45	16%	
	8	0		15	6%	35	8%	30	11%	34	12%	
	9	0		14	6%	25	6%	17	6%	13	5%	
	10	0		8	3%	17	4%	8	3%	7	2%	
		0	0	239	100%	428	100%	276	100%	287	100%	**9%**
1970–1979	0	0		0		2	1%	3	1%	1	0%	
	1	0		0		6	3%	5	2%	7	2%	
	2	0		0		3	2%	4	1%	5	2%	
	3	0		0		14	8%	10	3%	9	3%	
	4	0		0		27	15%	28	10%	15	5%	

	5	0		0		34	18%	42	15%	57	20%	
	6	0		0		53	28%	78	27%	78	28%	
	7	0		0		24	13%	57	20%	55	20%	
	8	0		0		14	8%	31	11%	35	12%	
	9	0		0		7	4%	22	8%	17	6%	
	10	0		0		2	1%	8	3%	3	1%	
		0	0	0	0	186	100%	288	100%	282	100%	**7%**
1980–1989	0	0		0		0		4	3%	1	0%	
	1	0		0		0		1	1%	3	1%	
	2	0		0		0		2	1%	12	4%	
	3	0		0		0		8	5%	12	4%	
	4	0		0		0		23	14%	22	7%	
	5	0		0		0		41	26%	64	20%	
	6	0		0		0		32	20%	80	25%	
	7	0		0		0		31	19%	53	17%	
	8	0		0		0		8	5%	45	14%	
	9	0		0		0		4	3%	19	6%	
	10	0		0		0		5	3%	5	2%	
		0	0	0	0	0	0	159	100%	316	100%	**7%**
1991–1996	0	0		0		0		0		0	0%	
	1	0		0		0		0		3	2%	
	2	0		0		0		0		8	5%	
	3	0		0		0		0		22	15%	
	4	0		0		0		0		22	15%	
	5	0		0		0		0		37	25%	

	6	0		0		0		0		27	18%	
	7	0		0		0		0		12	8%	
	8	0		0		0		0		13	9%	
	9	0		0		0		0		2	1%	
	10	0		0		0		0		1	1%	
		0	0	0	0	0	0	0	0	147	100%	**2%**
Total respondents who undertook the test		**1432**		**1471**		**1879**		**1413**		**1613**		

Source: NORC database, US General Social Survey, 1972–2014.
Note: In some cases, 1 sample-participant is rounded down to 0%.

American students read increasingly till grade 6 (11–12-year-olds). After that, the rate of reading drops off sharply.[62] After grade 5, the average reading level of the books-most-read rises very little. Individuals learn subtle difficult words by reading advanced-grade (10–12) literature (Dickens, Chesterton, Orwell, Turgenev, Conrad, Balzac, Greene, Stendhal and the like) in high school.[63] The less they do of this, the more author-usage and reader-comprehension of those words declines.

The problem underlying this is that high literacy cannot be attained institutionally. It requires an enormous commitment of student hours spent in silent reading and practicing writing. Classrooms eat into this time. Conversely, it is arguable that increasing reading and related activities would generate an increase in educational achievement along with a decrease in education public-sector costs. The key is silent-reading time. Unlike classroom time, silent reading is not expensive.[64] Also unlike classroom time it works. Silent-reading time represents the 'auto' in the age of auto-industrialism. Auto-industrialism is not just machine automation. The Internet in the 1990s brought machine automation to the sale of books. It disintermediated bookselling and made all of the world's classic reading available for instant access and at a zero or close-to-zero price. Today, a child's home library of 50 books would cost no more than $500 in total and in most cases much less. This is a tiny cost in contrast to classrooms. But the key to future learning is not just cheap-and-accessible books but behavioral change that increases the reading of books. This includes not just children reading more but also parents modelling reading for children with adults at home reading more. The logic of this is to move from '*ed*ucation to *read*ucation'.

True, not every child is a reader. But even the child who strongly prefers doing to reading, or making to reading, faces the same issues of the classroom that disrupts attention and undermines concentration and perseverance. For the 17 percent who constitute the sprawling modern professional-managerial class, though, reading and comprehension are essential. Just like the automobile in the age of horses, machine automation today has already transformed the nature of delivering and accessing educational materials. There is now literally almost no item of high literate culture that is not available online for either no cost or a minimal cost. That reflects the technological side of the modern self-organizing economy and autonomous society. But technology does not exhaust the 'auto' aspect of an autonomous society. In the case of learning, auto-industrialism implies the reorientation of learning toward autonomous reading. The auto-industrial era represents not just digital automation but even more crucially the increase in do-it-yourself activities and industries. The silent reader exemplifies a DIY culture. What does this mean for the public sector? It means a shift from class-time to reading-time.[65] From 1890 to 1960, America added 60 days of class-time a year, 40 percent more. Converting class time to silent-reading time implies reversing that and reducing class-time by 40 percent. That would, in effect, solve the productivity deficit of public education, reduce public-sector costs and expenditure and, most crucially of all, improve society's levels of communicative competency and learning outcomes.

Notes

1 NCES, 2012, Figure A. The mathematics score was similarly static: 304 in 1973; 306 in 2012.
2 NCES, 2012, Figure 34, 48.
3 See, e.g. OECD, 2003, Figure 1.2, 26.
4 Australia also has its own National Assessment Program for Literacy and Numeracy (NAPLAN), started in 2008, assessing Year-9 students (typically 14-year-olds). Between 2008 and 2016 test rounds, the mean scores of Australian students remained effectively flat-lined, with reading and numeracy ticking-up slightly from 578 to 580, and 582 to 588 while writing dipped from 569 to 549.
5 Triplett and Bosworth, Table A-1.
6 Richardson, 2014, Table 3.
7 Federal Reserve Bank of St Louis, Real Median Household Income in the United States; NCES, Estimated average annual salary of teachers in public elementary and secondary schools, by state or jurisdiction: Selected years, 1969–1970 through 2009–2010.
8 US Bureau of Labor Statistics, Contributions of Nonmanufacturing Industries to private nonfarm business productivity, June 22, 2016.
9 OECD, 2000, Table A2.1
10 OECD, 2009, Volume III, 48–49.
11 As well as Korea, versions of model 2 show up in the cases of Portugal and the Czech Republic in PISA 2000. In OECD, 2009, Figure III.1.16, student reading performance 'control' explained 19 percent of the variance in student reading achievement in Korea, 18 percent in Taiwan, 16 percent in Portugal and France, 14 percent in Australia, 12 percent in Jordan, 11 percent in Japan and New Zealand, 10 percent in Spain, Canada, Hong Kong and Trinidad, and 8 percent average across OECD countries as a whole. In comparison, 'elaboration' (Figure III.1.18) accounted for 10 percent of the variation in student reading performance in Taiwan, Korea 9 percent, Jordan 6 percent, Portugal 5 percent, and thereafter negligible.
12 OECD, 2000, Table A2.1
13 Chiu, 2007, especially Table 3. Fuchs and Wößmann, especially Table 4.
14 Chiu, 513.
15 Fuchs and Wößmann, Table 4.
16 OECD, 2003, Figure 2.6b, 59.
17 OECD, 2003, Table 2.4d, 391.
18 OECD, 2009, Volume III, 30.
19 OECD, 2009, Volume III, Figure III.1.3, 31.
20 OECD, 2009, Volume III, Figure III.1.5, 33.
21 OECD, 2009, Volume III, 30.
22 OECD, 2009, Volume III, Figure III.1.5, 33.
23 OECD, 2009, Volume III, Figure III.1.21, 54.
24 Evans, et. al., 2010, Table 2.
25 Evans, et. al., Table 3.
26 Evans, et. al., Table 1.
27 OECD, 2009, Volume II, Figure II.2.4, 44.
28 Nystrom, 1931.
29 Carsley, 1957.
30 Communications Management Inc., 2011, 24.
31 Australian Bureau of Statistics, Average weekly household expenditure at current prices(a), 1984 to 2009-10.
32 Galbi, 2007.
33 Galbi, 2007, Table 11.
34 Galbi, 2007, Tables 5 and 6.

35 IMLS, 2017.
36 NSLA, 2001, Table 1; NSLA, 2016, Table 3.
37 McKool, 2007. 199 fifth-grade students were surveyed for this study.
38 McKool, 2007, 111.
39 McKool, 2007, 112.
40 Anderson, et al., 1988.
41 The mean 5th-grade reading speed is 179 words a minute or 2 minutes a page (Anderson et al., 292). That is the equivalent of 5 hours for a standard 50,000 word book, or 20 minutes a day reading 25 books a year.
42 McKool, 118.
43 Carsley, 17.
44 Renaissance Learning, 2012, Table A1.
45 Bloom, 1987, 62. Bloom's first-hand observation was supported statistically a decade prior by Paul Copperman, 1980. Copperman noted the decline in SAT verbal scores through the 1960s and 1970s (beginning in 1964). He rejected the explanation, still recycled today, that this was the result of larger numbers of lower SES students taking the SATs. That social shift principally occurred in the 1960s, Copperman pointed out, leaving the sharp 1970s SAT decline (as well as a similar decline in grade school aptitude tests after 1964) begging an explanation. That the wave of doe-eyed political romanticism began in 1964 and accelerated in the 1970s is not a coincidence. It is causal. It replaced dogged book reading with infantile moral expressivism.
46 Carsley, 1957, 17.
47 McKool, 123. Cf. Csikszentmihalyi, 1990.
48 McKool, 123.
49 McKool, 111.
50 This point also echoes institutionally. The freedom or autonomy of schools to choose their own textbooks registers as a positive coefficient with science especially but also with reading scores and with school autonomy in determining course content. Fuchs and Wößmann, Table 4.
51 As Carsley (1957: 13) observed, for 95 percent of children 'the home provided the best environment for the private reading of books, there being less distraction and interruption than in school'. The study was based on over 2,000 students surveyed.
52 John Dewey, *The School and Society* (1899), *The Child and the Curriculum* (1902), *Moral Principles in Education* (1909), *Democracy and Education* (1916). The University of Chicago Laboratory Schools was founded by Dewey in 1896.
53 NCES, Historical summary of public elementary and secondary school statistics: Selected years, 1869-70 through 2005-2006.
54 See the General Social Survey 1972-2004 and the National Assessment of Adult Literacy, 1992 and 2003.
55 Nie, Golde and Butler, 2007; Nie, 2008.
56 Norman Nie, 2008, observed that: 'Our original hypothesis was that verbal ability would surely be one of those outcomes driven mainly by years in the classroom. As we looked deeper into the data on that ability, however, we came to the counterintuitive conclusion that increased education actually does *not* appear to cause an increase in verbal ability.'
57 Murphy, 2015, 8, 10, 168.
58 Dorius, Alwin and Pachecoc, 2016
59 Zhu, 2015, reviews the relevant literature.
60 Renaissance Learning, 2012, based on 2010-2011 book-reading records for 7.6 million grade 1-12 students in 24,465 schools across the 50 US states and Washington, D.C. The reading grade for a book means that an average-performing student in that school grade or higher would likely be able to read the text.
61 Renaissance Learning, 2012, Table 47.

62 Renaissance Learning, 2012, Table A1. From an average of 424,176 words per student per year in grade 6 to 302,441 words in grade 12.
63 Words like sedulous, cloistered, edible and chirrup—all from Edward Thorndike's 1942 vocabulary test, the precursor of the GSS test. His 1921 *The Teachers Word Book* pointed to the importance of English literature and the Bible in test-word selection. Rancorous critics of this now sneer at the thought of an old-fashioned 'humanist education' steeped in literature classics and the Bible (Bailin and Grafstein, 2016, chapter 2).
64 In Carsley's 1957 2,000+-size 30-school study of 10-11-year-old readers, in the UK Merseyside area, between 0.5 and 4 hours of student time weekly was set aside for silent reading (15). Two books per head were silently read per month. In most of the schools there was also periods of reading aloud by teachers. Most classes reported-on had their own class libraries, ranging from 50-450 books, which silent readers could borrow from (15). Some schools had central libraries, mainly stocked with reference materials, averaging 280 books per central collection. The read-out-aloud volumes typically consisted of a mix of children's classics (Lewis Carroll, Mark Twain, Robert Louis Stevenson), abridged adult books (Dickens, Cervantes, Dumas, Melville) and popular children's books of the time (Blyton, Crompton).
65 A model for this is the Acton Academy, the 'one-room schoolhouses for the twenty-first century'. The first one was founded in Texas in 2009. By 2016 the number had grown to 60 worldwide, created by interested parents and ranging in size from 7 students to a maximum of 120 students (Sandefer, 2017). The Academies blend online learning with a single onsite schoolhouse that has no classes and no teachers but instead adult guidance. The emphasis is on self-pacing, self-direction and self-efficacy in learning, hands-on studio-style science and arts directed at entrepreneurship and apprenticeship, and love of reading. Of the latter the Academy co-founder Laura Sandefer observed that '[what] you will see at Acton Academy [are] children who are late to group discussions because they cannot put their books down; children walking into walls because they are lost in books' (http://www.actonacademyparents.com/why-no-required-reading-lists/).

Bibliography

Anderson, R.C., P.T. Wilson and L.G. Fielding. 1988. "Growth in Reading and How Children Spend Their Time Outside of School." *Reading Research Quarterly* 23, no. 3: 285–303.

Bailin, A. and A. Grafstein. 2016. *Readability: Text and Context.* London: Palgrave Macmillan.

Bloom, A. 1987. *The Closing of the American Mind.* New York: Simon and Schuster.

Carsley, J.D. 1957. "The Interests of Children (Aged 10–11) in Books." *British Journal of Educational Psychology* 27, no. 1: 13–23.

Chiu, M.M. 2007. "Families, Economies, Cultures, and Science Achievement in 41 Countries: Country-, School-, and Student-Level Analyses." *Journal of Family Psychology* 21, no. 3: 510–519.

Communications Management Inc. 2011. *Sixty Years of Daily Newspaper Circulation Trends*, May 6.

Copperman, P. 1980. "The Decline of Literacy." *Journal of Communication* 30, no. 1: 113–122.

Csikszentmihalyi, M. 1990. *Flow: The Psychology of Optimal Experience.* New York: Harper and Row.

Dorius, S.F, D.F. Alwin and J. Pachecoc. 2016. "Twentieth Century Intercohort Trends in Verbal Ability in the United States." *Sociological Science* 3: 383–412.

Evans, M.D.R., J. Kelley, J. Sikora and D.J. Treiman. 2010. "Family scholarly culture and educational success: Books and schooling in 27 nations." *Research in Social Stratification and Mobility* 28, no. 2: 171–197.

Fuchs, T. and Wößmann, L. "What accounts for international differences in student performance? A re-examination using PISA data." *Empirical Economics* 32, 433–464, 2007.

Galbi, D.A. 2007. *Book Circulation per U.S. Public Library User since 1856*, July 29.

IMLS. 2017. *Public Libraries in the United States Survey: Fiscal Year 2014*. Washington, DC: Institute of Museum and Library Services, August.

McKool, S.S. 2007. "Factors that Influence the Decision to Read: An Investigation of Fifth Grade Students' Out-of-School Reading Habits." *Reading Improvement* 44, no. 3: 111–131.

Murphy, P. 2015. *Universities and Innovation Economies*. Farnham: Ashgate, 2015.

NCES. 2012. *NAEP 2012 Trends in Academic Progress*. Washington, DC: National Center for Education Statistics.

Nie, N.H. 2008. "Does Education Really Make You Smarter?" *Pacific Standard*, May 20.

Nie, N.H., S. Golde and D.M. Butler. 2007. *Education and Verbal Ability over Time: Evidence from Three Multi-Time Sources* Working Paper. Palo Alto: The Stanford Institute for the Quantitative Study of Society.

NSLA (National & State Libraries Australasia). 2015. *Australian Public Libraries Statistical report 2014–2015*. Brisbane: State Library of Queensland.

NSLA (National & State Libraries Australasia). 2001. *Australian Public Libraries Statistics 1996–97 to 1998–99*. Canberra: ACT Information Management and Libraries.

Nystrom, G.H. 1931. "A Study of Fifty Home Libraries with Special Reference to Their Function in Child Development." *Child Development* 2, no. 3: 230–233.

OECD. 2009. *PISA 2009 Results: Learning to Learn: Student Engagement, Strategies and Practices* Volume II and III. Paris: Organization of Economic Cooperation and Development.

OECD. 2003. *Learning for Tomorrow's World: First Results from PISA 2003*. Paris: Organization of Economic Cooperation and Development.

OECD. 2000. *Knowledge and Skills for Life: First Results from the OECD Programme for International Student Assessment (PISA)*. Paris: Organization of Economic Cooperation and Development.

Renaissance Learning. 2012. *What Kids Are Reading: The Book-Reading Habits of Students in American Schools*. Wisconsin Rapids, WI: Renaissance Learning.

Richardson, D. 2014. *Productivity in the Construction Industry*. Canberra: The Australia Institute.

Sandefer, L.A. 2018. *Courage to Grow: How Acton Academy Turns Learning Upside Down*. Austin, TX: Acton Press.

Triplett, J.E. and Bosworth, B.P. 2014. *Productivity in the U.S. Services Sector: New Sources of Economic Growth*. Washington, DC: Brookings Institution Press.

Zhu, Y. 2015. "Revisiting Word Exposure Frequency and Incidental Vocabulary Acquisition." *Theory and Practice in Language Studies* 5, no. 5: 968–973.

12 Income

Household income

In spite of the growth of public spending in the twentieth century, not all arguments for limited government fell on deaf ears. Far from it. The United States illustrates the point. Total US public spending was 39.9 percent of GDP in 1985 and 39.3 percent in 2015. It reached a marginally lower point in 2000 of 36.3 percent and a high of 45.2 percent in 2009 (Table 1.1). Across this undulating sequence, a number of categories of spending either remained constant or fell over time. In 1985, total US public welfare spending was 3.29 percent of GDP; in 2015 it was 2.57 percent. General government expenditure remained roughly constant, 0.99 percent in 1985 compared to 0.96 percent in 2015. Combined general government, transportation, protection and other spending—each relatively small fiscal items—amounted to 7.26 percent of GDP in 1985, falling to 6.65 percent in 2015. Defense spending fell from 6.79 percent of GDP to 4.45 percent over the same period as the military became more mechanized, less labor-intensive and increasingly auto-industrialized.

As government in many areas shrank, in other areas it swelled. The big increases occurred in education, healthcare and retirement-income-support. Public spending on healthcare rose dramatically from 3.43 percent of GDP in 1985 to 7.73 in 2015. Education spending grew substantially from 4.75 percent of GDP to 5.71 percent. In 1985, US Social Security-administered spending on retirement income was 4.34 percent of GDP; in 2015 it was 4.92 percent.[1] The size of government employee retirement pensions grew from 1.45 percent in 1985 to 2.29 percent.[2]

Retirement income schemes are designed to provide income after prime income-earning years. They spread income from the most productive adult years to the least productive ones.[3] Retirement income schemes fall into two types. There are taxation-and-benefit schemes and saving-and-investment schemes.

Employee retirement pension schemes are accumulation or 'funded' schemes (as are self-employed pension schemes). Payments are made from funds accumulated over the years. The funds are a mix of contributions (employer and employee contributions) and earnings on the investment of the fund's assets. In contrast, government-administered social security schemes are contributory but not accumulative. Inputs are in the form of taxes paid by employees and employers.

Payouts are calculated not on the basis of the amount accumulated in an individual's retirement fund but rather according to the government's definition of an 'entitlement' or benefit. The state defines a payment formula or rate payable. Taxes that are paid-in by contributors are not saved and invested for the future. Instead, they are used to fund each year's current pension obligations. America's Social Security, the UK's National Insurance and Germany's State Pension Insurance are built around employment tax contributions, though their payout formulas vary. Australia, in contrast, has a compulsory savings-and-accumulation style superannuation system based on employee and employer contributions as well as a means-tested Age Pension scheme funded out of general tax revenue.[4]

The models of retirement income are a fractal of income in general. They reflect two very different ways of thinking about income. One is accumulative, the other allocative. According to the latter, income is a benefit. The term 'benefit' derives from the Roman word *beneficium*. This was the benefit a person received in exchange for services to Rome's imperial state. Medieval European powers similarly granted *benefices* for military and administrative services. The modern era democratized the duty-and-allotment-entailed by a *benefice*. Modern companies provide benefits in the form of wages and salaries in return for employees working under direction. The modern state also provides benefits. It does so for military service. In the case of 'social insurance' schemes, state benefits are allotted in return for 'tax contributions' rather than military or administrative 'services rendered'. This trade-off developed in the course of the last century (Table 8.1). Those who possess the status of a democratic citizen (or its proxy, the legal resident) receive benefits in exchange for paying income or payroll taxes (Table 8.1).[5] Citizenship or legal residency status normally also entails welfare benefits subject to eligibility rules. Some citizens or residents are unable to pay taxes due to unemployment, disability, sickness or age. In those cases, welfare benefits (income transferred from taxpayers to non-taxpayers) are provided, subject to admissibility criteria.

That said, most benefits in the modern 'welfare state' are not welfare benefits but rather benefits (retirement, health, etc.) that are provided in exchange for paying taxes on income and employment. These are 'earned entitlements'. As money moves from taxpayers to the state and back to taxpayers varying degrees of non-transparent redistribution of income occurs. In the case of social insurance schemes, such transfers happen not just between income-classes but also between generations of recipients (Table 12.1). In addition, social insurance systems are susceptible to a collective delusion. Namely, that total benefits can exceed total contributions. This occurs when a population's total tax contributions over time are less than total recipient benefits (Table 12.1). The lack of equilibrium between taxation and benefits, in the end, will either cause a Ponzi-like collapse of the scheme or else further generational disparity as more recent recipient generations are obliged to pay-in more taxation and receive lower benefits than early recipient generations did.[6]

In short, income that takes the form of a benefit is provided 'in exchange for' a service or a status. There is, though, a second kind of income. Conceptually it is

Table 12.1 US social security and Medicare contribution-benefit ratios, 1940–2030

Year	Social Security, ratio of covered workers to beneficiaries	Year cohort turns 65	Two-Earner Couple: Average Wage/Low Wage ($44,600/$20,000 in 2012 dollars)		Non-contributory gain/loss	Benefit: tax ratio	Two-Earner Couple: Average Wage ($44,600 each in 2012 dollars)		Non-contributory gain/loss	Benefit: tax ratio	Two-Earner Couple: High Wage/ Average Wage ($71,400/$44,600 in 2012 dollars)		Non-contributory gain/loss	Benefit: tax ratio
			Total lifetime Social Security + Medicare benefits, 2012 dollars	Total lifetime Social Security and Medicare taxes, 2012 dollars			Total lifetime Social Security + Medicare benefits, 2012 dollars	Total lifetime Social Security and Medicare taxes, 2012 dollars			Total lifetime Social Security + Medicare benefits, 2012 dollars	Total lifetime Social Security and Medicare taxes, 2012 dollars		
1940	159.4													
1950	16.5													
1960	5.1	1960	269,000	26,000	243,000	1:10.3	305,000	36,000	269,000	1:8.4	319,000	42,000	277,000	1:7.6
1970	3.7													
1980	3.2	1980	545,000	155,000	390,000	1:3.5	612,000	213,000	399,000	1:2.9	685,000	251,000	434,000	1:2.7
1990	3.4													
2000	3.4													
2010	2.9	2010	877,000	523,000	354,000	1:1.8	966,000	722,000	244,000	1:1.3	1,080,000	921,000	159,000	1:1.2
2030	2.3	2030	1,257,000	716,000	541,000	1:1.7	1,367,000	988,000	379,000	1:1.4	1,504,000	1,284,000	220,000	1:1.2

Sources: Social Security Administration, Ratio of Social Security Covered Workers to Beneficiaries Calendar Years 1940–2013; Social Security Administration, 2017 Report of the Board of Trustees; C. Eugene Steuerle and Caleb Quakenbush, Social Security and Medicare Taxes and Benefits over a Lifetime, 2012 Update, Urban Institute, October 2012.

quite different. This is income derived from accumulation. It is a function of the growth of capital. Its roots lie in the Renaissance era. 'Benefit'-type income can always be rated, i.e. presented in a schedule of benefits. Persons receive a given rate of payment. In contrast, income from capital cannot be rated. Rather, it is contingent. It depends on the sale of products or services, the licensing or rental of property, the return on investments and the scale of savings. This kind of income is not the function of a status society but rather a contract society.[7]

Contract and status are powerful ways of conceiving the world. They vie constantly in contemporary societies. An example is funded retirement schemes. Their pay-outs in principle are based on the size of funds accumulated in employee retirement accounts. But in the twentieth century, many of these 'defined contribution' schemes were over-written by 'defined benefit' plans with retirement pay-outs based on social-security-like formulas (involving, for example, an employee's age, earning history and length of service). The number of the 'defined benefit' schemes has declined significantly over the past half-century, as their long-term financial unviability became apparent. But they signify just how much even in a contract society the pull of the status-tax-beneficiary model persists.

Just as the two models of income (accumulation and allocation) have different historical origins and are the expression of different concepts of society, over time the relation of the two fluctuates.

We can view these shifts in the case of the United States over the past thirty years (Table 12.2). Across those three decades, the share of US household income represented by wages has fallen while the share of household income represented by capital has remained constant. A related expression of this relative change is the net worth of US households. In constant dollars, the net worth of wage-earner-headed households grew 436 percent between 1962 and 2016 compared with 484 percent for self-employed-headed households (Table 12.2). Over the glacial-scale time-period of social transformation (far removed from the four-year electoral cycle), this gap is significant. Doubly so as the net worth of self-employed households (with income from sole proprietorships, partnerships and closely held corporations) in 1962 was five times that of waged households and by 2016 it was nearly six times (Table 12.2). This occurred even as farm households, once the mainstay of self-employment, shrank markedly.

This expresses an even-deeper shift in the relation between income from labor and capital (Table 12.5). In 1992 non-employing entities were 74 percent of all US business. In 2004, 77 percent. In 2013, 80 percent. As a percentage of the total (employee and self-employed) workforce, they grew from 12.8 percent in 1997 to 16.4 percent in 2014 (Table 12.4). Yet also between 1992 and 2014 companies with workforces larger than 500 grew from 40.7 percent to 43.6 percent of the total (employee and self-employed) workforce.[8] This kind of contradictory change is typical of the antipodal motion of social development. In short, as the corporate leviathans of US business have grown in recent decades so also has the self-employed segment (Tables 12.3, 12.4 and 12.5).

Sole proprietors and partnerships' share of business receipts nearly doubled between 1980 and 2013, from 10.6 percent to 19.3 percent of total US business

Table 12.2 Household income, US, 1962–2016

Percentage of household income by income source			1989	1992	1995	1998	2001	2004	2007	2010	2013	2016
Retirement income (total)			*8.2%*	*7.7%*	*8.6%*	*8.1%*	*7.8%*	*10.9%*	*9.6%*	*12.0%*	*13.0%*	*13.5%*
Labor	Wages		65.8%	63.0%	69.9%	68.5%	69.3%	69.7%	64.5%	68.1%	62.4%	60.8%
Capital	Interest, dividends, rents, royalties, estate/trust income		6.4%	5.2%	5.0%	4.2%	4.2%	3.5%	3.7%	3.6%	3.7%	3.4%
	Business, farm, self-employment*		10.9%	13.2%	11.6%	12.8%	11.7%	10.9%	13.6%	12.2%	12.7%	13.5%
	Capital gains		5.2%	1.9%	2.6%	4.5%	5.5%	3.2%	6.7%	0.9%	4.8%	5.5%
	Total Capital		*22.5%*	*20.3%*	*19.2%*	*21.5%*	*21.4%*	*17.6%*	*24.0%*	*16.7%*	*21.2%*	*22.4%*
State	Transfers#		3.5%	9.0%	2.3%	1.8%	1.6%	1.8%	1.9%	3.2%	3.4%	3.3%
	State-administered retirement income (pensions, social security)		4.1%	4.1%	4.8%	4.0%	4.0%	5.6%	4.5%	6.0%	6.1%	6.1%
	Total State		*7.6%*	*13.1%*	*7.1%*	*5.8%*	*5.6%*	*7.4%*	*6.4%*	*9.2%*	*9.5%*	*9.4%*
Age 65-and-over income by source		1962	1989	1992	[1994]	1998	2001	2004	2007	2010	2013	[2015]
State (Social Security)		31%	39%	41%	43%	38%	39%	39%	36%	37%	34%	33%
Government employee pensions		6%	8%	8%	9%	8%	9%	9%	8%	9%	9%	8%
Transfers#		16%	3%	4%	4%	3%	3%	3%	3%	4%	4%	4%
Govt pensions + income-support total		***53%***	***51%***	***53%***	***55%***	***49%***	***51%***	***51%***	***47%***	***50%***	***47%***	***45%***
Asset Income		15%	21%	22%	17%	20%	16%	13%	16%	11%	11%	9%
Earnings**		29%	18%	16%	17%	24%	24%	26%	29%	30%	33%	34%
Private earnings/asset income total		44%	39%	37%	34%	44%	40%	39%	45%	41%	44%	43%

Private pensions	**3%**	**9%**	**9%**	**10%**	**10%**	**9%**	**10%**	**9%**	**9%**	**9%**	**12%**
Private income total	**47%**	**48%**	**46%**	**44%**	**54%**	**49%**	**49%**	**54%**	**50%**	**53%**	**55%**
TOTAL (the sum of rounded components may be less or greater than 100%)	100%	99%	99%	99%	103%	100%	100%	101%	100%	100%	100%
Average household net worth (thousands of 2016 US$)	1962	1989	1992	1995	1998	2001	2004	2007	2010	2013	2016
Wage-earner-headed household (WEHH)	95	212	205	215	248	306	343	408	330	325	413
Net worth (WEHH) compared to previous survey		224.0%	96.8%	104.6%	115.6%	123.3%	112.2%	118.7%	81.0%	98.3%	127.4%
2016 net worth (WEHH) compared to 1962											*436.5%*
Self-employed-headed household (SEHH)	495	1216	1006	1098	1366	1710	1813	2274	1927	2235	2398
Net worth (SEHH) compared to previous survey		245.5%	82.8%	109.1%	124.4%	125.2%	106.0%	125.5%	84.8%	116.0%	107.3%
2016 net worth (SEHH) compared to 1962											*484.4%*
Self-employed-headed household net worth as % of wage-earner headed household	523%	573%	490%	511%	550%	559%	528%	558%	584%	689%	580%

Source: US Federal Reserve, Survey of Consumer Finances, Amount of before-tax family income, distributed by income sources, by percentile of net worth, 1989–2016 surveys; Family net worth, by selected characteristics of families, 1989–2016 surveys; Dorothy S. Projector, Survey of Changes in Family Finances, 1968, Supplementary Table 1 Net Worth of Consumers within Specified Groups, December 31, 1962; Fast Facts & Figures About Social Security series, Shares of aggregate income by source based on Social Security Administration, The Aged Population of the United States: The 1963 Social Security Survey of the Aged 1967 and the Annual Social and Economic Supplement to the Current Population Survey; US Department of Labor, Employee Benefits Security Administration, Private Pension Plan Bulletin Historical Tables and Graphs 1975–2014, Table E16. Pension Plan Benefits Disbursed by type of plan, 1975–2014; US Census Bureau, Money Income in the United States, Current Population Reports 1998, 1992, 1995 (Table 11, Table 34, and Table 11 respectively).

Government income assistance such as the post-1974 SSI Supplemental Security Income (SSI) providing cash assistance for over-65 low-income low-asset cohort and not part of the payroll-tax-based US Social Security [Old-Age, Survivors, and Disability Insurance, OASDI] program, family assistance payments, veterans benefits, TANF payments, government employees workers compensation, public assistance. Also includes judicially directed transfers such as alimony, child support, and private workers compensation payments. The latter are tiny percent of the total, around 0.7% of income.

*Farm and nonfarm sole proprietorships, partnerships, and closely held corporations.

**In 2017 23 percent of older Americans earned income from work. The median income earned by these retirees was $25,000 a year.

Table 12.3 Size of independent workforce, US, 2011–2017

Year	Full-time (15 hours a week or more) independent workers, millions	Part-time (1 to 15 hours, 11 hours average) independent workers, millions	Full-time equivalent [FTE] independent workers, millions	US workforce total, millions	Full-time independents as % of total workforce	FTE independents as % of total workforce
2011	15.9	N/A		140.9	11.28%	
2012	16.9	N/A		143.3	11.79%	
2013	17.7	N/A		144.7	12.23%	
2014	17.9	12.1	26.8	147.5	12.14%	18.15%
2015	17.8	12.4	26.9	150.1	11.86%	17.92%
2016	16.9	12.4	26.0	152.2	11.10%	17.08%
2017	16.2	11.8	24.9	154	10.52%	16.14%

Sources: MBO Partners, *The State of Independence in America reports 2011-2017*. Based on annual surveys of 1,100–2,000 Americans; Bureau of Labor Statistics, Labor Force Statistics from the Current Population Survey, 2011–2017.

Definitions: *BLS definition of employed person*: 'Persons 16 years and over in the civilian noninstitutional population who, during the reference week, (a) *did any work at all (at least 1 hour) as paid employees*; worked in their own business, profession, or on their own farm or worked 15 hours or more as unpaid workers in an enterprise operated by a member of the family; and (b) all those who were not working but who had jobs or businesses from which they were temporarily absent because of vacation, illness, bad weather, childcare problems, maternity or paternity leave, labor-management dispute, job training, or other family or personal reasons, whether or not they were paid for the time off or were seeking other jobs'. *MBO Partners definition of the independent worker*: 'people who work at least 15+ hours per week in non-traditional, non-permanent full or part-time employment and includes workers who identify themselves as consultants, freelancers, contractors, self-employed, and on-call workers, among others'. The others include microbusiness owners (fewer than four employees), temps, and solopreneurs working at least 15 hours per week. Full-time equivalent number of independent workers combines full-time count with 11/15 fractional count of part-timers. The MBO 2017 Report identifies that part-time independents work an average of 11 hours per week.

Table 12.4 Rate of self-employment, US, 1948–2014

Year	US workforce, combined number of employees and non-employer entities, US Census	Number of non-employer entities, US Census	Non-employer entities as percentage of total workforce	*Comparison data: BLS/CPS Percentage of US workforce self-employed in unincorporated and incorporated entities#*	Total number of employing firms and non-employing entities, US Census	Non-employing entities as percentage of total entities, US Census
1948				*18.5%*		
1955				*15.4%*		
1960				*13.8%*		
1966				*11.1%*		
1990				*11.4%*		
1992	107,150,797	14,325,000	13.4%		19,420,356	74%
1994				*12.1%*		
1997	120,738,732	15,439,609	12.8%	*11.5%*	20,981,527	74%
2002	130,046,716	17,646,062	13.6%	*10.6%*	23,343,821	76%
2007	142,312,286	21,708,021	15.3%	*11.1%*	27,757,676	78%
2012	138,674,383	22,735,915	16.4%	*10.4%*	28,462,075	80%
2014	144,906,881	23,836,937	16.4%	*10.1%*	29,662,395	80%

#Note: Bureau of Labor Statistics data is drawn for the Current Population Survey, which asks 'last week were you self-employed', a question that excludes, as Fox notes, a lot of part-time self-employed workers (J. Fox, Where Are All the Self-Employed Workers? Harvard Business Review, 7 February 2014).

Sources: U.S. Small Business Administration, Office of Advocacy, Private Firms, Establishments, Employment, Annual Payroll and Receipts by Firm Size, 1988–2014 based on data provided by the U.S. Census Bureau, Statistics of U.S. Business and Nonemployer Statistics; S. Hipple, 'Self-employment in the United States', Monthly Labor Review July 2004, Tables 1 & 2; S. Hipple, 'Self-employment in the United States: an update', Monthly Labor Review, September 2010, Tables 1 & 2; S. Hipple & L. Hammond, 'Self-employment in the United States', US Bureau of Statistics, March 2016; Labor Force Statistics from the Current Population Survey, 1948–2014.

Table 12.5 Self-employed entities (nonfarm), US, share of business receipts and profits, 1980–2013

1980–2013					
Sole proprietors and partnerships, share of total business receipts, 1980 (IRS)	10.6%				
Sole proprietors and partnerships, share of total business receipts, 1997 (IRS)	10.5%	Nonemploying entities 1997*	15,439,609	% of all entities	74%
Sole proprietorships and partnerships, share of total business receipts, 2004 (IRS)	16.4%	Nonemploying entities 1997*	22,735,915	% of all entities	77%
Sole proprietorships and partnerships, share of total business receipts, 2013 (IRS)	19.3%	Nonemploying entities 1997*	23,005,620	% of all entities	80%
	Number of companies with >500 employees, 1997*		16,079	% of all entities	0.08%
	Number of companies with >500 employees, 2004*		17,047	% of all entities	0.09%
	Number of companies with >500 employees, 2013*		18,636	% of all entities	0.08%
2004					
Total US business receipts, 2004 millions	$25,999,000				
Sole proprietor business receipts, millions	$1,140,000				
Sole proprietor % of total business receipts	4.38%				
Sole proprietor profits, millions	$242,449				

Sole proprietor returns by industry sector, 2004

Industry Sectors	*Sole proprietor receipts, millions*	*% of sole proprietor receipts*	*Sole proprietor profits, millions*	*% of sole proprietor profits*
Construction	$198,364	17%	$31,038	12.8%
Manufacturing	$25,825	2%	$3,018	1.2%
Wholesale Trade	$40,850	4%	$5,129	2.1%
Retail Trade	$187,077	16%	$8,102	3.3%
Transportation and warehousing	$65,304	6%	$8,756	3.6%
Information	$8,044	1%	$1,902	0.8%
Finance and insurance	$73,126	6%	$17,599	7.3%
Real estate and rental and leasing	$70,504	6%	$27,907	11.5%
Professional, scientific and technical services	$137,682	12%	$56,862	23.5%
Administrative and support services	$49,987	4%	$14,075	5.8%
Education services	$6,926	1%	$2,456	1.0%
Health care and social assistance	$104,159	9%	$41,963	17.3%
Arts, entertainment and recreation	$26,359	2%	$5,793	2.4%
Accommodation and food services	$39,721	3%	$1,391	0.6%
Other services	$73,006	6%	$16,458	6.8%
Partnership business receipts, millions	$3,142,000			
Partnership % of total business receipts	12.09%			
Partnership profits, millions	$183,157			

Partnership returns by industry sector, 2004				
Industry Sectors	*Partnership receipts, millions*	*% of partnership receipts*	*Partnership profits, millions*	*% of partner profits*
Construction	$226,165	7%	$18,351	10%
Manufacturing	$616,213	20%	$33,033	18%
Wholesale Trade	$357,070	11%	$9,763	5%
Retail Trade	$281,853	9%	$1,550	1%
Transportation and warehousing	$71,204	2%	$4,689	3%
Information	$178,121	6%	$1,639	1%
Finance and insurance	$149,980	5%	$32,741	18%
Real estate and rental and leasing	$117,900	4%	$9,254	5%
Professional, scientific and technical services	$231,711	7%	$54,159	30%
Administrative and support services	$52,851	2%	$3,158	2%
Education services	$3,084	0%	$148	0%
Health care and social assistance	$119,105	4%	$15,685	9%
Arts, entertainment and recreation	$34,543	1%	–$1,450	–1%
Accommodation and food services	$114,480	4%	–$104	0%
Other services	$17,497	1%	$541	0%

* U.S. Census Bureau, Statistics of U.S. Business and Nonemployer Statistics.

Sources: U.S. Small Business Administration, Office of Advocacy, Private Firms, Establishments, Employment, Annual Payroll and Receipts by Firm Size, 1988–2014 based on data provided by the U.S. Census Bureau, Statistics of U.S. Business and Nonemployer Statistics; Quantria Strategies, Effective Federal Income Tax Rates Faced By Small Businesses in the United States. US Small Business Administration, Office of Advocacy, April 2009, Table 9 and 12 based on IRS Statistics of Income; Statistical Abstract of the United States, 2008, Table 271, Number of Returns, Receipts and Net Income by Type of Business: 1990–2004 based on IRS Statistics of Income; SOI Integrated Business Dataset (IBD), Number of Returns, Total Receipts, Business Receipts, Net Income (less deficit), Net Income, and Deficit, 1980–2013.

receipts (Table 12.5). If S Corporations ('pass-through' entities whose owners report profits or losses on their personal income returns) were included as well, that would add a further approximate 1.5 percent share. DIY capitalism tends to be weak in the transport, information, education, arts and entertainment fields, and not very profitable in the retail industries (Table 12.5). Manufacturing and real estate are mixed cases. In other sectors, however, the self-employed cohort is strong. Construction and professional-scientific-and-technical services industries are prime examples. Healthcare along with finance and insurance are notable for DIY profitability.

That's labor and capital as sources of household income. What about the state? The share of income represented by explicit 'transfer payments' at times has fluctuated sharply up and down since 1989, but in the long run it has been constant and really quite modest. Its share of total 'benefit' income is often exaggerated. In contrast, state-administered retirement income as a portion of household income is both large and has risen significantly over time (Table 12.2). Yet, paradoxically, as it has grown it has also shrunk. The state provided half of US retirement income in 1989. In 2016, the figure was 45 percent. As state-administered spending has risen, its capacity to meet income needs has fallen. Consequently, retiree earnings from (part-time) work have increased sharply as a percentage of retirement income. As the income of over-65s from earnings (employee and self-employed earnings) has gone up, income from assets and private pensions has gone down (Table 12.2).

What a lifetime costs

The other side of income is spending. Income analysis only makes sense if we also look at who spends how much and for what. Again, the case of the United States is instructive. In 2015, Americans spent an average of $4,342 per household on healthcare (including $2,997 on health insurance), $1,315 on education and $6,016 on pension and social security contributions for future retirement.[9] That's a total of $11,673 per household. The average income before taxes of these units was $69,629. There were 128,437,000 such households, accounting for a total spend on health, education and income security of $1,499 billion. Total US tax revenue (including each level of government and including company taxes) in 2015 was $6,380 billion. Governments at all levels in the US spent 7 percent of revenue on welfare, 19 percent on pensions and social security, 22 percent on health care, and 15 percent on education.[10] In other words, 63 percent of public spending ($3,828 billion) went to the big three (income-support, health care and education). If we combine household spending and government spending, Americans in 2015 overall allocated $5,327 billion to the big three. That is $41,475 per household. The combined private-public spend on the big three was equal to 60 percent of average US household income before tax.

Another way of coming at this is to ask how much do the big three cost per US household? In 2015 dollars, the cost of educating a child in K-12 public schools is $100,000; the lifetime health cost for an adult is $476,000; the cost of healthcare for a child under 18 is $36,793; the average social security pension is $16,000 a year or, with a life expectancy of 20 years post-retirement, a life-time payout of $320,000.[11] For a household of two adults and two children that amounts to a life-time cost $1.6 million. Dispersed over 40 working years, that's the equivalent of $41,600 a year—virtually the same figure arrived at above.

That, though, leaves unaddressed whether the expenditure figure is 'good value for money'? So what 'in principle' should Americans properly spend on health, education and income-security? Is the $41,000 average per household too much? Too little? What is the prudential amount? The difficulty in answering this question is the difficulty of establishing whether the $41,000 of private and public money represents good value for money or whether bundled with good value is waste, low productivity and inefficiency.

The average US household that owns a home today pays $14,000 in income, sales and real estate taxes, amounting to 27 percent of total income. 2015 payroll taxes for 'social insurance and retirement receipts' represents another $8,294 average per household. If this $22,294 tax revenue was ring-fenced and allocated back to individual prudential savings accounts and then combined with the $11,673 of existing household self-funding that represents just under $34,000 in prudential savings per year for the average household, it would be a major boost to the fiscal power of first-party payers.

The hypothetical $34,000 is about 80 percent of the existing cost of the big three. But *existing* is the keyword. For, arguably, much of that *existing* expenditure is wasteful, inefficient, unnecessary and the function of low productivity in the public sector.

Three problems

The question then is to what degree and in what manner is the growth of expenditure on income-support, health and education a function of necessity or a function of inessential spending or low productivity or both?

Take the case of government pensions or government-mandated social insurance systems. These have been reluctant to follow the model of contribution-based superannuation schemes. The latter invest employee and employer contributions in prudential stocks and bonds so that the value of the contributions grow over time. This amplifies productivity by making savings-for-retirement 'work'. Another word for this is 'capitalism', which state-based systems tend to be allergic to but which is very productive over the medium and long-term so long as it is understood that investment returns are subject to cycles and naturally move up and down and up and down. As they have grown across the last century, state and government-mandated income-support systems have tended to be linear in their assumptions and expectations in sharp contrast to the cyclical nature of modern economies (Table 2.1). This has meant that poor-but-linear returns—for a lifetime of tax-paying into various types of government-defined retirement-income systems—have been preferred to the considerably larger returns on investment in cyclical markets.[12]

As major economies entered the twenty-first century, it became increasingly apparent that economic growth and productivity growth over the long-run was declining (Table 1.2). This is hardly surprising as typically a larger and larger percentage of the GDP in these economies was being devoted to low-productivity government, health and education sectors (Tables 9.1, 9.2, 9.3, 9.4 and 11.5).

The post-industrial-era health, education and income-support systems suffer from three debilitating syndromes.

The first is the outsized role of *third parties in paying for services*. This grew in the second half of the twentieth century, especially after 1970. In the health sector, third parties include the state, insurance companies and businesses that pay for employee insurance. In education, the principal third party is the state that pays for public schools and subsidizes private schools. Third parties are either poor at controlling costs or else they use paradoxically costly paperwork systems to try and control costs.

The second enervating syndrome is *low productivity*. Health, education and state-administered income systems in different ways are resistant to productivity improvements. First, the health and education sectors systematically resist labor-saving technology.[13] Typically in the case of each of these sectors the introduction of new technology increases costs rather than reduces costs. Second, government-mandated social insurance systems and state 'old age pension' systems (not to be confused with state employee pension schemes) have been reluctant to look on the taxes paid into these systems as investments that generate income by working hard. Third, the twentieth-century system of state-provided or state-subsidized education and health was wasteful. It committed substantial social resources to classrooms that delivered little added educational value over the long-term. Likewise, health: its organizational matrix frustrates productive work in a myriad microscopic ways, the macroscopic effect of which is to frustrate efficient effort and satisfying engagement.

The third problem is *greater expenditure than income*. Over a lifetime, a portion of society earns markedly less in aggregate than they spend on normal outgoings. What do we do about this? The response of the welfare state is to subsidize the spending of these citizens. This is done by reducing the tax on low-income earners to zero or less-than-zero and providing public goods to low-income earners whose value exceeds what these income earners pay in tax. The problem with these solutions is that they are both very costly. Even wealthy states struggle to cover the gap between the lifetime income and expenditure of low and very low-income groups. As populations live longer, the amount of state-funded retirement income-support expands. The real costs of hospitals and education likewise expands.

Three solutions

One solution to these problems is to reduce the persistently rising costs of public goods. This approach has been discussed in previous chapters. In essence, it means reducing the role of third-party payers, increasing the role of autotelic work in place of process-driven organization in healthcare and downscaling spending on classroom instruction and upscaling the emphasis on literate auto-didacticism.[14]

A second solution is to lift the pensionable retirement age, expecting people to work longer to match longer life-spans. State pensions were created on the basis of 45 years work and 2 years of retirement. They now have to bear the weight of 45 years of work and 20 years of retirement. Even 50 years of work—assuming that is either desirable or practical—still means retired persons would work 2.5 years for every year retired rather than working 2.25 years for each year retired. Even the most affluent societies struggle to sustain these ratios if prime working age income is not invested and remains inactive over time. The model of the self-managed retirement fund, built on tax-exempt savings and subject to simple prudential rules, is part of the necessary 'auto' in emerging auto-industrial societies alongside factors such as autotelic work, autodidactic learning, automated industry and autonomic pattern cities.

A third solution is to reduce in relative terms the size of the low-income cohort. During the post-industrial age, major industrial countries, among them the United States, Australia and Britain, chose to increase the levels of immigration. Economists routinely point to the benefits of immigration. These are real though often also paradoxical.[15] Yet there are also down-sides, less frequently observed. The importing of low-skill or semi-skilled labor fills gaps in the labor market. But it also, as a consequence, discourages the replacement of labor with machines, the long-term driver of economic productivity and social affluence. What this means is that the low-wage unskilled or semi-skilled social cohort is preserved at an artificially high level instead of being naturally scaled back over time. It is the low-productivity labor cohort that bears the burden of a pronounced gap between lifetime income and expenditure. This is inevitable simply because the kind of work it does of necessity is low-productivity in nature. Conversely, each skill increment represents an increase of income. This is because higher-skilled work is more productive and thus more valuable to both the employer and the employee.

In high-skill industries, immigration makes economic sense. These industries want to attract the best talent, which means the most productive people, from around the world. In low-skill industries, the obverse applies. Take the case of the United States.[16] The 2000 US Census reported that 61 percent of non-immigrant Americans were high-skilled by virtue of having 'more than a high school education' compared with 49 percent of immigrants.[17] Twenty-nine percent of adult immigrants in the United States do not have a high school diploma compared with seven percent among the US-born population.[18] In sharp contrast, local- and foreign-born adults possess bachelor's degrees in comparable proportions.

In the US, migrant labor is concentrated in private household service, hospitality, warehousing, agricultural and food service industries.[19] Migrant workers make up more than 20 percent of employees in these industries. Conversely, they make up 20 percent or more in management, high-tech manufacturing and infotech fields. Low-skill labor may be useful in the short-run. Employers may want it, sometimes desperately. Yet the larger it is as a percentage of the workforce, the more it represents an impediment to the kind of machine-based economy that leads to high productivity, economic growth and social prosperity in the long run.[20] The paradox is that replacing labor by machines is key not only to economic prosperity and higher-wage employment but to the long-term growth of jobs. What is saved by not paying for unskilled or semi-skilled work is reinvested not just in machines but also in complementary higher-skilled employees. As categories of work disappear, others appear.

Low-productivity work is inherently low-income work. Over the long-term, even though this cohort works, the income it earns falls significantly short of the cost of the health, education, pension and government services it consumes. As noted, the public–private cost of providing schools, health and retirement income for an average American household with two adults and two children is around $41,000 a year (in 2015 dollars). That's simply unaffordable for those in low-skill, low-income labor cohorts. Twenty-seven percent of Americans work in jobs that typically require less education than a high school diploma. These include taxi drivers, bar tenders, housekeeping cleaners, groundskeepers and amusement attendants. In 2013 this group earnt a median annual wage of $20,350. Two working adults in this skill-band would have earnt between them barely more than the cost per average household for schooling, healthcare and retirement income without anything left over for all other expenses. Other taxpayers cover the gap.

In 2016, 12.7 percent of Americans were poor—meaning that a household of two adults and two children had an income of $24,399 or less.[21] Many of these were working poor. In 2016, 5.8 percent of American workers were in poverty. They had incomes that fell significantly short of meeting major unavoidable life-cycle expenditures. In 2010, 46.2 million people—over 15 percent of the US population—lived below the poverty line; 10.5 million of these were working poor, or 3.3 percent of the population.[22]

So then how to deal with this? The orthodox approach is subsidization. Over a lifetime, the no-earned-income and low-earned income cohort receives substantially more in services and benefits than it pays in taxes. That was the solution of the twentieth-century welfare state. Higher-income earners (private individuals and businesses) are taxed while low-income earners and no-income earners are not. Money is redistributed—via government services and payments—from one group to the other. Over time, this has become less and less viable as the real cost of health, schooling and retirement income has risen. The perverse paradox of affluent societies is that the richer they get, the more unaffordable the mix of administered services and income transfers becomes. This is because the cost of these over time rises faster than the rate of inflation.[23]

Auto-industrialization is part of the answer to reducing the size of the low-skill workforce. From agriculture to manufacturing to services, routine work is increasingly being done by a mixture of robots and software automation.[24] The policy corollary of this is to reduce low-skill labor migration along with immigration programs based on family re-unions. The latter pay little or no attention to an incoming migrant's skills. The pivotal issue is whether a person's work ability is sufficiently productive such that the person's lifetime earned-income can plausibly match normal life-time expenditures.

Not all 'jobs' are the same. For example, a state for a time can run ultra-low interest rate policies. These underwrite mal-investment in under-performing low-productivity marginal firms and ventures. The jobs created are mal-investment jobs. The long-term net cost of these to the taxpayers, including low-income taxpayers, is substantial. Weighting the occupational profile of a society toward mid-skill and high-skill occupations, that is, higher-productivity jobs, is essential for affluent high-growth economies. These countries struggle to afford to subsidize low-income earners' lifetime cost-of-living so long as the real costs of health and education increase and retirement years continue to extend. Like anything else, 'jobs' are not an unalloyed good. Lots of persons on $20,000 a year or less an advanced economy does not make.

But if a society shrinks its pool of low-income work—if, for example, it replaces taxi-driving with automated driverless cars or substitutes computer-controlled factory-style manufacture of buildings for on-site construction—will it just make things worse by expanding the pool of unemployed no-income persons? The American experience with immigration suggests not. There, lower-paid migrants do displace local workers—just as machines do. What then happens to the local workers? They move into alternate employment that requires different and higher levels of skill.[25] That's a metaphor for the whole history of automation since the Industrial Revolution. Routine work is replaced by machines. Labor is replaced by capital. The more that routine work is done by machines, the more non-routine work grows to complement the machines.[26] The more machines, the more productive labor is, the more prosperous business is and the greater is the growth of high-wage work.

Notes

1 C. Chantrill, US Social Security Spending Fiscal Years 1935 to 2020 http://www.usgovernmentspending.com/

2 C. Chantrill, Government Employee Pensions Fiscal Years 1950 to 2020 http://www.usgovernmentspending.com/

3 Barr, 2002.

4 Some proposals to rescue social-security schemes envisage the state investing up to 40 percent of funds in the stock market using automated, passively managed and political-lobbying-free tracking of major market indexes (Burtless, Chen, Hou, Munnell, 2017). The counter-argument envisages decentralized first-party rather than centralized third-party investing of mandatory retirement funds (Tanner, 2017). The latter view rests tacitly on the idea that the aggregate of large-scale decentralized decision-making produces the best overall outcomes (Surowiecki, 2004).

5 The British sociologist and social liberal, T.H. Marshall, 1950, was the first to explicitly identify the link that had emerged between 'social rights' and having the status of a citizen in a modern democratic state. 'Citizenship,' as he put it, 'is a status bestowed on those who are full members of a community' (28).

6 The scheme's Board of Trustees suggests that already the scheme needs to increase payroll tax by 2.5 percent or reduce benefits by 16 percent, or some combination of both to remain solvent for the next 75 years. Actuarial projections rest on assumptions about future mortality, fertility, real wages, inflation and unemployment. Accordingly there are high-cost, intermediate and low-cost projections. The 2016 US Social Security

trustees report anticipates that costs will exceed income by 2029 and 2034 in the first and second scenarios. In the high-cost scenario, by 2030 the scheme would be able to fund only 69 percent of 'scheduled benefits'; in the intermediate scenario income will be sufficient to pay 77 percent of benefits in 2035. The non-calamitous low-cost scenario requires a miraculous combination of high fertility, minimal reduction in age-adjusted death rates, high immigration rates, high productivity, high wage rates, low unemployment, a high interest-rate return on the trust fund's Department of Treasury securities, low disability incidence, and high disability recovery rates. The intermediate scenario is presented as the most likely one. However, including interest-income in these scenarios is a fiction. Social security funds are 'invested' in low-risk, low-interest Treasury bonds. But this is a pseudo-investment. In reality the 'bonds' are not actual purchased assets but rather a redeemable claim on future general tax revenues. Since 2010 the scheme's cost has exceeded its non-interest income. Board of Trustees, 2016, 2, 5, 6, 9, 67–68.

7 The distinction between a status society and a contract society was coined by the British jurist Henry Maine (1822–1888). The Danish-born German socialist philosopher and sociologist Ferdinand Tönnies (1855–1936) drew a parallel distinction between *Gemeinschaft* (community) and *Gesellschaft* (society).

8 U.S. Small Business Administration, Office of Advocacy, Private Firms, Establishments, Employment, Annual Payroll and Receipts by Firm Size, 1988-2014 based on data provided by the U.S. Census Bureau, Statistics of U.S. Business and Nonemployer Statistics.

9 Bureau of Labor Statistics, Consumer Expenditures—2015.

10 http://www.usgovernmentspending.com/

11 Health: Alemayehu and Warner, 2004, Table 2; Education: National Center for Education Statistics average per-student expenditure in public schools; AARP, Social security income, AARP analysis of data from the Census Bureau, 2012. The Kaiser Family Foundation (Table 10.8) estimates life-time healthcare costs at $390,000 in 2015 dollars.

12 The historic return on US stocks is 6.7 percent per annum (1802–1870), 6.6 percent pa (1871–1925), 6.4 percent pa (1926–2012). Government bonds earnt 4.8, 3.7, 2.6 percent pa in comparison. Siegel, Table 5.1, 5.2

13 On occasions it has been frivolously argued that free-market advocates are logically defenders of child labor. But modern free-market capitalism is also industrial capitalism. The logic of industrialism is to replace labor with machines while generating new industries. Well-functioning markets and industries remove inefficient labor and replace it with machines. One of the last vestiges of child labor is after-school teenagers working limited hours in low-wage fast-food outlets. In a decade or two, due to auto-industrialization, much of this for-experience labor will disappear, replaced by automated order and delivery.

14 A companion of lowering the cost of public goods is to reduce the taxation and increase the automation of domestic housing industries. See Murphy, forthcoming.

15 See for example the comprehensive review of literature on US immigration by NASEM, 2016. One of the paradoxes of migrant labor is that while it does apply downward pressure on wages it also simultaneously expands employment. This is because as the labor supply expands the cost of recruiting labor declines—so employers then advertise more positions (146–147).

16 Singer, 2012.

17 NASEM, 2016, 141.

18 Singer, 2012, 4.

19 Bureau of Labor Statistics, Foreign-born workers: labor force characteristics—2016, Table 4; Singer, 2012, Figure 4.

20 'Firms that use relatively labor-intensive technology benefit more from immigration' concludes NASEM, 2016, 143. If we compare capital-intensive methods of production

(A) with less capital-intensive methods (B), then an 'influx of new immigrants now causes the amount produced using technology B to increase and the amount produced using technology A to decline.' Lewis (2011: 1,029) concluded that US metropolitan areas that have experienced fast growth in the supply of less-skilled immigrant labor have 'adopted significantly less machinery per unit output'.

21 Semega, Fontenot, Kollar, 2017, Figure 4; US Census Bureau, Poverty thresholds by Size of Family and Number of Children, 2016.

22 Stevens, 2013.

23 A classic example of why this occurs is provided by the 2010 US Patient Protection and Affordable Care Act (aka Obamacare) that heavily regulated the American personal health insurance market. In doing so it compelled millions of individuals who did not have group insurance to buy government-approved personal health insurance plans. The intent of this was force otherwise healthy people who did not want insurance to purchase it in order to cross-subsidize those in poor health. Consequently a large number of persons who either did not want or need insurance in the first place signed up for insurance plans (to avoid paying a government tax penalty). Many of those unwilling conscripts to insurance were low-income earners. That entitled them to financial subsidies under the legislation to enable them to pay for insurance that they didn't want. As a result, cross-subsidization of sick people by healthy people turned into government subsidization of both the sick and the healthy.

24 Murphy, 2017.

25 They move into jobs that are more communicative and language-intensive. Alternatively they are motivated to up-skill (such as get more training and education). The mobile members of the workforce move to other job markets in other cities. NASEM, 2016, 146.

26 Capital-skill complementarity is a driving force of industrial societies. Higher-skilled work complements machines; whereas lower-skilled work is more likely to be substituted for by machines. As automation progresses it is evident that some work thought to be skilled is in fact much more routine and thus replicable by machines than previously thought. Murphy, 2017.

Bibliography

Alemayehu, B. and K.E. Warner. 2004. "The Lifetime Distribution of Health Care Costs." *Health Services Research* 39, no. 3: 627–642.

Barr, N. 2012. *The Pension Puzzle: Prerequisites and Policy Choices in Pension Design*. Washington, DC: International Monetary Fund, March.

Board of Trustees. 2016. *The 2016 Annual Report of the Board of Trustees of the Federal Old-Age and Survivors Insurance and Federal Disability Insurance Trust Fund*, Washington, DC: US Government Publishing Office.

Burtless, G., A. Chen, W. Hou and A.H. Munnell. 2017. *How Would Investing In Equities Have Affected The Social Security Trust Fund?* Working Paper. Centre for Retirement Research, Boston College, May.

Lewis, E. 2011. "Immigration, Skill Mix, and Capital Skill Complementarity." *The Quarterly Journal of Economics* 126, no. 2: 1029–1069.

Marshall, T.H. 1950. *Citizenship and Social Class and other Essays*. Cambridge: Cambridge University Press.

Murphy, P. Forthcoming. "Housing Affordability and Tax Gluttony." *Connor Court Quarterly*.

Murphy, P. 2017. *Auto-Industrialism: DIY Capitalism and the Rise of the Auto-Industrial Society*. London: Sage.

NASEM (The National Academies of Sciences, Engineering, and Medicine). 2016. *The Economic and Fiscal Consequences of Immigration*. Washington, DC: The National Academies Press.

Quantria Strategies. 2009. *Effective Federal Income Tax Rates Faced By Small Businesses in the United States*. Washington, DC: US Small Business Administration Office of Advocacy, April.

Seigel, J.J. 2014. *Stocks for the Long Run*. 5th edition. New York: McGraw-Hill.

Semega, J.L., K.R. Fontenot and M.A. Kollar. 2017. *Income and Poverty in the United States: 2016 Current Population Reports*, Washington, DC: US Census Bureau, September.

Singer, A. 2012. *Immigrant Workers in the U.S. Labor Force*. Washington, DC: Brookings Institution, March 15.

Stevens, A.H. 2013. *Transitions into and out of Poverty in the United States*. Center for Poverty Research Policy Brief 1:1. Davis, CA: University of California Davis.

Surowiecki, J. 2004. *The Wisdom of Crowds*. New York: Doubleday.

Tanner, M. 2017. "Should the Social Security fund be invested in the stock market? It's complicated". *Marketwatch*, April 18.

13 Conclusion

Auto-industrial society

The pattern of nature

John Locke thought that every human being had the natural right to life, liberty and property. Thomas Jefferson replaced the natural right to property with the pursuit of happiness. In the twentieth century, these elegant formulas were inflated. Innumerable, often pretentious, social rights—to health, education, housing, food and work—were coined. The state, it was supposed, could provide and pay for these things (with tax-payer's money). Social liberalism and socialism provided philosophical grounds for these claims. Big government lobbies circled in the background.

Locke's liberalism dealt with the natural rights of individuals in relation to other individuals. Locke sensibly held that a person had the natural right not to be murdered, molested, attacked or defrauded by someone else. Through the courts and the armed forces, governments had a key role in upholding the natural rights of individuals. From Adam Smith onwards it was widely observed that individuals not only interact with other individuals but also with larger-scale social phenomena. Individuals have to deal not only with violent spouses, miscreant neighbors, untruthful witnesses and dishonest traders but also with big-picture social mechanics. Edmund Burke (1730–1797) called this 'working after the pattern of Nature'.[1]

'By a constitutional policy working after the pattern of Nature,' Burke wrote, 'we receive, we hold, we transmit our government and our privileges, in the same manner in which we enjoy and transmit our property and our lives.' Nature is the collective correlate of Locke's individual rights. By following the order of nature '[the] institutions of policy, the goods of fortune, the gifts of Providence, are handed down to us, and from us, in the same course and order'. Government (=policy) does not conflict with personal fortune or necessity. In this way, the 'political system is placed in a just correspondence and symmetry with the order of the world, and with the mode of existence decreed to a permanent body composed of transitory parts'. Society changes yet remains the same. It is dynamic and conservative.

This is due to its collective wisdom: 'a stupendous wisdom, molding together the great mysterious incorporation of the human race, the whole, at one time'.

What this wisdom does is 'never old or middle-aged or young [but manifests] in a condition of unchangeable constancy [that] moves on through the varied tenor of perpetual decay, fall, renovation, and progression'. Thus, concluded Burke, 'by preserving the method of Nature in the conduct of the state, in what we improve we are never wholly new, in what we retain we are never wholly obsolete'. And by 'adhering in this manner and on those principles to our forefathers, we are guided, not by the superstition of antiquarians, but by the spirit of philosophic analogy'. Each good change is an analogue of a pattern that is permanent.

From the tax state to the savings nation

In our own age, acting 'after the pattern of nature' includes adapting prudently to the cycles of employment and technology and establishing the delicate balances that have to be struck between the cost and quality of goods like education and health. Two questions follow from this. How does the theory of limited government deal with the social laws (the in-built cycles and ratios) of modern life? Conversely how does it respond to pressures on government to provide goods close to zero price?

First, it observes that government provision of goods—however these are nominally priced for the end-consumer—is typically expensive, bureaucratic, status-driven and wasteful.

Second, it observes that rather than providing goods or subsidizing 'approved organizations' to provide goods, government can organize individual saving accounts for its citizens and residents, and subject these to simple prudential rules and guarantees. This means replacing the taxation state in substantial part with a savings state.[2]

The effect of this kind of approach is to institute, in a structured manner, a providential system allowing everyone to meet inescapable life-cycle and social-cycle needs by tax-exempt savings supplemented by tax credits for those whose low income makes prudential saving impossible. The point of savings is that the user pays. This increases pressure on providers to meet actual needs and with a minimum of wasteful bureaucracy and virtue-signaling status-seeking. Yet to do so effectively requires more than a system of savings and market payments.

Third, it also requires industries, publics and cities to 'innovate' in the sense of provide low-cost, high-quality goods for purchase. Autonomic market pressure and market demand is a necessary but not sufficient condition to achieve this. Seamless, autotelic work in big institutions like hospitals is a corollary condition. Education, whether private or public, can't achieve what it could without deep autodidactic learning. Good-value housing requires cities to reduce cumbersome rule-based planning and increase the quotient of swift aesthetic-style decision making based on pattern-order.[3] As an example, the relative size of Australian cities follows a golden-ratio pattern (Table 13.1). The urban population distributes itself 'after the pattern of nature' into large, medium and small cities. Urban planning or legislative schemes aimed at altering such a pattern by means of planning, incentives, directions or subsidies invariably fail.

Table 13.1 Australian city size

City Size by tier	Number of cities in Australia by tier size	City	Percentage of population	Population	Population divided by the golden ratio, phi, 1.618	Combined population of the next two largest cities by tier	City	Percentage of population	Population	Population divided by the golden ratio, phi, 1.618	Combined population of the next two largest cities by tier
4 million+	2	Sydney	20.74%	5,029,768	3,108,633	3,684,520	Melbourne	19.24%	4,725,316	2,920,467	2,669,027
2 million+	2	Brisbane	9.74%	2,360,241	1,458,740	1,971,262	Perth	8.56%	2,022,044	1,249,718	941,983
1 million+	1	Adelaide	5.50%	1,324,279	818,467	942,652					
0.5–1 million	1	Gold Coast-Tweed Heads	2.64%	646,983	399,866	441,585	Gold Coast-Tweed Heads	2.64%	646,983	399,866	396,588
0.25–0.5 million	4	Wollongong	1.23%	295,669	182,737	216,226	Wollongong	1.23%	295,000	182,324	180,383
100,000–500,000	7	Darwin	0.60%	145,916	90,183		Ballarat	0.42%	101,588	62,786	
30,000–100,000	28	Bundaberg	0.29%	70,310	43,455		Rockhampton	0.33%	78,795	48,699	

Source: Australian Bureau of Statistics, Greater Capital City Statistical Areas/Significant Urban Areas by population, 2016.

The auto in auto-industrial

In the late eighteenth century the rise of industrial society started. In the mid-twentieth century the rise of post-industrial society began. Now another shift is upon us. The auto-industrial society is emerging.[4] The first sign of it, evident as far back as the mid-1990s, is automation. Industrial society rests on automation. First, it was the mechanization of agriculture. Then, after the 1960s, manufacturing began to be automated. Now it is turn of the post-industrial service industries. A fusion of computer algorithms and electronic sensing will make much routine no-collar, white-collar, pink-collar, professional and managerial work redundant. It already has bitten quite deeply into such work over the past two decades. It will continue to do so in the next four decades. Technological automation is slow but persistent. The 'auto' in auto-industrial is not just machine intelligence, though. It also points to a different kind of political economy.

'Auto' also means an autonomous economy and society. This is different from, sometimes complementary to, sometimes in competition with, the world of organizations. Schools and universities, hospitals, firms and corporations and the state grew remarkably in the twentieth century. These were all purposive organizations. They operated on the basis of rules, codes and procedural hierarchies. Their social dominance was historically unique. They elevated a new class of managers to social prominence. The ascendancy of organizations remains. But it is fraying at the edges. It is being challenged. The challenge comes from increasing numbers of persons who prefer to be immersed in the rhythms and patterns of self-regulating systems rather than subject to the rules and directions of organizations. Among these are increasing numbers who choose self-employment in place of organizational employment.[5]

A long-term shift is occurring. This is not a rupture or a breach. Rather, it is an incremental turn. Mostly, it is invisible. But its small increments add up over the long-term to a big transformation. One of the biggest long-run effects will be on the state. In the major economies over the past century, states have increased spending dramatically. They have financed large increases in retirement income-support, healthcare and education. Publicly funded or subsidized employment in health and education has been enormous. Auto-industrialization represents a challenge to this. Technologically, it means the invention of machines to undertake routine work in hospitals and schools. It is regularly denied that work in the 'people professions' can be automated. Yet the development of artificial intelligence machines that can support or replace the routine work of surgeons, doctors, nurses, teachers and teaching assistants suggests otherwise.[6] I discussed this in a previous book, *Auto-Industrialism*. 'Auto' however is not just a signifier of machines. It is also an index of autopoietic, do-it-yourself, pattern-based social systems. These offer plausible and powerful alternatives to organizations.

Why would we want an alternative to organizations? Surely they do a great job? Don't they 'educate children' and 'save lives'? Are they not therefore saintly? Perhaps not after all. Governments struggle to pay for them. So much so that they have to borrow money to fund them. Having spent so much on them, what then is the result? No matter how much is spent on post-industrial organizations, they almost never deliver what they promise. Public-funded education promises a 'knowledge society'. Yet learning scores stagnate or decline over the long-term in states that spend the most on education and that increase real spending year after year. Public-funded health has delivered much longer life-spans compared with a century ago. Yet the real cost of this in the past half century has risen and risen. Why? Clinically, medicine works. Organizationally, though, it produces a large amount of wasted time and energy. The big organizational leviathans in education and health have been less than spectacular success stories.

Not that we are supposed to say this. There is a fairytale that everyone is meant to repeat. The fairytale says that state-funded education and health bring great benefits—and that the vehicles for delivering for those benefits (the hospital bed and the classroom) are the acme of human endeavor. These organizational systems, their staff and especially their managers represent the zenith of social achievement. Except they do not. Unfortunately, a substantial part of what they do produces waste and poor results. That seems a harsh thing to say. After all, are not those who work in these systems sacrificing themselves for the 'public good'? Aren't classrooms and hospital beds 'public goods'? Isn't it mean and churlish to criticize them? Aren't critics Dickensian? Don't they want to deny children an education? Don't they want to condemn the sick to untold suffering? No. What critics want from education and healthcare are systems that work in the sense of not producing waste and futile action.

The term 'public goods' came into vogue in the mid-1950s.[7] It hides all sorts of human futility. And not just wasted effort alone. But also missed opportunity. One of the big steps taken in expanding early twentieth-century state expenditure was the state provision of pensions. When recipients lived for two years after ending work, the effect of this all-round was modest. Today, when recipients live on for two decades after stopping work, the public retirement income-support system is much more consequential. It supports more people for longer, putting enormous strain on public finances. To say so is impolite. It rubs up against the pieties of political life. These, though, disguise the fundamental inadequacy of state pension systems. The funds underlying these systems are not productive. Even if they earn interest from the government the interest is only a transfer from one part of the government's pool of tax revenue to another part. The funds are not investable in productive assets that grow over time. This is in contrast to superannuation funds that purchase assets that do grow over time. The income that superannuation funds produce is largely derived from this asset growth. Investment growth means a larger end-pension compared with state-pensions that lack a productive growth basis.

The prudential maxims of auto-industrial public policy

What is the alternative to the managerial society? Autopoietics. Self-making. Self-reliance. Self-management. The meaning of such terms vary from sector to sector. In education they mean decreasing classroom time and increasing silent-reading time, moving from education to 'readucation'. In health they mean shifting from lethargic waste-prone organizations to lean sinewy systems conducive to autotelic work. In income-support they mean moving from a taxation state to a savings state.

Education: From education to 'readucation'
Health: From wasteful process-based organizations to lean pattern-based systems
Income: From the taxation state to the savings nation

Each one of these represents an increase in do-it-yourself, self-managed behavior. In each case though, this happens in different ways.

The child who reads widely is engaged in a do-it-yourself activity contrasted with the instruction mode of the classroom. The organization that gravitates to lean patterns moves away from procedure and direction. It becomes a system that models itself instead on efficient aesthetic-like shapes and patterns. It begins to think in terms of ratios rather than rules, proportions rather than procedures, flow rather than stoppage.

The same applies to the taxation state and the savings nation. The taxation state takes a given amount of today's tax money and allocates it as income-support. The money is not made to work. It does not grow through its productive use. The prudent investor, in contrast, takes savings and invests them in industries that over time will provide an accumulating return on investment. In a savings system, the emphasis is on the productive growth of assets. The focus is the future. In a tax system, the stress is on the distribution of receipts. The emphasis is on today. Saving systems are accumulative; tax systems are extractive and allocative. Extraction and allocation creates nothing and adds nothing to what exists. Saving and investment build and generate. The political problem posed by this is how to achieve a transition from one to other without disruption. The simplest scenario is to begin with new entrants into the workforce. Convert their tax-based retirement accounts into accumulation accounts. Then offer the option to older workers to do the same.

The savings approach applies not only to retirement-income but also education and health spending. Why tax money for these rather than mandate it to savings accounts? Why move money in a circumlocution through third-parties rather than have it spent directly? This would mean repatriating a sizable portion of taxation to a prudentially structured, flexibly linked lifetime system of individual education, health and retirement-income savings accounts. A system of spending based on accumulation rather than allocation increases liberty, expands choice and boosts first-party paying, encouraging competition and innovation. Taxation would not disappear. It would continue to fund core government activity. That includes boosting low incomes and insufficient savings with tax credits as needed.

The core of government though is not large. It is a complement to, not a replacement for, society's larger more flexible, more creative, deeper and richer self-organizing social systems. The state is an administered organization. It is like the firm or the university, the church or the charity, the school or the hospital department. All are functional to a point but beyond that point their positives gradually turn into negatives. Process erodes time, purpose consumes economy, and rules devour grace.

Underlying this is a philosophical view. A lot of contemporary government would like to treat the billions of decisions that everyday millions of individuals make as if these decisions were like a big organization subject to rules, procedures and directions. But they are not. Regulation is supposed to produce beauty and coherent meaning. Yet it does not. Rules and directives instead tend to produce ugliness, incoherence and insignificance. Doubtless they are not meant to. But they do. Intuitive, instinctive symmetries, ratios and proportions, and the multitude of aesthetic-like shapes and patterns built into nature and imitated by society and art, create beauty. Organizations untouched by pattern thinking fashion, in the main, awkward, discomfiting, graceless structures and profiles.[8] The challenge for public policy is to avoid this.

Notes

1 Burke, 2009 [1790], 35.
2 A shift from a tax state to a savings state necessarily involves transitional difficulties. Bosworth and Burtless, 1997, neatly summed up the problems. They noted that America's Social Security system had 'accumulated trillions of dollars in liabilities to workers who are already retired or who will retire soon. To make room for a new private system, policymakers must find funds to pay for these liabilities while still leaving young workers enough money to deposit in new private accounts.'
3 Outcome-based or principle-based regulation is an alternative to rule-based planning. On the former, see Di Lorenzo, 2012; Black, 2010; Black, Hopper and Band, 2007. Principle-based regulation requires safe, sound results such as structural integrity in construction but leaves building firms to decide how to achieve the outcome.
4 Murphy, 2017.
5 It was Adam Smith in *The Wealth of Nations*, III.4.19, who observed the superior capacity of small proprietors for productive improvement. Of all the kinds of improvers, the small-scale property owner is 'the most industrious, the most intelligent, and the most successful'. See also Smith, III.2.7 and III.2.20.
6 Murphy, 2017.
7 Google N-gram search.
8 The management thinker J.M. Juran (1992: 114) observed how in business much of customer behavior was shaped by cultural patterns and that 'a great deal of failure to determine what customer needs are is traceable to failure to understand the nature and even existence of the cultural pattern of the customers'.

Bibliography

Black, J. 2010. "The Rise, Fall and Fate of Principles Based Regulation." *LSE Law, Society and Economy Working Papers* 17. London: London School of Economics and Political Science Law Department.

Black, J., M. Hopper and C. Band. 2007. "Making a Success of Principles-Based Regulation." *Law and Financial Markets Review* 1, no. 3: 191–206.

Bosworth, B.P. and G. Burtless. 1997. *Privatizing Social Security: The Troubling Trade-Offs*. Washington, DC: Brookings Institution, March 1.

Burke, E. 2009 [1790]. *Reflections of the Revolution in France*. Overland Park, KS: Digireads.

Di Lorenzo, V. 2012. "Principles-Based Regulation and Legislative Congruence." *New York University Journal of Law and Public Policy* 15, no. 1: 45–108.

Juran, J.M. 1992. *Juran on Quality by Design*. New York: Free Press.

Murphy, P. 2017. *Auto-Industrialism: DIY Capitalism and the Rise of the Auto-Industrial Society*. London: Sage.

Smith, A. 1996. *An Inquiry into the Nature and Causes of the Wealth of Nations*. London: Strahan and Cadell.

Index

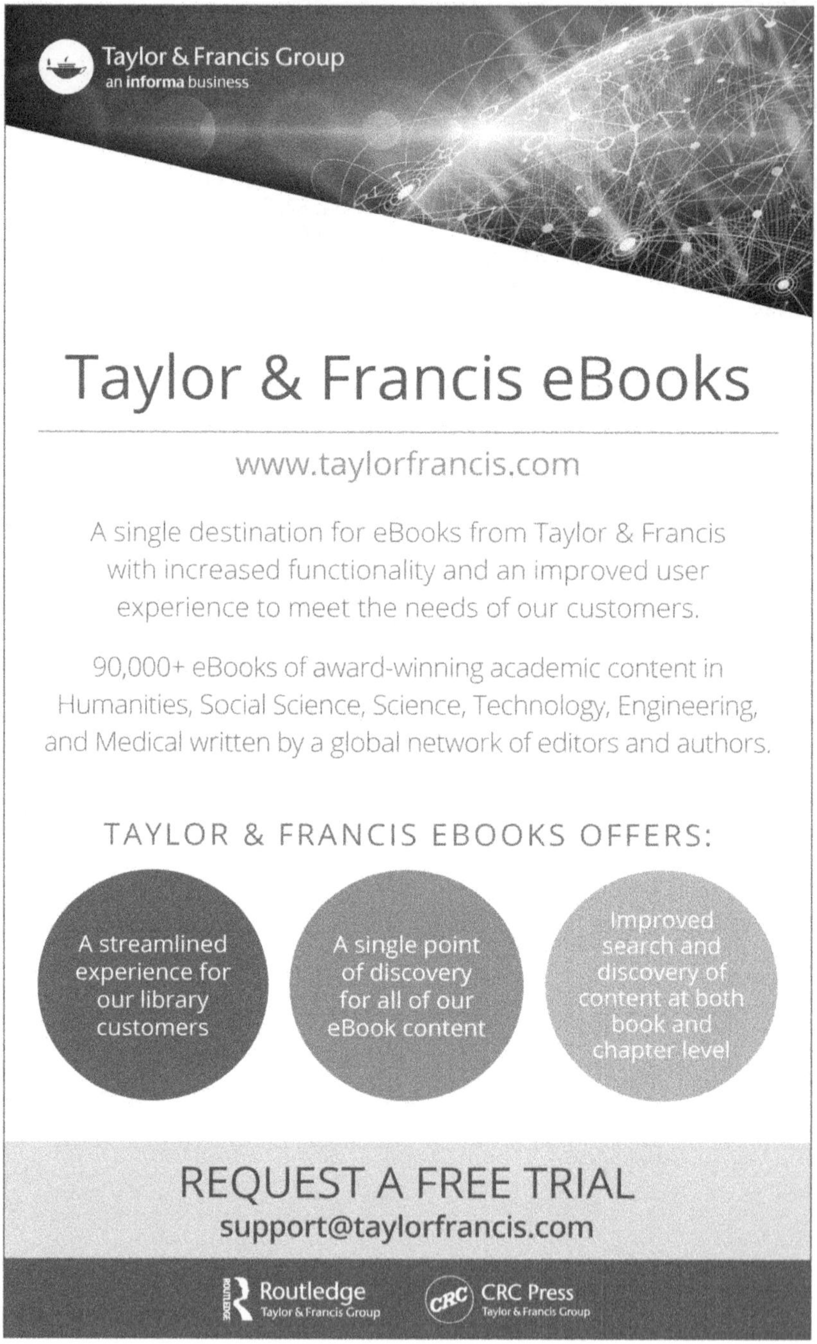
Taylor & Francis Group
an informa business
Taylor & Francis eBooks
www.taylorfrancis.com
A single destination for eBooks from Taylor & Francis with increased functionality and an improved user experience to meet the needs of our customers.
90,000+ eBooks of award-winning academic content in Humanities, Social Science, Science, Technology, Engineering, and Medical written by a global network of editors and authors.
TAYLOR & FRANCIS EBOOKS OFFERS:
A streamlined experience for our library customers
A single point of discovery for all of our eBook content
Improved search and discovery of content at both book and chapter level
REQUEST A FREE TRIAL
support@taylorfrancis.com
Routledge
Taylor & Francis Group
CRC Press
Taylor & Francis Group

For Product Safety Concerns and Information please contact our EU representative GPSR@taylorandfrancis.com
Taylor & Francis Verlag GmbH, Kaufingerstraße 24, 80331 München, Germany

www.ingramcontent.com/pod-product-compliance
Ingram Content Group UK Ltd.
Pitfield, Milton Keynes, MK11 3LW, UK
UKHW011007180926
475701UK00004B/602
* 9 7 8 0 3 6 7 5 8 5 0 9 9 *